PUERTO RICAN SOLDIERS SERVING WITH PRIDE

Norma Iris Pagan Morales

ISBN 978-1-959895-47-3 (paperback)
ISBN 978-1-959895-46-6 (ebook)

Printed in the United States of America

IN MEMORY OF MY FAMILY MEMBERS WHO SERVED WITH PRIDE

Sgt. Julio Pagan Torres, My Grandfather (Army)
CSM Juan Jose Pagan Rodriguez, My Dad (Army)
CPL Julio Pagan Rodriguez, My Uncle (Army)
PFC Jose Enrique Pagan Rodriguez, My Uncle (Army)
Sgt. Vicente Pagan Rodriguez, My Uncle (Army)
Petty Officer Ramon L. Pagan Rodriguez, My Uncle (Navy)
Sgt. Julio Pagan Morales, My Brother (Air Force)

OVERVIEW

THE MILITARY HISTORY OF PUERTO RICO

The military history of Puerto Rico goes back from the time Spanish conquistadores battled the native Taínos in the rebellion of 1511, to the present time.

PART OF THE SPANISH EMPIRE

Puerto Rico was part of the Spanish Empire for four centuries, during which the people of Puerto Rico defended themselves against invasions from the British, French, Dutch and many more.

The brave "Boricuas" warriors fought alongside General Bernardo de Gálvez during the American Revolutionary War in the battles of Baton Rouge, Mobile, Pensacola and St. Louis.

During the mid-19th century, Puerto Ricans residing in the United States fought in the American Civil War.

As you read this book, you will understand that Puerto Ricans have been fighting to keep the United States and Puerto Rico safe for more than a couple of centuries....

CONTENTS

CHAPTER 1

Taíno Rebellion of 1511

Christopher Columbus arrived in Puerto Rico on November 19, 1493, during his second voyage to the "New World".

The island was inhabited by the Arawak group of native people known as Taínos. The Taínos called the island "Borikén" or "Borinquen".

Before going on with the story of the Spaniards conquering the island, let me tell you a brief history of The Taínos in Puerto Rico.

Agüeybaná I

Agüeybaná I was the principal and most powerful cacique of the Taíno people in "Borikén" when the Spanish first arrived on the island on November 19, 1493.

Born: Puerto Rico
Died: 1510, Puerto Rico
Nickname(s): "The Great Sun"
Place of death Puerto Rico/"Borikén" in 1510
Rank Cacique
Commands held Taínos of "Borikén"
Relations Brother of Güeybaná, better known as Agüeybaná II

Agüeybana I, which has been interpreted by 19th and 20th century authors as meaning "The Great Sun", was the hereditary title shared by the family that ruled the theocratic monarchy of Borikén, governing the hierarchy over the rest of the regional chiefs or caciques.

Like other nobiliary recognitions within Taíno culture, it was passed down through the maternal bloodline.

The Spanish settlers Hispanicized the title to be the equivalent of the European concept of kings, with contemporary writers such as Juan de Castellanos and Gonzalo Fernández de Oviedo y Valdés employing the title of Rey Agüeybana, English: "King Agüeybana", when referring to the second monarch to lead the Taíno during the 1510s.

By the 1800s, the terms "king" and "cacique" were used exchangeable by both local and Spanish authors, but a revival in the interest concerning Taíno history during the 20th century led to the popularization of native words and later the term gained more verbal fame.

Agüeybaná I received the Spanish conquistador Juan Ponce de León upon his arrival in 1508. According to an old Taíno tradition, Agüeybaná I practiced the "guatiao," a Taíno ritual in which he and Juan Ponce de León became friends and exchanged names.

Ponce de León then baptized the cacique's mother into Christianity and renamed her Inés.

The cacique joined Ponce de León in the exploration of the island. After this had been accomplished, Agüeybaná accompanied the conquistador to the island of La Española.

Today is what comprising the nations of the Dominican Republic and Haiti. This is the place where Ponce de Leon was well received by the Governor Nicolás de Ovando.

Agüeybaná's actions helped to maintain the peace between the Taíno and the Spaniards, a peace which was to be short-lived.

The hospitality and friendly treatment that the Spaniards received from Agüeybaná I made it easy for the Spaniards to deceive and conquer the island.

After a short period of peace, the Taínos were forced to work in the island's gold mines and in the construction of forts as slaves. Many Taínos died because of the cruel treatment which they received.

Upon Agüeybaná's death in 1510, his brother Güeybaná, better known as Agüeybaná II, became the most powerful Cacique in the island. Agüeybaná II was troubled by the treatment of his people by the

Spanish and attacked them in battle. The Taíno were ultimately defeated at the <u>Battle of Yagüecas</u>.

Some Taínos in Puerto Rico abandoned the island. The ones that stayed, were forced to labor as slaves and the rest were killed by the Spaniards.

Recent genetic studies published between 2018 and 2019 revealed that Taíno blood ancestry is still present in, many Puerto Ricans. The analyses revealed a narrative more suggestive of assimilation and migrations to nearby islands rather than extinction.

Although many died to the smallpox epidemic that attacked the islanders in 1519, others survived the genetic bottleneck to produce offspring's.

Agüeybaná II

There is a Statue of Agüeybaná II, "El Bravo", in Ponce, Puerto Rico in his honor. <u>The Agüeybaná II,"El Bravo". sector Caracoles, Barrio Playa, Ponce, Puerto Rico</u>

<u>Rank: "Cacique of Borikén</u>
Reign 1510 - 1511
Predecessor Agüeybaná I
Born 1470 in "Borikén"
Died 1511, aged 40–41
Puerto Rico
Military career
Nickname(s) "El Bravo" (The Brave)
Commands held Taínos of "Borikén"
Battles/wars Taíno rebellion of 1511
Relations Brother of Agüeybaná I

<u>Agüeybaná II 1470 – 1511</u>, born <u>Güeybaná</u> and known as Agüeybaná El Bravo, <u>English: Agüeybaná the Brave</u>, was one of the two principal and most powerful caciques of the Taíno people in "Borikén" when the Spaniards first arrived in Puerto Rico on November 19, 1493.

Agüeybaná II led the Taínos of Puerto Rico in the <u>Battle of Yagüecas</u>, also known as the "<u>Taíno rebellion of 1511</u>" against Juan Ponce de León and the Spaniards.

In 1511, in the region known as <u>Yagüecas</u> some 11,000 to 15,000 Taínos had assembled against some 80 to 100 Spaniards.

Before the start of the battle, a Spanish soldier using an <u>arquebus</u> shot and killed a native. It is presumed this was Agüeybaná II, because the warrior was wearing a golden necklace which only a cacique wore.

After the death of Agüeybaná II, the native warriors withdrew and became disorganized.

Agüeybaná II's followers chose for engaging the Spaniards via guerilla tactics. Such guerilla warfare rebellion lasted for the next 8 years, until 1519.

A second round of raids erupted in 1513 when Ponce de Leon departed the island to explore Florida. The settlement of Caparra, the seat of the island government at that time, was sacked and burned by an alliance between Taínos and natives from the northeastern Antilles.

By 1520 the Taíno presence in the Island had almost disappeared. A government census in 1530 reports the existence of only 1,148 Taínos remaining in Puerto Rico.

However, harsh conditions for the surviving Taíno continued. Many of those who stayed on the island soon died of either the cruel treatment that they had received or of the smallpox epidemic, which had attacked the island in 1519.

Let me remind you that our Taínos were very peaceful, therefore, the Spaniard took advantage of them.

The Spaniards arrival...

The Taínos were known as peaceful people, however, they were also warriors and often fought against the Caribs, who in more than one occasion attempt to invade Puerto Rico.

Columbus named the island San Juan Bautista in honor of Saint John the Baptist. The main port was named Puerto Rico which means Rich Port.

Eventually the island was renamed Puerto Rico. The port was to change into the capital of the island and was renamed San Juan. The conquistador Juan Ponce de León accompanied Columbus on this trip.

Here is some information about Güeybaná, better known as Agüeybaná II, The Brave...

When Ponce de León arrived in Puerto Rico, he was well received by the Cacique, the Tribal chief Agüeybaná, The Great Sun, chieftain of the island Taíno tribes.

Besides the conquistadors, some of the first colonists were farmers and miners in search of gold.

In 1508, Ponce de León became the first appointed governor of Puerto Rico, founding the first settlement of Caparra. This area is known today as cities of Bayamón and San Juan.

After being named Governor, Ponce de León and the conquistadors forced the Taínos to work in the mines and to build defenses. Many Taínos died because of cruel treatment during their labor.

In 1510, upon Agüeybaná's death, his brother Güeybaná, better known as Agüeybaná II, The Brave, and a group of Taínos led Diego Salcedo, a Spaniard, to a river. Salcedo was drowned. This was to prove to the Taínos people that the white men were not Gods.

Upon realizing this, Agüeybaná II led his people in the Taíno rebellion of 1511. This was the first rebellion in the island against the better armed Spanish forces.

Guarionex, cacique of Utuado, attacked the village of Sotomayor, present day known as Aguada…

In this attack, eighty of its inhabitants were killed. Cacique Guarionex died during the attack which was considered a Taíno victory.

After the Taíno victory, the colonists formed a citizens' militia to defend themselves against the attacks. Juan Ponce de León and one of his top commanders, Diego de Salazar led the Spaniards in a series of offensives which included a massacre of the Taíno forces in the domain of Agüeybaná II.

The Spanish offensive ended in the Battle of Yagüecas against Cacique Mabodomoca. Agüeybaná II was shot and killed, ending the first recorded military action in Puerto Rico.

After they failed the rebellion, the Taínos were forced to give up their customs and traditions'. These were order by Royal decree, approved by King Ferdinand II. It required that they adopt and practice the values, religion, and language of their conquerors.

According to the "500th Florida Discovery Council Round Table", on March 3, 1513, Juan Ponce de León, organized and initiated an expedition with a crew of 200. This expedition included women and free blacks.

They departed from "Punta Aguada" Puerto Rico. Puerto Rico was the historic 1st gateway to the discovery of Florida which opened the doors to the advanced settlement of the U.S.A.

They introduced Christianity, cattle, horses, sheep, the Spanish language and more to Florida. Later, Florida, became the United States of America. This was 107 years before the Pilgrims landed.

The Taíno were Arawak people who were the indigenous people of the Caribbean and Florida.

During that time, the European were the first contact in the late 15th century. They were the principal inhabitants of most of Cuba, Jamaica, Hispaniola, the Dominican Republic, Haiti, and Puerto Rico.

In the Greater Antilles, the northern Lesser Antilles, and the Bahamas, they were known as the Lucayans and spoke the Taíno language, a derivative of the Arawakan languages. The Tano's ancestors entered the Caribbean from South America.

At the time of contact, the Taíno were divided into three broad groups, known as the Western Taíno Jamaica, most of Cuba, and the Bahamas, the Classic Taíno Hispaniola and Puerto Rico.

Also, the Eastern Taíno, northern Lesser Antilles. A fourth, lesser-known group went on to travel to Florida and divided into tribes.

At the present time, we know that there are four named tribes: the Tequesta, Calusa, Jaega and Ais. Other tribes are known to have settled in Florida, but their names are not known.

During Columbus' time, in 1492, there were five Taíno chiefdoms and territories on Hispaniola, each led by a principal Cacique chieftain, to whom tribute was paid.

Ayiti "land of high mountains" was the indigenous Taíno name for the mountainous side of the island of Hispaniola, which has retained its name as Haiti in French.

Cuba, the largest island of the Antilles, was originally divided into 29 chiefdoms. Most of the native settlements later became the site of Spanish colonial cities retaining the original Taíno names.

For instance, Havana, Batabanó, Camagüey, Baracoa and Bayamo are still recognized by their Taíno names. Puerto Rico also was divided into chiefdoms.

As the hereditary head chief of Taíno tribes, the cacique was paid significant tribute.

At the time of the Spanish conquest, the largest Taíno population centers may have contained over 3,000 people each.

The Taíno were historically enemies of the neighboring Carib tribes, another group with origins in South America. The Carib lived principally in the Lesser Antilles. The relationship between the two groups has been the subject of much study.

For most 0f the 15th century, the Taíno tribe was being driven to the northeast in the Caribbean and out of what is now South America, because of raids by the Carib, resulting in Women being taken in raids and many Carib women speaking Taíno.

The Spaniards, who first arrived in the Bahamas, Cuba, and Hispaniola in 1492, and later in Puerto Rico, did not bring women in the first expeditions. They took Taíno women for their common-law wives, resulting in mestizo children.

Sexual violence in Hispaniola with the Taíno women by the Spaniards was also common. Scholars suggest there was substantial racial and cultural mixing in Cuba, as well, and several Indian pueblos survived into the 19th century.

The Taíno became nearly extinct as a culture following settlement by Spanish colonists, primarily due to infectious diseases to which they had no immunity.

The first recorded smallpox outbreak in Hispaniola occurred in December 1518 or January 1519. The 1518 smallpox epidemic killed 90% of the natives who had not already died.

Warfare and harsh enslavement by the colonists had also caused many deaths....

By 1548, the native population had declined to fewer than 500. Starting in about 1840, there have been attempts to create a quasi-indigenous Taíno identity in rural areas of Cuba, the Dominican Republic, and Puerto Rico. This trend accelerated among the Puerto Rican community in the United States in the 1960s.

<u>Terminology</u>

The Taíno people, or Taíno culture, has been classified by some authorities as belonging to the Arawak, as their language was considered to belong to the Arawak language family, the languages of which were present throughout the Caribbean, and much of Central and South America.

The early cultural historian, Daniel Garrison Brinton, called the Taíno people the "<u>Island Arawak"</u>. Nevertheless, contemporary scholars have recognized that the Taíno had developed a distinct language and culture.

Modern historians, linguists and anthropologists now hold that the term Taíno should refer to all the Taíno/Arawak tribes except for the Caribs, who are not seen to belong to the same people.

Linguists continue to debate whether the Carib language is an Arawakan dialect or creole language, or perhaps an individual language, with an Arawakan lingo used for communication purposes.

<u>Here are some Taíno words in the Puerto Rican Vocabulary</u>
areito - Taíno ceremony that includes song, music, dance, and history
barbacoa - a 4-legged stand made of sticks used for cooking
batea: large tray
batey - yard area -
bohio - typical round home of Taínos
Boricua - valiant people
Borikén - Great Land of the Valiant and Noble Lord
burén - flat cooking plate or griddle
cabuya - fishing line
cacique - chief
canarís: water vessels
caney - square house for Chiefs and Shammans only
canoas/piraguas/cayucas/kurialas: canoes
Caribe -strong people
casabi - yuca bread
cibucanes: used to extract poisonous juice from Yuca
coa - farming tool - a wooden stick used to work the soil

cokie - coquí - small tree frog
colibri - hummingbird
conuco - farming area - mounds of loose soil
cucubano - lightning bug
ditas y jitacas: food vessels made from higüero
dujo - chair with short legs
fotuto - sea shell trumpet
guanín - chief's medallion
Guaraguao - red tailed hawk
guatiao - exchanging named and becoming blood brothers
iguana - lizard
Inrirí - Wood Pecker
jamaca - hammock
jicotea - land turtle
jurakan - storm
jutía - small rabbit-like creature
Lukiyó - sacred mountain
mabí - fermented drink made from Mabí tree
macana - weapon - club
mime - small fly
nagua - loin cloth used by married women
nasa: fishing mesh or net
natiao - brothers
tabacú - tobacco
uguaca - parrot
Yocahú - God
yucayeque - Taíno village

CHAPTER 2

Puerto Ricans United States Citizens

As citizens of the United States, Puerto Ricans have participated in every major United States military engagement from World War I onward, with the soldiers of Puerto Rico's 65th Infantry Regiment distinguishing themselves in combat during the Korean War.

While under Spanish rule, Puerto Rico fought alongside the American colonists in the Revolutionary War.

Bernardo de Galvez, the governor of Louisiana in 1779, was named general of the Spanish colonial army and led his troop. This troop was consisting primarily of Puerto Ricans and other Hispanics. They were ordered to capture the cities of Baton Rouge, Louisiana; Mobile, Alabama; Pensacola, Florida; and St. Louis, Missouri, from the British.

Spain ceded Puerto Rico to the U.S. under the 1898 Treaty of Paris, and Puerto Rico became a U.S. territory. The Army National Guard formed the Porto Rico Regiment on the island.

It has been 101 years since the citizens of Puerto Rico were collectively naturalized as U.S. citizens under the Jones Act of 1917. The act was meant to deal with the fact that Puerto Rico was neither a U.S. state nor an independent country. "It was foreign to the United States in a domestic sense," said a 1901 Supreme Court decision.

But guess what? Citizenship created contradictions. Puerto Ricans still feel something less than fully American. Puerto Ricans cannot vote for the U.S. president when they live in the territory, but they can when they reside in one of the 50 U.S. states or the District of Columbia.

In crisis, notably during Puerto Rico's 2017 bankruptcy, and the federal response to the devastation of the island by Hurricane Maria, the inequality of Puerto Rico is often expose. There are many questions asked again about the Jones Act.

Chief among them, what did the Jones Act do?

To understand the Jones Act, it is best to start with a clarification of what the law was not.

It was not the first Congressional statute conferring U.S. citizenship on persons born in Puerto Rico. It was not the last such statute. The law did not change Puerto Rico's status as a U.S. territory. The Jones Act, in its collective extensive of American citizenship to Puerto Rico residents, proved to be a crucial glue. The glue that is cementing and enduring relationships between residents of Puerto Rico and of the United States.

In the aftermath of the Spanish-American War of 1898, the United States annexed Puerto Rico. The terms of the annexation were outlined in the Treaty of Paris peace accords ratified in 1899.

Unlike prior treaties of territorial annexation, the Treaty of Paris did not contain a provision extending or promising to extend U.S. citizenship to the inhabitants of Puerto Rico.

As documented in the so-called Red Book files, the official correspondence of the negotiations between the United States and Spain, President McKinley opposed granting citizenship to the "less civilized" non-Anglo-Saxon inhabitants of Puerto Rico and the other annexed Spanish territories.

Instead, Section Nine of the Treaty invented a local "nationality" that barred island-born inhabitants from either retaining their Spanish citizenship or acquiring U.S. citizenship.

This local nationality required Puerto Ricans to establish a new allegiance with the United States, while simultaneously barring their membership in the U.S. political community. It allowed the federal government to selectively rule Puerto Ricans as foreigners in a domestic or constitutional sense.

However, the Treaty established that Congress could subsequently enact legislation to determine the civil and political status of Puerto Ricans.

In 1900, Congress enacted the Foraker Act, which established the island's territorial status and affirmed the citizenship provision of the Treaty of Paris.

Even though the United States had annexed Puerto Rico, Section Three of the Foraker Act treated Puerto Rico as a foreign territorial possession for purposes of imposing tariffs, duties, or taxes on merchandise trafficked between the island and the mainland.

Section Seven invented a Puerto Rican citizenship to describe the status of island-born Puerto Ricans. A year later, the Supreme Court affirmed Congress' power to selectively rule Puerto Rico as a foreign territorial possession in a domestic or constitutional sense.

It seems that the Puerto Rican citizenship was invented for Puerto Rico. It clashed with various federal citizenship and nationality laws.

For example, the prevailing passport law of the period limited the issuance of passports to U.S. citizens, so Puerto Rican merchants who sought to travel found themselves unable to acquire a U.S. passport.

In response to this and other administrative problems created by the Puerto Rican citizenship. Congress in 1906 began to enact legislation granting individual Puerto Ricans the ability to acquire U.S. citizenship by traveling to the mainland and undergoing the prevailing naturalization process.

In effect, Puerto Ricans were able to acquire citizenship individually, just like any other racially eligible immigrant. This was the first law granting Puerto Ricans U.S. citizenship.

This wasn't enough. Between the enactment of the Foraker Act of 1900 and the Jones Act of 1917, Congress debated upwards of 30 bills containing citizenship provisions for Puerto Rico.

The Federal lawmakers supported the collective naturalization of the inhabitants of Puerto Rico for a wide array of reasons. Some in Congress were concerned that depriving Puerto Ricans of U.S. citizenship would allow neighboring Latin American countries to describe the United States as a colonial empire.

Other lawmakers believed that depriving Puerto Ricans of U.S. citizenship was bad for business, and still others thought that preventing Puerto Rico inhabitants from acquiring a U.S. citizenship would foster disloyalty and threaten the U.S. military or strategic interests in Puerto Rico.

As members of Congress considered the issue, they decided that the risks of rectifying these problems were low. Most importantly, policymakers agreed that that extending U.S. citizenship to Puerto Rico did not bind Congress to grant statehood to the island.

While the Jones Act wouldn't pass until 1917, the legislative record shows that Congress had effectively decided to collectively naturalize the residents of Puerto Rico three years earlier. This was before the U.S. entered World War I.

Still, they didn't propose making Puerto Rico a state because most lawmakers opposed the admission of a state primarily inhabited by non-white citizens.

Meanwhile, in Puerto Rico, the debate centered on whether the residents of the island would acquire U.S. citizenship via individual or collective naturalization. This reflected a larger, longer-term discussion over whether Puerto Rico's future should be one of independence from the U.S., or of an autonomous entity within the U.S., or of statehood.

By 1914, both parties in Puerto Rico believed that the extension of citizenship to Puerto Rico was pending...

The leadership of the Partido Unión, who advocated either territorial autonomy and/or independence, sought to establish a pact supporting the extension of U.S. citizenship with the leadership of the Partido Republicano, which advocated for statehood as a way of demanding more democratic reforms to the prevailing territorial government.

Unlike the supporters of the Partido Republicano, who believed that the collective naturalization of Puerto Ricans could serve as a bridge to statehood. The leadership of the Partido Unión argued that individual citizenship would provide more civil liberties for Puerto Ricans and would be compatible with either territorial autonomy or independence. The Federal lawmakers took these debates into account when drafting the citizenship provision of the Jones Act.

Never had the country extended citizenship to an annexed, though unincorporated, territory that was not considered a state-in-the-making.

The Jones Act of 1917 amended the Foraker Act of 1900 to address several lasting problems in the local government. It also included a citizenship provision that incorporated the local political debates over the way citizenship was extended to Puerto Rico under the terms of Section Five.

The first clause of this citizenship provision granted individual Puerto Rican citizens a choice between retaining their status quo or acquiring U.S. citizenship.

Only 288 Puerto Ricans chose to retain their Puerto Rican citizenship. The second clause collectively naturalized island-born Puerto Ricans residing in the island who chose not to retain their Puerto Rican citizenship.

Two additional clauses granted different types of alien residents the ability to acquire U.S. citizenship by following simple legal procedures within various time frames. In the end, most Puerto Rican citizens residing in the island acquired U.S. citizenship by simply doing nothing.

Yet, while the Jones Act collectively naturalized the inhabitants of Puerto Rico, it did not change the island's territorial status.

Puerto Rico remained an unincorporated territory or a foreign territorial possession for citizenship and constitutional purposes. Since people born in Puerto Rico were born outside of the United States, they could only acquire a derived form of parental or just sanguinis citizenship.

For constitutional purposes, people born in Puerto Rico were not citizens at birth, but they were naturalized citizens like the child of any U.S. citizen born in a foreign country. This meant that only the children of citizens born in Puerto Rico could acquire U.S. citizenship.

The children of aliens, and of some mixed marriages, born in Puerto Rico could not acquire U.S. citizenship at birth. Even though the Jones Act granted U.S. citizenship to most of the inhabitants of Puerto Rico, it also created thousands of stateless residents of the island.

To address this problem, Congress subsequently amended the citizenship provision of the Jones Act on three occasions over the next two decades.

The 1927 amendment made it possible for the remaining 288 Puerto Rican citizens and other aliens residing in the island to naturalize through an expedited process.

In 1934, Congress introduced a territorial form of birthright citizenship permitting the children of Puerto Ricans born in the island to acquire U.S. citizenship at birth.

In addition, this amendment extended the Cable Act of 1922 to Puerto Rico and began to eliminate the application of the doctrine of Coverture in Puerto Rico. The doctrine of Coverture stipulated that a U.S. woman acquired the citizenship of her husband as a direct result of marriage.

The 1934 amendment allowed U.S. citizen women residing in Puerto Rico to retain their U.S. citizenship after marrying an alien.

Later, a 1938 amendment retroactively naturalized Puerto Rico-born residents. Taken together, these corrective amendments sought to collectively naturalize island-born Puerto Ricans who either did not acquire U.S. citizenship at birth or lost it along the way.

Two years later, Congress replaced the <u>Jones Act with the Nationality Act of 1940</u>. It extended a statutory form of birthright or just citizenship to Puerto Rico that was anchored in the Citizenship Clause of the Fourteenth Amendment.

According to the Nationality Act of 1940, birth in Puerto Rico was now equal to birth in the United States. Since 1940, Congress has enacted several laws that affirm the Nationality Act's citizenship provisions for Puerto Rico and grant all persons born in the island U.S. native-born citizenship status.

But even though the Nationality Act settled questions of citizenship, it did not deal with the larger question of the island's political future.

Even though the Jones Act citizenship was short-lived, 1917-1940, it was important historically. The Jones Act was not only the first law that collectively naturalized the majority of Puerto Ricans residing in the island, but also it was the first law that collectively naturalized the inhabitants of a territory that was not meant to become a state of the United States.

Although Congress had previously collectively naturalized individual Native American nations, and later all Native Americans, it had not treated the land they inhabited as territories or potential states for constitutional purposes.

To this extent, the Jones Act represented an advance for American citizenship:

Never had the country extended citizenship to an annexed, albeit unincorporated, territory that was not considered a state-in-the-making.

Finally, the Jones Act citizenship was an early affirmation of a permanent and irrevocable relationship between Puerto Ricans and the United States. Once Congress clothed Puerto Ricans with U.S. citizenship, it could not strip them of this right.

Read as a whole, this patchwork of citizenship laws illustrate the contradictory U.S. territorial law used to rule Puerto Rico for more than a century.

On the one hand, the United States continues to govern Puerto Rico as an unincorporated territory and that is a foreign possession in a domestic or constitutional sense. Simultaneously, federal citizenship laws treat Puerto Ricans as members of the U.S. political community.

In part, these territorial laws create a two-storied home. Citizens residing on the first floor, the mainland. They enjoy the full legal and political rights of membership in the U.S. political community, whereas citizens residing in the basement or Puerto Rico live with a second-class status determined by the laws and policies Congress and the Supreme Court extend to the island.

CHAPTER 3

Puerto Ricans in World War I

Puerto Ricans and people of Puerto Rican descent have participated as members of the United States Armed Forces in every conflict in which the United States has been involved since World War I.

One of the consequences of the Spanish American War was that Puerto Rico was annexed by the United States in accordance with the terms of the Treaty of Paris of 1898, ratified on December 10, 1898.

On January 15, 1899, the military government changed the name of Puerto Rico to Porto Rico.

On May 17, 1932, the U.S. Congress changed the name back to "Puerto Rico".

On March 21, 1915, the first shots by the United States in World War I were fired by the Porto Rico Regiment of Infantry from El Morro Castle at a German ship in San Juan Bay.

U.S. Citizenship was extended to the political body known as Porto Rican citizens via the Jones–Shafroth Act of 1917, the Puerto Rican House of Delegates had rejected an earlier bill in 1914 because it did not include universal male suffrage.

Even though Puerto Ricans were "American" nationals since 1900, due the Foraker Act, which made them eligible for the Selective Service Draft lottery, they were excluded from the initial draft law.

The Puerto Rican legislature and local leaders demanded that Puerto Ricans were included in the draft and allowed to fight in the war.

Puerto Ricans who resided on the island had been serving as volunteers in the "Porto Rico Regiment of Infantry," dating back to 1899. As was the case nationwide and under Spanish control, the Puerto Rican units created during WWI, the 94th Infantry Division, were racially segregated.

Puerto Ricans of African descent were assigned to the 375th Regiment which was part of the 94th Infantry Division which was the Puerto Rican contribution to what came to be known as the National Army.

Those who resided in the mainland served in regular units of one of the following branches of the United States military, the United States Marine Corps, Army, or the Navy.

As such, they were assigned to regular military units; however, Puerto Ricans of African descent were assigned to segregated all-black units and were subject to the discrimination which was rampant in the U.S. in those days.

It is estimated that 236,000 Puerto Ricans in the island registered for the World War I draft and that 18,000 served in the war.

It is, however, impossible to determine the exact number of Puerto Ricans residing on the United States mainland who served and died in the war because the War Department did not keep statistics regarding the ethnicity of its members.

Puerto Ricans have had a long history of defending their island, having fought off against attacks from Caribs and pirates, against invasions of other European powers at war with Spain which sought to capture Puerto Rico.

Enlisting alongside General Bernardo de Gálvez during the American Revolutionary War in the battles of Baton Rouge, Mobile, Pensacola and St. Louis, and fighting in Europe during the Napoleonic Wars against the forces of Napoleon Bonaparte at the Siege of Saragossa.

In the 19th Century, Puerto Ricans fought against the Spanish Empire. They fought for Mexico's independence and in the Latin American revolutions alongside Simón Bolívar.

Puerto Ricans who resided in the United States, such as LT Augusto Rodriguez, fought in the American Civil War...

In Puerto Rico they revolted against Spanish rule and fought for Puerto Rico's independence in "El Grito de Lares" and in the "Intentona de Yauco."

They also fought for Cuba's independence in the Ten Years' War alongside General Máximo Gómez and as members of the Cuban Liberation Army alongside Jose Marti.

At the end of the 19th century, Puerto Ricans fought alongside their Spanish counterparts in the Spanish American War against the United States in the Battle of San Juan Hill in Cuba and in Puerto Rico when the American military forces invaded the island in what is known as the Puerto Rican Campaign and against the Philippine Republic during the Philippine–American War.

Puerto Rico became a U.S. Territory in accordance with the 1898 Treaty of Paris which ended the Spanish American War. The United States appointed a military governor and soon the United States Army established itself in San Juan.

The Army Appropriation Bill created by an Act of Congress on March 2, 1899, authorized the creation of the first body of native troops in Puerto Rico.

On June 30, 1901, the "Porto Rico Provisional Regiment of Infantry" was organized.

On July 1, 1901, the United States Senate passed a Bill which would require a strict mental and physical examination for those who wanted to join the Regiment. It also approved the recruitment of native Puerto Rican civilians to be appointed to the grade of Second Lieutenants for a term of four years if they passed the required tests.

An Act of Congress, approved on May 27, 1908, reorganized the regiment as part of the "regular" Army. Since the native Puerto Rican officers were Puerto Rican citizens and not citizens of the United States, they were required to undergo a new physical examination to determine their fitness for commissions in the Regular Army and to take an oath of U.S. citizenship with their new officer's oath.

There were many military installations in Puerto Rico, however Camp Las Casas played an instrumental role in preparing the native Puerto Ricans for the military.

On January 30, 1908, the "Porto Rico Regiment of Infantry" was stationed at Camp Las Casas in Santurce, a section of San Juan, in what is now El Residencial Las Casas, a public housing complex.

Camp Las Casas served as the main training camp for the Puerto Rican soldiers prior to World War I.

Most of the men trained in this facility were assigned to the "Porto Rico Regiment of Infantry." Puerto Ricans were unaccustomed to the racial segregation policies of the United States which were also implemented in Puerto Rico and often refused to designate themselves as "white" or "black".

Such was the case of <u>Antonio Guzmán</u> who at first was assigned to a white regiment only to be reassigned to a black regiment at Camp Las Casas. He requested a hearing and argued his case to no avail.

<u>Captain Luis R. Esteves,</u> who on June 19, 1915, became the first Puerto Rican to graduate from the United States Military Academy, West Point, organized the 23rd Battalion which was composed of Puerto Ricans.

Esteves served as instructor at the Officers' Training Camps that were established soon afterwards. He was instructor or commander of three of these camps, which produced all the officers who would lead the more than 20,000 men trained in Puerto Rico during World War I.

Marine aviation was new. It came into existence on May 22, 1912, and he first major expansion of the Marine Corps' air component. Puerto Rico played a major role, came with America's entrance into World War I.

On January 6, 1914, First Lieutenant Bernard L. Smith established the Marine Section of the Navy Flying School in the island municipality of Culebra.

As the number of Marine Aviators grew, so did the enthusiastic desire to separate from Naval Aviation.

By doing so, the Marine Aviation was designated as separate from the United States Naval Aviation. The creation of a Marine Corps Aviation Company in Puerto Rico consisted of 10 officers and 40 enlisted men.

In addition, several local militia units called "Home Guard" units were organized in various cities and towns to defend and maintain domestic order in the island.

Virgil R. Miller, a native of San Germán, Puerto Rico, who in World War II served as the Regimental Commander of the highly decorated 442d Regimental Combat Team, served in the San Juan unit of the Puerto Rico Home Guard.

2nd Lt. Pedro Albizu Campos organized the Ponce unit of the Home Guard.

Lt. Teófilo Marxuach's unit of the Porto Rico Regiment of Infantry was stationed at El Morro Castle. It was then an Army base called Fort Brookeat San Juan Bay.

The United States tried to remain neutral when World War I broke out in August 1914. However, the Government of the United States in Washington, D.C. insisted on its neutral right to send ships to Europe and that therefore, the German U-boats must refrain from attacking them. The American ships carried food and raw materials to Britain.

On March 21, 1915, Lt. Marxuach was the officer of the day at El Morro Castle. The Odenwald, built in 1903, not to be confused with the German World War II war ship which carried the same name, was an armed German supply ship which tried to force its way out of the San Juan Bay and deliver supplies to the German U-boats waiting in the Atlantic Ocean.

Lt. Marxuach gave the order to open fire on the ship from the walls of the fort. Sergeant Encarnacion Correa then operated a machine gun and fired warning shots with little effect.

Marxuach fired a shot from a cannon located at the Santa Rosa battery of "El Morro" fort, in what is the first shot of World War I fired by the regular armed forces of the United States against any ship flying the colors of the Central Powers forcing the Odenwald to stop and to return to port where its supplies were confiscated.

The shots ordered by Lt. Marxuach were the first fired by the United States in World War I. Marxuach's actions became an international incident when the German Government accused the United States Government of the holding the Odenwald illegally against its will without firing the customary warning shot as required by international law.

The United States Government responded that the official report of the United States War Department made by the commander of the fortress of El Morro Castle, <u>Lt. Col. Burnham</u>, made it clear that only warning shots were made and that none were aimed at the Odenwald.

Eventually, the Odenwald was refitted and renamed SS Newport by the U.S. Government and assigned to the U.S. Shipping Board, where it served until 1924 when it was retired.

In 1917 the Germans resumed submarine attacks, knowing that it would lead to America's entry into the war.

On April 6, 1917, the United States Congress declared war on Germany.

By May 3, 1917, the Regiment was transferred to the regular Army and recruited 1,969 men and the 295th, 296, 373rd, 374th and 375th regiments of Puerto Rico were created.

The United States continued to apply their military segregation policies to the native Puerto Ricans. Puerto Ricans of African descent were assigned to all black units such as the 375th Regiment.

Puerto Ricans were to be sent to North Carolina to train for deployment overseas, however Senators from the southeastern states opposed and blocked these plans, citing that Puerto Ricans would be a problem to the laws and customs of the racist Jim Crow policies.

Southern politicians were alarmed of the idea of having armed African Americans in the south and believed that Puerto Ricans of mixed race, who did not understand their racial policies, would only add to their problems.

On May 17, 1917, the Porto Rico Regiment of Infantry was sent to guard the Panama Canal in defense of the Panama Canal Zone and other vital military installations while the other Puerto Rican regiments guarded Puerto Rico.

Puerto Ricans became U.S. citizens because of the 1917 Jones-Shafroth Act and two months later, when Congress passed the Selective Service Act, conscription was extended to the island.

Those who were eligible, except for women, were expected to serve in the military. About 20,000 Puerto Ricans were drafted during World War I.

<u>In November 1917, the first military draft</u>, mobilization, lottery in Puerto Rico was held in the island's capital, San Juan. The first

draft number pick was made by Diana Yager, the daughter of the U.S. appointed governor of Puerto Rico Arthur Yager.

The number she picked was 1435 and it belonged to San Juan native Eustaquio Correa. This made Correa became the first Puerto Rican to be "drafted" into the Armed Forces of the United States.

It is estimated that 236,000 Puerto Ricans in the island registered for the World War I draft and that 18,000 served in the war.

Prior to the Jones-Shafroth Act, Puerto Ricans in the mainland United States as all other non-citizens, who were permanent residents were required to register with the Selective Service System by law and could be drafted.

In New York City, many Puerto Ricans of African descent joined the 369th Infantry Regiment which was mostly composed of Afro-Americans. They were not allowed to fight alongside their white counterparts.

They were permitted to fight as members of a French unit in French uniforms. They fought along the Western Front in France, and their reputation earned them the nickname of "the Harlem Hell Fighters" by the Germans.

Among them was Rafael Hernández Marín, one of Puerto Rico's greatest music composer and his brother Jesus.

In 1917, Rafael Hernández was working as a musician in North Carolina, when the United States entered World War I. The Jazz bandleader James Reese Europe recruited brothers Rafael and Jesús Hernández, and 16 more Puerto Ricans to join the United States Army's Harlem Hell fighters' musical band, the Orchestra Europe.

The Hernández brothers enlisted and were assigned to the U.S. 369th Infantry Regiment, formerly known as the 15th Infantry Regiment, New York National Guard, created in New York City in June.

Hernandez toured Europe with the Orchestra. The 369th was awarded Croix de guerre by France for battlefield gallantry.

Pedro Albizu Campos was a Puerto Rican who volunteered in the United States Infantry. Albizu was commissioned a Second Lieutenant in the Army Reserves and sent to the City of Ponce where he organized the town's Home Guard. He was called to serve in the regular Army and sent to Camp Las Casas for further training.

Upon completing the training, he was assigned to the 375th Infantry Regiment. The 375th was a regiment of black Puerto Ricans who were trained by non-Puerto Rican officers for overseas deployment, but the war ended before it could join the fight in Europe.

Albizu was honorably discharged from the Army in 1919, with the rank of First Lieutenant. During the time that he served he was exposed to the racism of the day which left a mark in his beliefs towards the relationship of Puerto Ricans and the United States, thus becoming a leading advocate for Puerto Rican independence.

Another Puerto Rican of African descent who was sent to Camp Las Casas was Nero Chen. "El Negro," was Puerto Rico's first professional boxer to gain international recognition and served as a boxing instructor to the servicemen at the camp.

On June 2, 1918, the SM U-151, the first German U-boat to operate in U.S. territory in World War I, sank six ships and damaged two others off the coast of New Jersey in the space of a few hours in what is known by historians as "Black Sunday".

Among the ships sunk by torpedo was the SS Carolina, a Puerto Rican passenger vessel. Prior to the sinking, Captain Heinrich von Nostitz, the U-boat commander, issued a warning as to his intentions.

Captain T.R. Barbour of the SS Carolina then gave the order to abandon ship. There were no casualties amongst the 217 passengers aboard the vessel, mostly citizens of Puerto Rico, including men from the Porto Rico Regiment of Infantry, when it was sunk.

The SS Carolina was a cargo ship when it was purchased in 1905, by Juan Ceballos, the owner of the Porto Rico Line, later renamed New York & Porto Rico Steamship Co..

The company, which operated from 1885 to 1949, had a regular service route from Puerto Rico, Porto Rico, to Cuba involving several cargo vessels in the transportation of sugar.

In 1899, the company converted the SS Carolina into a passenger ship, providing services between San Juan, Puerto Rico, Havana, Cuba, and New York City.

Among the Puerto Ricans who distinguished themselves in combat during World War I was Lieutenant Frederick Lois Riefkohl of the US Navy.

On August 2, 1917, <u>Riefkohl</u>, a native of the town of Maunabo, became the <u>first Puerto Rican to be awarded the Navy Cross</u>. The Navy Cross, which is the second highest medal after the Medal of Honor, that can be awarded by the U.S. Navy, was awarded to Lt. Riefkohl for his actions in an engagement with an enemy submarine.

<u>Lt. Riefkohl</u>, who was also the first Puerto Rican to graduate from the United States Naval Academy, served as a Rear Admiral in World War II.

CHAPTER 4

WW II The PR WACS

PFC Carmen García Rosado born October 29, 1926, and died 2016.

She was an educator, author, and activist for the rights of women veterans who was among the first 200 Puerto Rican women to be recruited into the WAC's during World War II.

Her book "LAS WACS-Participacion de la Mujer Boricua En la Segunda Guerra Mundial", The WACs-The participation of the Puerto Rican women in the Second World War, is the first book to document the experiences of the first 200 Puerto Rican women who participated in said conflict as members of the armed forces of the United States.

García Rosado was the seventh of nine siblings born in Humacao, Puerto Rico to Jesus García Doble and Maria Rosado Arce de García. Her father was the foremen of a sugar plantation who would often be assigned to work in Cuba and the Dominican Republic.

Consequently, he will inspire his children the desire to travel and see the world beyond Puerto Rico.

She received her primary and secondary education in the towns of Las Piedras and Caguas. She continued her education in Santurce and graduated from Santurce Central High School.

In 1944, at the age of 18, she earned her teachers diploma from the University of Puerto Rico and worked in her profession in the mountainous areas between the towns of Las Piedras and Humacao.

On September 17, 1944, "El Mundo", a local newspaper, announced that the United States were seeking women volunteers for the Women's Army Auxiliary Corps, WAC's.

By this time the United States had entered World War II and needed to boost its military capabilities....

As a result, the Army ordered Puerto Rico's 65th Infantry Regiment to full war strength and drafted many Puerto Ricans even those whose knowledge of English was minimal.

The Army recognized the need for bilingual personnel to fill in the clerical positions left empty by the male soldiers who were sent to the front lines.

In 1944, the Army sent three WAC, Women's Army Corps, recruiters to Puerto Rico to organize a unit of 200 WACs. There were over 1,500 women that responded to the call and applied for different positions. Guess what, only 200 were selected, among them, against her parents' wishes, was García Rosado.

After being sworn in during the ceremonies held in San Juan, García Rosado and the other 199 women were sent to Fort Oglethorpe, Georgia for their basic training.

The women were tested for their abilities and were given further training. Their duties varied, some were assigned as dental assistants, others as clerks and so on.

García Rosado was assigned to the position of dental assistant. The women were assigned to Company 6, 2nd Battalion, 21st Regiment of the Women's Army Auxiliary Corps, a segregated Hispanic unit.

Upon the completion of their training, they were sent to the port of embarkation of New York City.

According to García Rosado, one of the hardships which the women were subject to be the social and racial discrimination against the Latino community which at the time was widespread in the United States.

The American participation in the Second World War came to an end in Europe on May 8, 1945, when the western Allies celebrated "V-E Day", Victory in Europe Day, upon Germany's surrender.

In the Asian theater on August 14, 1945 "V-J Day", Victory over Japan Day, when the Japanese surrendered by signing the Japanese Instrument of Surrender.

The women of Company 6, 2nd Battalion, 21st Regiment of the Women's Army Auxiliary Corps returned to Puerto Rico on January 6, 1946, where Garcia Rosado and the others were Honorably Discharged from the military.

After the war, Garcia Rosado, like so many other women in the military, returned to civilian life.

From 1946 to 1948, García Rosado continued in her profession as a teacher, during which time she earned her Bachelor of Arts degree from the Interamerican University, then known as the Polytechnic Institute at San German, Puerto Rico.

She traveled through various states of the U.S. to work on her thesis, titled "Career Education," and worked on her doctorate in supervision and administration in education.

García Rosado retired in 1979 but continued to work at Ana G. Mendez's Puerto Rico Institute Jr. College and later as the Resident Director of the "Señoritas de la Universidad del Sagrado Corazon", University of the Sacred Heart.

In 1989, she was named consultant to the Director of Veterans Affairs in Puerto Rico. In her position she became an activist and worked for the rights of the Puerto Rican women veterans.

CHAPTER 5

Korean War

About 61,000 Puerto Ricans served in the Korean War, including about 18,000 who enlisted in the continental United States.

The Puerto Ricans distinguished themselves as part of the 65th Infantry Division, the "Borinqueneers," receiving many awards and recognition, though they were involved in the largest court-martial of the Korean War.

The term "Borinqueneers" is a combination from "Borinquen," the Taino name for Puerto Rico, and "Buccaneers."

According to history reports, the 65th's soldiers fought off many attacks by the Chinese in Korea, even though they lacked warm clothing during harsh winters.

In December 1950, the Marines found themselves at the Chosin Reservoir area, and in June 1951, the 65th was able to help the Marines withdraw from the Hauack-on Reservoir.

CMS Juan Jose Pagan Rodriguez, my dad, told me that they were in Korea for almost a month before getting winter clothing.

When the Marines were encircled by the Chinese troops close to the Manchurian border, the 65th rushed to their defense. The 65th soldiers fought in many battles, such as Operation "Killer." They became the first regiment to cross the Han River.

The 65th were also instrumental in breaking the "Iron Triangle." They took part in the last recorded battalion-sized bayonet attack by the U.S. Army on Jan. 31, 1951. The assault took three days.

<u>Sgt. Ildelfonso "Pancho" Colon Jr.</u>, who has been the post and department commander of the American Legion in Cabo Rojo, Puerto Rico, off and on for 40 years, has spoken with many Puerto Rican veterans from various wars, some of them being 65th soldiers. That is where we are getting so much information about the different wars.

Sgt. Colon continues....

"All of the officers were in a bunker in a meeting when they took a direct hit from Chinese artillery. That ended that," he said. "There was no artillery, no air support. They couldn't dig in because the ground was all rock.

The Chinese had the higher ground. These guys all grew up with each other and trusted each other, and the Army brought in replacements they didn't know, who ordered them to take the hill that another unit had already lost."

The 65th's soldiers refused the order and were told they had to shave their mustaches off and told they could no longer eat their normal diet of rice and beans. They also had to wear signs that said, <u>"I am a coward."</u>

In December 1954, 162 Puerto Ricans of the 65th Infantry Regiment were arrested, 95 were court-martialed, and 91 were found guilty and sentenced to prison terms ranging from one to 18 years of hard labor.

It was the largest mass court-martial of the Korean War. Army Secretary Robert Stevens quickly remitted the sentences and granted clemency and pardons to all involved.

The 65th is credited with participation in nine campaigns, and its members have at least 10 Distinguished Service Cross awards, 256 Silver Stars and 596 Bronze Stars. More than 750 Puerto Ricans lost their lives in Korea.

Army <u>Pfc. Pedro Morales</u> said that after seven days of fighting at Jackson Heights, when his officers, team leaders and half of his team were dead, he didn't want to go back and continue to fight.

Operation Iraqi Freedom veteran <u>Marine Corps 1st Sgt. Ildefonso "Pancho" Colon Jr.</u> speaks about his military experience during an interview in Cabo Rojo, Puerto Rico, Aug. 12, 2016.

"They arrested me, sent me to California and put me in jail for six months," he said. "They divided us into groups and sentenced us. We had been waiting on backup, and the support just never came. That's why we didn't want to fight. It was like signing a death sentence."

The soldiers were given an honorable discharge, and in April 2016, President Barack Obama awarded them the Congressional Gold Medal.

"We waited all these years for this moment, Morales said. "It was so hard to really believe it was true. I couldn't sleep. It was such an honor to receive it. I'm so proud to have served my country. I would go back in the service and serve again and do it proudly."

During the Korean War, PFC. Fernando Luis Garcia also became the first Puerto Rican recipient of the Medal of Honor when he covered a grenade with his body, saving the lives of his fellow Marines.

CHAPTER 6

Vietnam War

Puerto Ricans in the Vietnam War

Commencing with World War I, Puerto Ricans and people of Puerto Rican descent have participated as members of the United States Armed Forces in every conflict in which the United States has been involved. Accordingly, thousands of Puerto Ricans served in the Armed Forces of the United States during the Vietnam War, also known as the Second Indochina War.

Hundreds of them died, either killed in action, KIA, or while prisoners of war, POW. The Vietnam War started as a Cold War and escalated into a military conflict that spread to Vietnam, Laos, and Cambodia from 1959 to April 30, 1975.

Puerto Ricans served in different positions throughout the military as commanders, fighter pilots and common foot soldiers.

Many of them distinguished themselves in combat and were awarded the highest honors conferred by the military. Five were awarded the Medal of Honor, the highest United States military decoration.

Six were awarded the Distinguished Service Cross, DSC, the second-highest military decoration of the United States Army. Three received the Navy Cross, the second-highest medal that can be awarded by the U.S. Navy. The Navy Cross is awarded to members of the U.S. Navy or U.S. Marine Corps for heroism or distinguished service.

At World War I, Puerto Ricans and people of Puerto Rican descent have participated as members of the United States Armed Forces in every conflict in which the United States has been involved.

One of the consequences of the Spanish American War was that Puerto Rico was annexed by the United States in accordance to the terms of the Treaty of Paris of 1898, ratified on December 10, 1898.

Puerto Ricans became U.S. citizens because of the 1917 Jones–Shafroth Act. The timing of the Jones Act was intentional. It enabled the United States to forcibly conscript Puerto Ricans into the U.S. military, and rapidly deploy them to the trenches of the European front.

Puerto Ricans who resided in the island were immediately assigned to the "Porto Rico Provisional Regiment of Infantry," organized on June 30, 1901, and served in World War I.

Those who resided in the mainland United States served in regular units of one of the United States militaries: the United States Marine Corps, Army, or the Navy.

The Porto Rico Regiment was renamed the 65th Infantry Regiment under the Reorganization Act of June 4, 1920 and went on to serve in World War II and the Korean War, as the only segregated Army unit, where its members distinguished themselves in combat.

On July 25, 1952, the Constitution of Puerto Rico was proclaimed by Gov. Luis Muñoz Marín and the island, which continues to be an unincorporated territory of the United States, adopted the name of Estado Libre Asociado, "Free Associated State".

Despite this "free association," the Puerto Rican government and military remained under complete U.S. jurisdiction.

The 65th Infantry was deactivated in 1956, however the Department of the Army was persuaded to transfer the 65th Infantry from the regular Army to the Puerto Rico National Guard.

Since then, Puerto Ricans have served in regular integrated units of the military.

The Vietnam War was fought between communist North Vietnam, supported by its communist allies, and the government of South Vietnam, supported by the United States and other nations.

The United States entered the war to prevent a communist takeover of South Vietnam as part of their wider strategy of containment. Military advisors arrived beginning in 1950.

U.S. involvement escalated in the early 1960s and combat units were deployed beginning in 1965. Involvement peaked in 1968 at the time of the Tet Offensive.

During the Vietnam War, an estimated 48,000 Puerto Ricans served in the four branches of the armed forces.

Amongst the highest-ranking Puerto Ricans who served in the United States Navy and had distinguished military careers were Admiral Horacio Rivero, Jr. and Vice Admiral Diego E. Hernández.

Admiral Horacio Rivero, Jr.

Admiral Horacio Rivero, Jr., the first Puerto Rican four-star Admiral in the United States Navy, oversaw the day-to-day work of the Navy as the Vice Chief of Naval Operations. He was a stern supporter of a "brown-water navy," or riverine force, on the rivers of South Vietnam.

Lieutenant Diego E. Hernández, who retired from the Navy with the rank of Vice Admiral, flew two combat tours in Vietnam during the war. He also served as Aide and Flag Lieutenant to Commander, Carrier Division 14.

At sea, he was the commander of a fighter squadron, a carrier air wing, and a fleet oiler, the USS Truckee. Hernández later became the first Hispanic to be named Vice Commander, North American Aerospace Defense Command, NORAD.

Among the Puerto Ricans who served in the United States Air Force and had distinguished military careers were Major General Salvador E. Felices, Brigadier General Antonio Maldonado, Brigadier General Antonio J. Ramos, Brigadier General José M. Portela, Brigadier General Ruben A. Cubero and Colonel Héctor Andrés Negroni.

Major General Salvador E. Felices held various positions within the military.

In June 1968, he was named commander of the 306th Bombardment Wing. He flew 39 combat bombing missions over North Vietnam during the Vietnam War in a B-52 aircraft.

In 1969, he became the commander of the 823rd Air Division which covered the regions of Florida, Puerto Rico, North Carolina, and Georgia.

On May 1970, Felices was named Assistant Deputy Chief of Staff at the Headquarters of Strategic Air Command, SAC. He was responsible for SAC's intercontinental ballistic missile, ICBM, operational testing programs."

Brigadier General Antonio Maldonado, who in 1967 became the youngest pilot and Aircraft Commander of a B-52 Stratofortress nuclear bomber, was assigned in January 1971 to the 432nd Tactical Fighter Reconnaissance Wing, Udon Royal Thai Air Force Base in Thailand. His active participation in the war included 183 air combat missions over North and South Vietnam, Laos and Cambodia, logging more than 400 combat flying hours in the F-4C Phantom.

Brigadier General Antonio J. Ramos, the first Hispanic to serve as commander, Air Force Security Assistance Center, Air Force Materiel Command, and dual-hatted as Assistant to the Commander for International Affairs, Headquarters Air Force Materiel Command, also served in Vietnam.

In November 1971, Ramos, who was then a lieutenant, was assigned to the 310th Tactical Airlift Squadron, Phan Rang Air Base and Tan Son Nhut Air Base, South Vietnam.

In August 1972, was transferred to U-Tapao Royal Thai Naval Airfield in Thailand where he was the Base Operations Officer until November 1972.

Brigadier General José M. Portela, as a first lieutenant, was sent to the Republic of Vietnam during the war and participated in numerous combat missions.

On June 8, 1972, he was promoted to captain and on September 1972, was reassigned to the 3rd Military Airlift Squadron at Charleston Air Force Base, South Carolina as a C-5 pilot. During his stint there he was assigned to the C-141s and in 1972 became the youngest C-141 Starlifter aircraft commander and captain at the age of 22.

He served at CAF until July 1973, when he joined the Air Force Reserve as a C-5A Initial Cadre at the 312th Airlift Squadron at Travis Air Force Base in California.

Brigadier General Ruben A. Cubero was a captain when sent to the Republic of Vietnam on May 1969. He was assigned to the 1st Brigade, 25th Infantry Division, 19th Tactical Air Support Squadron, Tay Ninh West, where he flew an OV-10 and served as a forward air controller.

In November 1969, he was reassigned to the 19th Tactical Air Support Squadron, at Bien Hoa Air Base. Cubero later became the first Hispanic graduate of the United States Air Force Academy, to be named Dean of the Faculty of the academy.

Colonel Héctor Andrés Negroni, the first Puerto Rican graduate of the United States Air Force Academy, was a captain when he participated in combat missions during the war and accumulated over 600 combat hours. During his tour he served in the 553rd Reconnaissance Squadron stationed in Korat, Thailand and as Chief of Combat Operation in the 7th Airborne Command and Control Squadron in Udon, Thailand.

The Medal of Honor

Five Puerto Ricans were awarded the Medal of Honor, the highest United States military decoration for heroism. They were Captain Humbert Roque Versace, Captain Eurípides Rubio, PFC Carlos James Lozada, Specialist Four Hector Santiago-Colon, and Staff Sergeant Felix M. Conde-Falcon. All five were members of the United States Army and their awards were posthumous.

Captain Humbert Roque "Rocky" Versace

Captain Humbert Roque "Rocky" Versace was a United States Army officer of Puerto Rican–Italian descent began his first tour of duty in the Republic of Vietnam as an intelligence advisor.

Versace was captured during his second tour and taken to a prison deep in the jungle along with two other Americans, Lieutenant Nick Rowe, and Sergeant Dan Pitzer.

He tried to escape four times but failed in his attempts. The Viet Cong separated Versace from the other prisoners. The last time the prisoners heard his voice, he was loudly singing "God Bless America".

On September 26, 1965, North Vietnam's "Liberation Radio" announced the execution of Captain Humbert Roque Versace. Versace's remains have never been recovered.

On July 8, 2002, in a ceremony in the White House East Room, Versace was posthumously awarded the Medal of Honor by President George W. Bush for his heroism, the first time an Army POW had been awarded the nation's highest honor for actions in captivity.

Captain Eurípides Rubio was a member of H&H Co., 1st Battalion, 28th Infantry, 1st Infantry Division, RVN.

On November 8, 1966, Rubio's company came under attack from the North Vietnamese Army, leaving the safety of his post, Rubio received two serious wounds as he braved the intense enemy fire to distribute ammunition, re-establish positions and render aid to the wounded.

Despite his pain, he assumed command when a rifle company commander was medically evacuated. He was then wounded a third time as he tried to move amongst his men to encourage them to fight with renewed effort.

While aiding the evacuation of wounded personnel, he noted that a U.S. smoke grenade, which was intended to mark the Viet Cong's position for an air strike, had fallen dangerously close to friendly lines. He ran to move the grenade but was immediately struck to his knees by enemy fire.

Despite his wounds, Rubio managed to collect the grenade and run through enemy fire to within 20 meters of the enemy position and throw the by-then already smoking grenade into the enemy before he fell for the final time. Using the now-repositioned grenade as a marker, friendly air strikes were directed to destroy the hostile positions.

PFC Carlos James Lozada

PFC Carlos James Lozada was assigned to Co. A 2nd Battalion, 503 Infantry, 173rd Airborne Brigade. On November 20, 1967, at Dak To, Lozada spotted a North Vietnamese Army company rapidly approaching his outpost.

He alerted his comrades and opened fire with a machine gun, killing at least twenty enemy soldiers and disrupting their initial attack.

He realized that if he abandoned his position there would be nothing to hold back the surging North Vietnamese soldiers and that his entire company withdrawal would be jeopardized, as a result he told his comrades to move to the back and that he would supply cover for them.

Lozada continued to deliver a heavy and accurate volume of suppressive fire against the enemy until he was mortally wounded and had to be carried during the withdrawal.

Specialist Four Héctor Santiago-Colón, on June 28, 1968, members of Santiago-Colon's Company B of the 5th Battalion, 7th Cavalry, 1st Cavalry Division were engaged in combat at Quảng Trị Province.

An enemy, North Vietnamese, soldier lobbed a hand grenade into Santiago-Colon's foxhole. Realizing that there was no time to throw out the grenade, he tucked it in to his stomach and turning away from his comrades, absorbed the full impact of the blast, sacrificing his life to save his fellow soldiers from certain death.

Staff Sergeant Felix M. Conde-Falcon was awarded the Medal of Honor posthumously in a special ceremony held in the White House on March 18, 2014, for his courageous actions while serving as an acting Platoon Leader in Company D, 1st Battalion, 505th Infantry Regiment, 3d Brigade, 82d Airborne Division during combat operations against an armed enemy in Ap Tan Hoa, Republic of Vietnam on April 4, 1969.

Further information: List of Puerto Rican recipients of the Medal of Honor.

The Navy Cross

Three Puerto Ricans were awarded the Navy Cross, the second highest medal that can be awarded by the U.S. Navy and are awarded to members of the U.S. Navy or U.S. Marine Corps for heroism or distinguished service. They were Sergeant Angel Mendez and Corporal Miguel Rivera-Sotomayor. Both men were members of the United States Marine Corps.

Sgt. Angel Mendez

Corporal Angel Mendez, 1946–1967, was among the many men who volunteered to join the Marine Corps right after graduating from high school. He was assigned to Company F, 2nd Battalion, 7th Marines, 1st Marine Division on March 16, 1967, and conducting a search and destroy mission with his company when his company came under attack from a Viet Cong battalion.

Half of a platoon was pinned down under enemy fire and Mendez, volunteered to lead a squad to assist the pinned-down Marines in returning to friendly lines with their two dead and two seriously wounded.

Mendez exposed himself and opened fire on the enemy. His platoon commander, Lieutenant Ronald D. Castille was seriously wounded, and he fell, unable to move.

Mendez shielded him with his body as he applied a dressing to the wound; he picked up the Lieutenant and started to carry him to friendly lines, which were more than seventy-five meters away.

Mendez was hit in the shoulder, yet he chose to act as rear man, and he continued to shield his lieutenant with his own body until he was mortally wounded. Mendez was posthumously awarded the Navy Cross and promoted to sergeant.

For saving the life of his platoon commander, Lieutenant Castille, (now one of the seven justices of the Supreme Court of Pennsylvania U.S. Senator Charles Schumer recommended in 2003 that Mendez' award be upgraded to Medal of Honor.

Corporal José L. Rivera, born in Ciales, Puerto Rico. His parents moved from Puerto Rico to the United States and settled in Waukegan, Illinois.

He was a member of the United States Marine Corps and belonged to Company L, Third Battalion, 5th Marines, 1st Marine Division, Reinforced, Fleet Marine Force.

When the enemy forces threw a grenade at his position, he covered it with his helmet and smothered the explosion with his own body, thereby saving the lives of his comrades.

Corporal Miguel Rivera-Sotomayor, born in Philadelphia, Pa. to Puerto Rican parents, belonged to Company F, 2nd Battalion, 9th Marines, 3rd Marine Division.

Rivera-Sotomayor silenced enemy machine guns and allowed his platoon to move from its pinned down position to establish an effective base of fire against the enemy.

The Distinguished Service Cross

Seven Puerto Ricans were awarded the Distinguished Service Cross. The second highest military decoration of the United States Army. Actions which merit the Distinguished Service Cross must be of such a high degree to be above those required for all other U.S. combat decorations but not meeting the criteria for the Medal of Honor.

They were Sergeant Eddie Edwin Chervony, Staff Sergeant Efraín Figueroa-Meléndez, Spc4 Fruto James Oquendo, Sergeant First Class Wilfredo Pagan-Lozada, First Sergeant Ramiro Ramirez and Private First-Class Reinaldo Rodriguez. Five of the awards were posthumous.

Sergeant Eddie E Chervony, died May 5, 1968, was born in Hormigueros, Puerto Rico.

He was a member of Alpha Battery, 1st Battalion, 77th Field Artillery, 1st Cavalry Division.

On separate trips, he evacuated five seriously wounded across one hundred meters of open terrain to a place of safety. When carrying a sixth man to the friendly lines he was cut off by enemy force and was attacked with grenades and satchel charges.

While protecting his wounded companion from the satchel charge by covering him with his own body, he received a mortal wound.

Staff Sergeant Efraín Figueroa-Meléndez, died March 5, 1969, was born in Cataño, Puerto Rico. He was a member of Company D, 3d Battalion, 8th Infantry Regiment, 4th Infantry Division.

On three occasions Staff Sergeant Figueroa-Meléndez purposely drew communist volleys on himself to permit his men to draw back to protected positions.

Spc4 Fruto James Oquendo, died May 6, 1969, of Puerto Rican descent, was born in New York City. Oquendo was a member of the US Army and in Vietnam served with Company C, 2d Battalion, 8th Cavalry Regiment, 1st Brigade of the 1st Cavalry Division. He was mortally wounded while defending his area during a hand-to-hand struggle.

Sergeant First Class Wilfredo Pagan-Lozada, died February 9, 1967, born in New York City to Puerto Rican parents, Pagan-Lozada was a member of the US Army and served in Vietnam with Company D, 2d Battalion, 5th Cavalry Regiment, 1st Cavalry Division.

At the cost of his life, Sgt. Pagan-Lozada, charged into a through a hail of bullets to save an officer's life.

First Sergeant Ramiro Ramirez was a member of Company C, 1st Battalion, 18th Infantry Regiment, 2d Brigade, 1st Infantry Division.

First Sergeant Ramirez despite being wounded pulled one of his men to the safety of a bomb crater and refused aid until all others had been treated. Receiving word that another man had been severely wounded; Sergeant Ramirez volunteered to rescue him and was hit in the arm and chest as he left the crater.

Private First-Class Reinaldo Rodríguez, died January 15, 1971, was born in Guanica, Puerto Rico. He belonged to Company C, 1st Battalion, 27th Infantry Regiment, 2d Brigade, 25th Infantry Division. Private Rodriguez provided cover fire for his comrades maintaining suppressive fire upon the adversary until he was wounded a third time.

Although evacuated immediately to the rear medical facilities, Private Rodriguez succumbed to his wounds.

Corporal Aristides Sosa, died March 2, 1968, was born in Puerto Rico. His parents moved to New York City in 1947 when he was one year old.

In 1967, he received a draft notice while attending Baruch College of Business Administration. He was drafted into the Army via the Selective Service system during the Vietnam War.

He served in Company A, 65th Engineer Battalion, 25th Infantry Division in the U.S. Army. On March 2, 1968, Corporal Sosa rolled on top of a grenade to save another soldier from its blast and was mortally wounded by the exploding grenade.

The Most Decorated Soldier
Sergeant First Class Jorge Otero Barreto

Sergeant First Class Jorge Otero Barreto was born in the town of Vega Baja, Puerto Rico, t the son of Eloy Otero-Bruno and Crispina Barreto-Torres.

His father named him "Jorge", Spanish for George, after George Washington whom Otero-Bruno admired. In Vega Baja, Otero Barreto received his primary and secondary education. He attended college for three years, studying biology until 1959 when he joined the U.S. Army, which he chose over medical school in Spain.

After his basic training, he continued to train with the 101st Airborne Division in Fort Campbell, Kentucky, graduating in 1960.

In 1961 to 1970, Otero Barreto served five tours in Southeast Asia, starting as an advisor who helped train Vietnamese troops.

According to the documentary "Brave Lords", Otero Barreto served in various military units during his military career. He served in the 101st Airborne Division and the 25th Infantry Division "Tropic Lightning".

He also served in the 82nd Airborne Division, an active airborne infantry division of the United States Army specializing in parachute landing operations and in the 173rd Airborne Brigade Combat Team.

He participated in 200 combat missions. Otero Barreto was wounded five times in combat and was awarded 38 military decorations.

Among his many decorations are 2 Silver Stars, 5 Bronze Stars with Valor, 4 Army Commendation Medals, 5 Purple Hearts and 5 Air Medals, one each for every 5th mission which involved a helicopter.

He was referred to as Puerto Rican Rambo or Sergeant Rock. Otero Barreto has been called "the most decorated Puerto Rican veteran," and the news media and various organizations have called him "the most decorated soldier in the Vietnam War."

However, NBC News said that Robert L. Howard may have been the most highly decorated American soldier of the modern era, [while KWTX-TV states that he was "said to be the most decorated service member in the history of the United States".

John Plaster in his 1998 book SOG: The Secret Wars of America's Commandos in Vietnam states that Howard "remains to this day the most highly decorated American soldier."

Otero Barreto was highly decorated during Vietnam and is possibly the most decorated Puerto Rican Vietnam War veteran living today.

Platoon Sergeant Jorge Otero-Barreto, ASN: RA-50156967, United States Army, was awarded the Silver Star for conspicuous gallantry and intrepidity in action against the enemy while serving with Company A, 1st Battalion, Airborne, 502d Infantry Regiment, 101st Air Cavalry Division, in the Republic of Vietnam.

His gallant actions and dedicated devotion to duty, without regard for his own life, were in keeping with the highest traditions of military service and reflect great credit upon himself, his unit, and the United States Army.

The President of the United States of America, authorized by Act of Congress July 9, 1918, amended by an act of July 25, 1963, takes pleasure in presenting a Bronze Oak Leaf Cluster in lieu of a Second Award of the Silver Star to Platoon Sergeant Jorge Otero-Barreto, ASN: RA-50156967, United States Army, for gallantry in action in the Republic of Vietnam on 1 May 1968.

Platoon Sergeant Otero distinguished himself while serving as a squad leader on a combat operation in the Republic of Vietnam. Company A, 1st Battalion, Airborne, 502d Infantry Regiment, 101st Air Cavalry Division, was occupying defensive positions around a village north of Hue, Republic of Vietnam.

The village was occupied by elements of the 8th Battalion, 90th North Vietnamese Army Regiment and had defied all offensive attempts for two days. Because of clear weather, the enemy had been subject to constant air strikes and artillery.

At 0415 hours, the enemy began a series of human wave attacks against Company A in a desperate attempt to break out of the village. After the human wave assaults had twice been driven back and fifty-eight enemy lay dead, the enemy forces withdrew into the village for their final stand.

The first platoon led Company A into the village to destroy the remainder of the North Vietnamese Army forces and Sergeant Otero was the leader of the point element of the first platoon.

Suddenly the point came under fire from rocket propelled grenades, machine guns, and small arms firing from enemy bunkers and spider holes. With complete disregard for his own safety, Platoon Sergeant Otero immediately assaulted the nearest machine gun emplacement and killed all three of its crew members.

He then led his squad through enemy fire in assaulting three more enemy positions, overrunning them and killing or incapacitating all the enemy.

Platoon Sergeant Otero swiftly moved his squad to occupy vacated enemy positions and place effective fire on the remaining enemy so that other Company A platoons could maneuver.

Platoon Sergeant Otero's extraordinary heroism in close combat against a numerically superior force was in keeping with the highest traditions of the military service and reflect great credit upon himself, his unit, and the United States Army.

On 22 June 2012, Otero Barreto was the keynote speaker at a Vietnam Veterans Memorial Dinner in Lorain, Ohio.

On 1 September 2006, the Coalición Nacional Puertorriqueña, National Puerto Rican Coalition, honored Otero Barreto with a "Lifetime Achievement Award" in a Conference held at the Hotel Hilton of Chicago. The keynote speaker was U.S. Congressman Luis Gutierrez.

A transitional home for veterans in Springfield, Massachusetts, the SFC Jorge Otero-Barreto Homeless Veterans Transitional Home, was also named after Otero Barreto.

The home is managed by the Vietnam Veterans of America Chapter #866 in Springfield, Massachusetts. The home is part of a program named the "Jorge Otero Barreto Homeless Veterans Transitional Program" which houses twelve veterans.

The program offers counseling, DVA services from the Western Massachusetts Bilingual Veterans Outreach Center, assistance in obtaining Chapter 115 financial assistance, AA/NA meetings, and Christian Rehabilitation Substance Abuse meetings.

The town of Vega Baja dedicated its military museum to Otero Barreto and named it the "Jorge Otero Barreto Museum."

On 2 October 2011, Otero Barreto was named Vegabajeño del Año En Civismo, Civic Citizen of Year of Vega Baja.

Otero Barreto was featured in the documentary film Brave Lords, a perspective on the war in Vietnam, as experienced by Puerto Rican soldiers.

In June 2016, Lieutenant General Joseph Anderson presented the "Distinguished Member of the 502nd Infantry Regiment" award to Otero Barreto, honoring him for his valor in the Vietnam War. Otero Barreto's name is one of those displayed on a wall of honor at Fort Campbell in Kentucky

During the Vietnam War, it is estimated that 48,000 Puerto Ricans served in the four branches of the armed forces.

There is a total of 345 Puerto Ricans who died in combat. There were 18 listed as MIA's. They were all members of the Army with the exceptions of First Lieutenant Jose Hector Ortiz who was the only Puerto Rican MIA member of the United States Air Force and PFC Jose R. Sanchez who was a member of the United States Marine Corps.

Of the 18 Puerto Rican MIA's, PFC. Humberto Acosta-Rosario is the only one whose body has never been recovered and is currently still listed as Missing in Action.

Friendly forces captured documents from the Vietnam People's Army 7th Infantry Division dated August 23, 1968. The documents were analyzed by US intelligence agencies.

The reports documented that Humberto Acosta-Rosario was in fact captured by NVA forces during the battle near the Ben Cui Rubber Plantation.

However, the US military chose not to upgrade his status to Prisoner of War…..

It's been 56 years since the ground campaign of the Vietnam War began. It was a conflict that would go slowly on for a decade. It took thousands of lives. It changed America's mentality about war.

Following the 1964 Gulf of Tonkin incident, the U.S. increased its military presence in South Vietnam. The first U.S. regular combat units arrived in Vietnam on March 8, 1965.

When the conflict ended 10 years later, 58,220 of the 3 million Americans involved had lost their lives. The weary troops who returned faced a largely unwelcome homecoming.

American flag reflected in Vietnam Veterans Memorial wall.

When they came back, there was a lot of anger about the war. Some veterans were seen arguing on in airports.

Humberto Acosta-Rosario, a Puerto Rican soldier, whose body has never been recovered and is currently still listed as Missing in Action.

Friendly forces captured documents from the Vietnam People's Army 7th Infantry Division dated August 23, 1968. The documents were analyzed by US intelligence agencies. The reports documented that

Humberto Acosta-Rosario was in fact captured by NVA forces during the battle near the Ben Cui Rubber Plantation.

However, the US military chose not to upgrade his status to Prisoner of War.

In 1979, the Vietnam Wall was built. It's commonly known, as a tribute to the war's veterans, who consider it a tangible symbol that the American people recognized and honored for their service.

More than 340 Puerto Ricans died in combat, and 17 were listed as missing in action.

Army Sgt. Jorge Zambrana has post-traumatic stress disorder from his two tours in Vietnam. He remembers picking up service members killed or wounded in action and taking them and their belongings to the South Vietnamese capital of Saigon. He also had to work at a cemetery.

He said he did face some racism during his time in Vietnam, but he would just work harder to prove himself. "I would tell my friends to follow the rules," he said. "We couldn't shine our boots because we were in the mud. We didn't have time for inspections."

He said he didn't care what race someone was, and that in Vietnam, soldiers learned whatever job was needed. "If the guy got killed, who else was going to do it? Wherever they needed you, forget about your specialty. Your job was whatever," he said.

Zambrana said he's proud of his service and would do it all over again. "Even though I'm 65, I'm pretty healthy," he said. "I could still handle an M50 or M60. I'm still willing to fight for my freedom. Those of us who served in Vietnam served with honor."

Missing in Action

A total of 18 Puerto Ricans were listed as Missing in Action (MIA). This number does not include those who resided in the United States mainland, only those who resided in Puerto Rico.

They were all members of the Army with the exceptions of First Lieutenant Jose Hector Ortiz who was a member of the United States Air Force and PFC. Jose Ramon Sanchez a U.S. Marine. PFC. Humberto Acosta-Rosario is the only one whose body has never been recovered and is currently still listed as MIA.

PFC Humberto Acosta-Rosario

PFC Humberto Acosta-Rosario was born and raised in the city of Mayagüez, Puerto Rico, which is in the western coast of Puerto Rico. He joined the Army after graduating from high school. He was a member of Company B, 1st Battalion, 5th Infantry, Mechanized, 25th Infantry Division, United States Army.

On August 22, 1968, Acosta-Rosario accompanied some members of his unit during a reconnaissance mission. His unit was attacked by North Vietnamese Army, NVA, regulars in the vicinity of Bến Củi Rubber Plantation, east of Tay Ninh City, Tay Ninh Province. His unit, Company B, was forced to withdraw from the battlefield under heavy enemy attack.

The unit regrouped and discovered that PFC Acosta-Rosario and another machine gunner, PFC Philip T. DeLorenzo, Jr., were missing. Acosta-Rosario's platoon sergeant stated that he believed PFC Acosta-Rosario had been hit by enemy fire prior to the unit's withdrawal.

The NVA forces were driven back after artillery fire and helicopter gunships were called in and Company B returned to its original position.

An extensive ground search was conducted by members of Company B for the two missing soldiers. The only body recovered was that of PFC DeLorenzo's, along with the two M60 machine guns.

A search by two battalions who were brought in to sweep the area of only enemy activity did not produce Acosta-Rosario's body and he was officially listed as Missing in Action.

Friendly forces captured documents from the NVA 7th Infantry Division dated August 23, 1968. The documents were analyzed by U.S. intelligence agencies.

The reports documented that Humberto Acosta-Rosario was in fact captured by NVA forces during the battle near the Ben Cui Rubber Plantation. However, the U.S. military chose not to upgrade his status to Prisoner of War.

Acosta-Rosario's name was listed in the United States Government's "Last Known Alive" list. This list, which was released by the U.S. Government in April 1991, includes missing Americans whom the U.S. believed might have survived their initial loss incident.

In March 1978, Acosta-Rosario was declared dead/body not recovered based on a presumptive finding of death.

Acosta-Rosario was posthumously promoted to the rank of Staff Sergeant. His name is on panel 47W, line 030 of the Vietnam Memorial Wall in Washington, D.C. and he is also list in El Monumento de la Recordación located in San Juan, Puerto Rico. There is a headstone with his name inscribed Plot: MB 0 6 of the Puerto Rico National Cemetery in Bayamón, Puerto Rico.

PFC Jose Ramon Sanchez

PFC. Jose Ramon Sanchez born in Brooklyn, NY was assigned to Company D, 1st Battalion, 4th Marines, 3rd Marine Division. On June 6, 1968, he was among a group of fellow Marines who comprised a patrol operating in the rugged jungle covered mountains southwest of Khe Sanh, Quảng Trị Province, South Vietnam.

Their mission was to block NVA troops and supplies from infiltrating toward Khe Sanh. The Marines engaged a communist force of unknown size in heavy combat. As the fierce firefight raged around them, the Marines, who were outnumbered and rapidly running low on ammunition, requested an emergency extraction.

A CH46A Sea Knight helicopter was sent for Sanchez and the rest of the patrol who were on Hill 672. As the helicopter gained altitude, it was immediately struck by intense and accurate enemy ground fire causing it to enter a nose-low attitude and crash onto an east/west mountain ridgeline, roll down to the bottom of the hill and burst into flames.

Within an hour and a half, a search and recovery, SAR, team was inserted into the crash site. The team members pulled the charred bodies of the aircrew and passengers from what was left of the burned-out helicopter and placed them in body bags.

Of the 12 of the 23 Marines aboard who were killed, 4 were reported as MIA/KIA, besides Sanchez the other three were L/Cpl. LaPlant, L/Cpl. Palacios, and L/Cpl. Harper. Various attempts to recover the bodies of the four were made to no avail.

In 2006, a team began excavating the site and recovered human remains and non-biological material evidence including La Plant's identification tag. While at the site, a Vietnamese citizen turned over to the team human remains that he claimed to have found amid the wreckage.

In 2007, another team completed the excavation and recovered additional human remains, life support material and aircraft wreckage.

On November 5, 2008, The Department of Defense POW/ Missing Personnel Office, DPMO announced that the remains of four U.S. servicemen, including Sanchez, were identified. The remains of the four men share a single casket along with a box engraved with their names which was buried with full military honors at Arlington National Cemetery.

On April 23, 1975, President Gerald Ford gave a televised speech declaring an end to the Vietnam War. During the Vietnam War, an estimated 48,000 Puerto Ricans served in the four branches of the armed forces.

Some sources state that a total of 345 Puerto Ricans who resided in the island died in combat, however according to a report by the Department of Defense, titled "Number of Puerto Ricans serving in the U.S. Armed Forces during National Emergencies" the total number of Puerto Ricans who died was 455 and that were wounded was 3,775.

Because of lack of separate documentation, the total number of Puerto Ricans who lived in the mainland United States and died is unknown.

At the time, Puerto Ricans were not tabulated separately, but were generally included in the general white population census count. Separate statistics were kept for African Americans and Asian Americans.

The names of those who died are inscribed in both the Vietnam Veterans Memorial located in Washington, D.C. and in El Monumento de la Recordación, The Wall of Remembrance, located in San Juan, Puerto Rico.

According to a study made by the Department of Epidemiology and Public Health and the Department of Psychiatry, Yale University, Puerto Rican Vietnam veterans, have a higher risk for posttraumatic stress disorder, PTSD, and experience more severe PTSD symptoms than non-Hispanic white Vietnam veterans.

However, despite the hardships suffered by the experiences of war, many went on to live normal everyday lives.

Among the Puerto Ricans who served in Vietnam and held important presidential administrative positions in the Administration of President George W. Bush were <u>Major General William A. Navas</u> Jr., who was awarded the Bronze Star Medal and was named Assistant Secretary of the Navy on June 6, 2001, and <u>Dr. Richard Carmon</u>a, a former Green Beret who was awarded two Purple Hearts and was appointed Surgeon General in March 2002.

CHAPTER 7

Gulf, Iraq, Afghanistan Wars

In 1990, about 1,700 Puerto Rican National Guardsmen were among the 20,000 Hispanics deployed to the Persian Gulf in Operations Desert Shield and Desert Storm as part of the Gulf War.

In the military campaigns in Iraq and Afghanistan, three Puerto Rican women, <u>Army SPC Frances M. Vega</u>, <u>Army SPC Lizbeth Robles</u> and <u>Army SPC Ramirez Gonzalez</u> were among U.S. service members killed.

<u>SPC Lizbeth Robles</u>

In the 21st century, Puerto Ricans have participated in the military campaigns of Afghanistan and Iraq, in what the United States and its allies refer to as the War on Terror.

Among those killed in Iraq are the first three Puerto Rican women to die in a foreign combat zone. They are SPC Frances M. Vega, SPC Lizbeth Robles and SPC Aleina Ramirez Gonzalez.

On November 2, 2003, SPC Frances M. Vega became the first female Puerto Rican soldier born in the United States to die in a war zone. A ground-to-air missile fired by insurgents in Fallujah hit the Chinook transport helicopter Vega was in; she was one of 16 soldiers who lost their lives in the crash that followed.

On March 1, 2005, SPC Lizbeth Robles became the first female Puerto Rican soldier born on the island to die in Iraq when her Humvee was involved in an accident.

On July 10, 2007, Captain María Inés Ortiz, who was assigned to a hospital in an area known as the "Green Zone" in Baghdad, Iraq, became the first Puerto Rican nurse to die in combat and the first Army nurse to die in the Iraq War after the area came under a heavy mortar attack.

SPC Hilda I. Ortiz Clayton, who was of Puerto Rican descent, was a U.S. Army combat photographer killed in 2013 when a mortar exploded during an Afghan training exercise. She was able to photograph the explosion that killed her and four Afghan soldiers.

The 55th Signal Company named their annual competitive award for combat camera work "The SPC Hilda I. Clayton Best Combat Camera, COMCAM, Competition" in her honor.

On Nov. 2, 2003, Vega became the first female Puerto Rican soldier born in the United States to die in a war zone when a ground-to-air missile fired by insurgents in Fallujah, Iraq, hit the Chinook transport helicopter Vega was in. She was one of 16 soldiers who lost their lives in the crash that followed.

Marine Corps Sgt. Alexander Munoz, who was in the second push in Fallujah, Iraq, in 2004, was part of the team that assisted wounded Marine 1st Bradley Kasal out of Fallujah's famous "House of Hell."

"It was pretty rough," he said. "The Marines were trapped inside the house. We were trying to figure out how we were going to get them out." He said his squad was tight knit, which made it harder when he saw his fellow Marines get hit. His PTSD stems from that and from having the enemy combatants constantly trying to kill him, he said.

"At Hell House, the house crumbled, and the guy still threw a grenade to kill us," he said. "They just wanted to destroy us."

Munoz said he's proud to have served, and to be Puerto Rican.

"A lot of my friends stay in the states and come to visit me," he said. "They don't even know where Puerto Rico is. Come on man; we've been with you guys since 1898.

We're proud, and we know how to serve. We know how to say thanks. We're part of the nation. You're my brothers. We're here to fight ."

Colon, who also served in Iraq and as a Marine drill instructor, said he is also proud to have served.

"Even though I was born and raised in New York, I came to Puerto Rico every summer and spoke Spanish at home," Colon said. "I'm super-proud of my heritage.

Like any soldier from Texas who loves his Texas flag and loves his state, Puerto Ricans, we love our flag, we love our state, we call it a state. I've wanted to be a soldier all my life. It's so motivational being around all these veterans. We're proud Americans. We love our country, but we love Puerto Rico, too."

As of 2010, the Veterans Affairs Department listed Puerto Rico's veterans at 116,029. More than 1,225 Puerto Ricans have died while serving for the United States.

The names of those who died in combat are inscribed in "El Monumento de la Recordación", the Monument of Remembrance, which was unveiled May 19, 1996, and is in front of the capital Building in San Juan, Puerto Rico.

CHAPTER 8

Remarkable Puerto Ricans Soldiers

The Puerto Rico movement was the American military sea and land operation on the island of Puerto Rico during the Spanish American War. The attack began on May 12, 1898, when the United States Navy attacked the capital, San Juan.

The war officially ended four months later, when the U.S. and Spanish governments signed the Treaty of Paris on December 10, 1898.

Apart from guaranteeing the independence of Cuba, the treaty also forced Spain to cede Guam and Puerto Rico to the United States.

Upon the outbreak of World War I, the U.S. Congress approved the Jones–Shafroth Act, which extended United States citizenship, the Puerto Rican House of Delegates rejected US citizenship, with limitations upon Puerto Ricans and made them eligible for the military draft.

As citizens of the United States, Puerto Ricans have participated in every major United States military engagement from World War I onward. The soldiers of Puerto Rico's 65th Infantry Regiment distinguishing themselves in combat during the Korean War.

There are currently some 330,000 veterans and some 35,000 Puerto Ricans in active-duty service. The Puerto Rico Army/Air National Guard and the Reserve components represent another 10,000 Puerto Ricans in uniform.

At least, more than 375,000 Puerto Ricans are veterans or are still wearing the uniform.

The following is a list of names from A thru Z of distinguished Puerto Rican men and women who served and some still serving in the ARMED FORCES.

A

Joseph M. Acaba, U.S. Marine Corps Reserve - Astronaut, scientist, and educator. He is the First Puerto Rican Astronaut.

Doris Acevedo, Major PRANG She was the commander of the Language Center

Sharon Acosta, PRANG FORMER Drill Sgt. At the Language Center

Johnny Albino, U.S. Army - bolero singer

Pedro Albizu Campos, U.S. Army - Politician. President and principal leader of the Puerto Rican Nationalist Party.

Carlos Albizu Miranda, U.S. Army - Psychologist, educator. First Hispanic Educator to have a North American University renamed in his honor and one of the first Hispanics to earn a Ph.D. in Psychology in the United States.

Roberto Angleró, U.S. Air Force - Music composer and singer.

B

Ray Barreto, U.S. Army - Percussionist, jazz, and salsa leader

Víctor Manuel Blanco, U.S. Army Air Force - astronomer.

In 1959, Blanco discovered "Blanco 1," a galactic cluster. He was the second Director of the Cerro Tololo Inter-American Observatory in Chile, which has the largest 4-m telescope in the Southern Hemisphere.

In 1995, the telescope was dedicated in his honor and named the "Víctor M. Blanco Telescope" and is also known as the "Blanco 4m".

Elba Bonilla, U.S. Army National Guard. Worked as a Drill Sgt. At the Puerto Rico Language Center. She was then transferred to Camp Santiago. Supply Sgt., Safety Range Inspector, Sgt. Bonilla still active.

Frank Bonilla, U.S. Army - Academic of Puerto Rican descent. Bonilla became a leading figure in Puerto Rican Studies.

C

Elias Cabrera U.S.S ARMY PRANG SSC Recruiting /Retention Former Language Center Cadre. He still active.

Juan Cancel Ríos, U.S. Army - 7th President of the Senate of Puerto Rico.

David Childs, U.S. Army Puerto Rico National Guard Retired Drill Sgt. Worked at the Language Center, Paratrooper.

Byron Chique Sanchez, retired SPC, U.S. Army

Byron Omar Chique Carreras, Active Lt. U.S. Army, Doctor

Gary Chique Sanchez, retired U.S. Army Colonel served in Iraq, Afghanistan

Roberto Clemente, U.S. Marine Corps Reserve - Major League baseball player. First native Puerto Rican to be inducted into the Baseball Hall of Fame.

Francisco J. Collazo, U.S. Army - businessman. Founder of "COLSA Corporation", a provider of engineering and support services in Huntsville, Alabama.

Luis Cora CSM PRNG was a Drill Sgt. And First Sgt. At the LANGUAGE CENTER.

D

Carlos Del Castillo, U.S. Army - scientist. Recipient of the Presidential Early Career Award for Scientists and Engineers (PECASE) award, the highest honor bestowed by the United States government on scientists and engineers beginning their independent careers.

E

Sixto Escobar, U.S. Army - Boxer. First Puerto Rican world champion and member of Boxing Hall of Fame.

Nicholas Estavillo, U.S. Marine Corps - Former Chief of Patrol, NYPD. In 2002, Estavillo became the first Puerto Rican and the first Hispanic in the history of the NYPD to reach the three-star rank of Chief of Patrol.

Noel Estrada, U.S. Army - Composer. Composer of "En Mi Viejo San Juan."

F

Pedro Flores, U.S. Army - Composer. One of Puerto Rico's best-known composers of Ballads and Boleros.

G

Joxel García, U.S. Department of Health and Human Services – Physician García is a former four-star admiral in the U.S. Public Health Service Commissioned Corps. He served as the thirteenth Assistant Secretary for Health (ASH).

José Gautier Benítez, Spanish Army – Poet
Considered by many to be Puerto Rico's best poet of the Romantic Era.

Anibal González Irizarry, U.S. Army - Journalist
Former newscaster for "Telenotaicias en accion."

H

Rafael Hernández, U.S. Army - Composer
Composer of "Preciosa" and "Lamento Borincano"

Lorenzo Homar, U.S. Army - Visual artist
Considered by many to be Puerto Rico's greatest graphic artist.

L

Jacob Lozada, U.S. Army - Management Consultant
Nominated by President George W. Bush to be Assistant Secretary of Veterans Affairs.

M

José "Aguila Blanca" (White Eagle) Maldonado Román, Cuban Liberation Army - Puerto Rican revolutionary
His controversial exploits in Puerto Rico have contributed to making him part of Puerto Rican tradition.

Hugo Margenat, U.S. Army - Poet
Margenat was the founder of the political youth pro-independence organizations "Acción Juventud Independentista" and "Federación de Universitarios Pro Independencia"

Abraham Márti Battle, U.S. Army - Served during the Vietnam War. He received the purple heart medal for his heroic performance.

Federico Medina, U.S. Marine was killed in the Vietnam War.

Ángel Mislan, Spanish Army - Composer of Danzas

William Miranda Marín, Puerto Rico Army National Guard PRNG – Politician. Miranda was the former mayor of Caguas, Puerto Rico from 1996 till 2010. He was also the Adjutant General, Mayor General, for the Puerto Rico National Guard from 1990 till 1992.

Luis Morales, U.S. Marine is presently serving with pride."

Wendy Montero U.S. ARMY PRANG Former Drill Sgt. At Language Center.

O

Samuel Ortiz U.S. ARMY National Guard former Drill Sgt. Language Center.

P

Pvt. Julio Pagan Perez, U.S. Army served during the Vietnam War

Staff Sgt. Julio Pagan Torres Puerto Rico Army National Guard retired after 30 yrs. of service, as Staff Sgt. (served in WW II and Korea)

CSM Juan Jose Pagan Rodriguez, Puerto Rico Army National Guard-- retired after 33 yrs. (served in the Korean war and Vietnam)

CPL Julio Pagan Rodriguez, Puerto Rican Army National Guard served during the Korean War (eight years) retired from NYC Transit worked for 30 yrs.

Sgt E7 Vicente Pagan Rodriguez Army Reserve Retired after 30 years of service (Vietnam War) Worked as an MVO in NYPD, retired from the NYC TRANSIT as a Bus Driver.

Petty Officer Ramon Luis Pagan Rodriguez Navy Reserve retired active duty over 30 yrs. of service. He also retired as a Correction Officer. Worked in Rikers Island in New York for 25 years.

Sgt. Julio Manuel Pagan Morales retired active Air Force (Vietnam) Composer/Singer

Antonio Paoli, Spanish Army - Tenor, opera singer
First person in history to record an entire opera

Pedro Pietri, U.S. Army - Nuyorican poet and playwright
Pietri co-founded the Nuyorican Poets Café.

Q

Miguel Quiles U.S. ARMY PRANG Former Sgt. At the PRANG
   Language Center

R

Adolfo Ramos, U.S. ARMY served in the Korean War

Rigoberto Ramos Ramos, U.S. Army served during the Vietnam war

Eliot Ramos Ramos, U.S. Army served during the Vietnam war

Sylvia Rexach, U.S. Women's Army Corps - Singer, composer

Marie Teresa Ríos, U.S. Women's Army Corps - Author
Author of the novel "The Fifteenth Pelican," which was the basis for the
   popular 1960s television sitcom, The Flying Nun.

Tomás "Maso Rivera" Rivera Morales, U.S. Army – Composer
Composed over 1,000 instrumental compositions for the cuatro.

Juan "Chi-Chi" Rodríguez, U.S. Army - Professional golfer
He is the first Puerto Rican to be inducted into the World Golf Hall of
   Fame.

Pete "El Conde" Rodríguez, U.S. Army - Singer/Composer

Noris Rodriguez Major, PRANG Retired Major, was supervisor for all
   English Instructors at the Language Center. Still working for the
   guard, as a civilian.

S

Enrique Sanchez, PFC U.S. Army served during WWI

Joe Sánchez, U.S. Army - Author and former New York City police officer
Sánchez is a highly decorated former New York City police officer, and
   author whose books give an insight as to the corruption within the
   department.

Soraya Suarez PRANG CSM She was a Drill Sgt. First Sgt. At the
   Language Center.

Victor Sanchez Astacio, Sgt. Served served in Panama

Tony Santiago, U.S. Marine Corps - Military historian.

Salvatore Santiago Sgt. U.S. ARMY PRANG former Cadre at the PRNG
   Language Center

Daniel Santos, U.S. Army – Composer, Singer of boleros

Efrain Soto Santiago, Puerto Rico Army National Guard. Retired Colonel. Educator... As a major, he served as Commander at the Language Center Fort Allen, Juana Diaz PR

Miguel Ángel Suárez, U.S. Navy - Actor, playwright, stage director
Acted in various films such as Stir Crazy and Under Suspicion.

Ray Suarez, U.S. Marine Corps - Politician
Alderman of the 31st ward in Chicago.

T

Francisco Torralbo, Spanish Army - Politician
Torralbo served as Spanish acting governor of Puerto Rico on two occasions, 1789 and 1792–1793, both ad interim.

Guillermo José Torres, U.S. Army - Journalist
Television reporter and news anchorman

José "Chegui" Torres, U.S. Army - Boxer
Light Heavyweight Championship and member of Boxing Hall of Fame.

Wilson Torres Col. PRANG was a former commander at the Language Center

Rafael Tufiño, U.S. Army - Painter and printmaker

V

Carlos Vázquez, Captain Active Army
He was a former educator at the Language Center, Juana Diaz PR

Pedro Vázquez, U.S. Marine Corps - 8th Secretary of State of Puerto Rico

Antonio J. Vicens, Puerto Rico Army National Guard PRNG - Adjutant General of the Puerto Rico National Guard.

Juan Emilio Viguié, U.S. Army - Pioneer movie producer who produced Romance Tropical, the first Puerto Rican film with sound.

Z

David Zayas, U.S. Air Force - Theatrical, film, and television actor

He is most known for his roles as Angel Batista on Showtime's series Dexter and as Enrique Morales on the HBO prison drama Oz.

CHAPTER 9

Puerto Rican women in the U.S. Military

In 1944, the U.S. Army sent recruiters to the island to recruit no more than 200 women for the Women's Army Corps (WAC). Over 1,000 applications were received for the unit, which was to be composed of only 200 women....

The Puerto Rican WAC unit, Company 6, 2nd Battalion, 21st Regiment of the Women's Army Auxiliary Corps, a segregated Hispanic unit, was assigned to the New York Port of Boarding, after their basic training at Fort Oglethorpe, Georgia. They were assigned to work in military offices that planned the shipment of troops around the world.

Among the women recruited was PFC Carmen García Rosado, who in 2006, authored and published a book titled "LAS WACS-Participacion de la Mujer Boricua en la Segunda Guerra Mundial", The WACs-The participation of the Puerto Rican women in the Second World War. This is the first book to document the experiences of the first 200 Puerto Rican women who participated in said conflict.

In 1989, she was named consultant to the Director of Veterans Affairs in Puerto Rico. In her position she became an activist and worked for the rights of the Puerto Rican women veterans.

Puerto Rican Army nurses, 296th Station Hospital, Camp Tortuguero, Vega Baja, PR.

That same year the Army Nurse Corps (ANC) decided to accept Puerto Rican nurses so that Army hospitals would not have to deal with the language barriers.

Thirteen women submitted applications, were interviewed, underwent physical examinations, and were accepted into the ANC.

Eight of these nurses were assigned to the Army Post at San Juan, where they were valued for their bilingual abilities.

Five nurses were assigned to work at the hospital at Camp Tortuguero, Puerto Rico. Among the nurses was Second Lieutenant Carmen Lozano Dumler, who became one of the first Puerto Rican female United States Army officers.

Not all the women served as nurses. Some of the women served in administrative duties in the mainland or near combat zones. Such was the case of Technician Fourth Grade (T/4) Carmen Contreras-Bozak who belonged to the 149th Women's Army Auxiliary Corps.

The 149th Women's Army Auxiliary Corp, WAAC, Post Headquarters Company was the first WAAC Company to go overseas, setting sail from New York Harbor for Europe in January 1943.

The unit arrived in Northern Africa on January 27, 1943 and rendered overseas duties in Algiers within General Dwight D. Eisenhower's theater headquarters, T/4.

Carmen Contreras-Bozak, a member of this unit, was the first Hispanic to serve in the U.S. Women's Army Corps as an interpreter and in numerous administrative positions.

Another was Lieutenant Junior Grade (LTJG) María Rodríguez Denton, the first woman from Puerto Rico who became an officer in the United States Navy as a member of the WAVES. The Navy assigned LTJG Denton as a library assistant at the Cable and Censorship Office in New York City. It was LTJG Denton who forwarded the news, through channels, to President Harry S. Truman that the war had ended.

Some Puerto Rican women who served in the military went on to become famous in fields outside of the military. Among them, are Sylvia Rexach, a composer of boleros, Marie Teresa Rios, an author, and Julita Ross, a singer.

Sylvia Rexach, dropped out of the University of Puerto Rico in 1942 and joined the United States Army as a member of the WACS where she served as an office clerk. She served until 1945, when she was honorably discharged.

Marie Teresa Rios was a Puerto Rican writer who also served in World War II. Rios, mother of Medal of Honor recipient, Capt. Humbert Roque Versace, and author of The Fifteenth Pelican, which was the basis for the popular 1960s television sitcom "The Flying Nun", drove Army trucks and buses.

She also served as a pilot for the Civil Air Patrol. Rios Versace wrote and edited for various newspapers around the world, including places such as Guam, Germany, Wisconsin, and South Dakota, and publications such the Armed Forces Star & Stripes and Gannett.

During World War II, Julita Ross entertained the troops with her voice in "USO shows", United Service Organizations.

Chief Warrant Officer, CWO3, Rose Franco, was the first Puerto Rican woman to become a Warrant Officer in the United States Marine Corps. With the outbreak of the Korean War, Franco surprised her family by announcing that she was leaving college to join the United States Marine Corps.

In 1965, Franco was named Administrative Assistant to the Secretary of the Navy Paul Henry Nitze by the administration of President Lyndon B. Johnson.

Dr. Antonia Coello Novello

Is a pediatrician who served as the 14th Surgeon General of the United States from 1990 to 1993.

In 1978, Dr. Novello joined and received a commission in the Public Health Service Commissioned Corps, PHSCC, rising all the way up to flag officer/medical director grade. Her first assignment being as a project officer at the National Institute of Arthritis, Metabolism and Digestive Diseases of the National Institutes of Health, NIH.

She held various positions at NIH, rising to the medical director/flag rank in the PHSCC and to the job of deputy director of the National Institute of Child Health and Human Development, NICHD, in 1986.

She also served as Coordinator for AIDS Research for NICHD from September 1987. In this role, she developed a particular interest in pediatric AIDS.

Dr. Novello made major contributions to the drafting and enactment of the Organ Transplantation Procurement Act of 1984 while assigned to the United States Senate Committee on Labor and Human Resources, working with the staff of committee chairman Orrin Hatch.

She was the first woman and the first Hispanic, Puerto Rican, to hold the position of Surgeon General.

Dr. Milagros, Mili, J. Cordero is a licensed, registered occupational therapist with board certification in Pediatrics. She is the founder and President of ITT'S for Children, a professional group that assists and empowers parents to develop a better understanding of the strengths and needs of their children and to enhance their children's development to the full extent of their capability.

Dr. Cordero is certified in the use of SAMONAS and Tomatis sound therapies. She is a member of the national DIR Institute faculty and serves as vice-chair to Georgia 's State Interagency Coordinating Council for the Babies Can't Wait Program, the professional advisory council of the National Cornelia De Lange Association, and the board of the Frazer Center in Atlanta, Georgia.

Helen Rodriguez-Trias

Dr. Helen Rodríguez-Trías was a pediatrician and activist. She was the first Latina president of The American Public Health Association, a founding member of the Women's Caucus of the American Public Health Association and the recipient of the Presidential Citizen's Medal.

She testified before the Department of Health, Education, and Welfare for passage of federal sterilization guidelines. The guidelines, which she drafted, require a woman's written consent to sterilization, offered in a language they can understand, and set a waiting period between the consent and the sterilization procedure.

She is credited with helping to expand the range of public health services for women and children in minority and low-income populations in the United States, Central and South America, Africa, Asia, and the Middle East.

Puerto Rican women have also excelled in the fields of Physics and Physiology. Among them Prof. Mayda Velasco and Dr. María Cordero Hardy.

Physics is the study of the laws and constituents of the material world and encompasses a wide variety of fields, including condensed matter physics, biological physics, astrophysics, particle physics, and others.

Prof. Mayda Velasco (PhD) is a professor of physics at Northwestern University. Her research is centered in particle physics. She plays a leadership role in the CMS experiment at the CERN LHC. She is currently the director of the "Colegio de Física Fundamental e Interdiciplinaria de las Ámericas", College of Fundamental and Interdisciplinary Physics of the Americas, located in San Juan, Puerto Rico.

Dr. María Cordero Hardy is a physiologist. Physiology is the study of life, specifically, how cells, tissues, and organisms' function. She is a scientist who did her research on vitamin E. Her work helped other scientists understand about how vitamin E works in the human body.

She is now a professor at Louisiana State University and teaches students how to be medical technologists. A medical technologist is a person who studies your blood and other body fluids in the human body.

CHAPTER 10

Puerto Rican Women Revolt against United States

In the 1930s, the Puerto Rican Nationalist Party became the largest independence group in Puerto Rico.

Under the leadership of Dr. Pedro Albizu Campos, the party opted against electoral participation and advocated violent revolution. The women's branch of the Puerto Rican Nationalist Party was called the Daughters of Freedom.

Some of the militants of this women's-only organization included Julia de Burgos, one of Puerto Rico's greatest poets.

The arrest of Carmen María Pérez Gonzalez, Olga Viscal Garriga, and Ruth Mary Reynolds; three women involved with the Puerto Rican Nationalist Party who were arrested because of violations to the "Ley de la Mordaza", Gag Law. The law was later repealed as it was considered unconstitutional.

Plaque honoring the women of the Puerto Rican Nationalist Party...

Various confrontations took place in the 1930s in which Nationalist Party supporters were involved and that led to a call for an uprising against the United States and the eventual attack of the United States House of Representatives in 1954.

One of the most violent incidents was the 1937 Ponce massacre, in which police officers fired upon Nationalists who were participating in a peaceful demonstration against American abuse of authority.

About 100 civilians were wounded and 19 were killed, among them, a woman, Maria Hernández del Rosario, and a seven-year-old child, Georgina Maldonado.

On October 30, 1950, the Nationalist Party called for a revolt against the United States. Known as the Puerto Rican Nationalist Party Revolts of the 1950s, uprisings were held in the towns of Ponce, Mayagüez, Naranjito, Arecibo, Utuado, San Juan and most notably in Jayuya, which became known as the Jayuya Uprising.

Various women who were members of the Nationalist Party, but who did not participate in the revolts were falsely accused by the U.S. Government of participating in the revolts and arrested.

Among them Isabel Rosado, a social worker and Dr. Olga Viscal Garriga, a student leader and spokesperson of the Puerto Rican Nationalist Party's branch in Río Piedras.

Other women who were leaders of the movement were Isabel Freire de Matos, Isolina Rondón and Rosa Collazo.

The military intervened and the revolts came to an end after three days on September 2, 1954, two of the most remarkable women, who bore arms against the United States, were Blanca Canales and Lolita Lebrón.

Blanca Canales is best known for leading the Jayuya Revolt. Canales led her group to the town's plaza where she raised the Puerto Rican flag and declared Puerto Rico to be a Republic.

She was arrested and accused of killing a police officer and wounding three others. She was also accused of burning down the local post office. She was sentenced to life imprisonment plus sixty years of jail.

In 1967, Canales was given a full pardon by Puerto Rican Governor Roberto Sanchez Vilella.

Lolita Lebrón was the leader of a group of nationalists who attacked the United States House of Representatives in 1954. She presented her attack plan to the New York branch of the Puerto Rican Nationalist Party where Rosa Collazo served as treasurer.

Lebrón's mission was to bring world attention to Puerto Rico's independence cause...

When Lebrón's group reached the visitor's gallery above the chamber in the House, she stood up and shouted "¡Viva Puerto Rico Libre!","Long live a Free Puerto Rico!", and unfurled a Puerto Rican flag. Then the group opened fire with automatic pistols. A popular legend claims that Lebrón fired her shots at the ceiling and missed.

In 1979, under international pressure, President Jimmy Carter pardoned Lolita Lebrón and two members of her group, Irvin Flores, and Rafael Cancel Miranda.

CHAPTER 11

Puerto Rican Female as Military leadership

Lieutenant Colonel Custodio climbing down from the cockpit of a T-38

Changes within the policy and military structure of the U.S. armed forces helped expand the participation and roles for women in the military, among these the establishment of the All-Volunteer Force in the 1970s.

Puerto Rican women and women of Puerto Rican descent have continued to join the Armed Forces, and some have even made the military a career. Among the Puerto Rican women who have or had high ranking positions are the following:

Lieutenant Colonel Olga E. Custodio, USAF, became the first Hispanic female U.S. military pilot. She holds the distinction of being the first Latina to complete U.S. Air Force military pilot training. Upon retiring from the military, she is also the first Latina commercial airline captain.

In 2017, Custodio was inducted into the San Antonio Aviation and Aerospace Hall of Fame for being the first Hispanic Female Military pilot in the United States Air Force.

Major Sonia Roca was the first Hispanic female officer to attend the Command and General Staff Officer Course at the Army's School of the Americas.

In 2007, United States Air Force <u>Captain Hila Levy</u> became the first Puerto Rican to be awarded a Rhodes Scholarship.

She was honored with a plaque that has her name, squadron name and graduation date, which was placed in the ballroom balcony of the United States Air Force Academy's Hall of honor. The plaque recognizes Levy as the top former CAP cadet in the Class of 2008.

<u>Colonel Maritza Sáenz Ryan</u>, U.S. Army, is the head of the Department of Law at the United States Military Academy. She is the first female and the first Hispanic West Point graduate to serve as an academic department head. She also has the distinction of being the most senior-ranking Hispanic Judge Advocate.

As of June 15, 20<u>11, Colonel Maria Zumwalt</u>, U. S. Army, served as commander of the 48th Chemical Brigade.

<u>Captain Haydee</u> Javier Kimmich (U.S. Navy) from Cabo Rojo, Puerto Rico was the highest-ranking Hispanic female in the Navy. Kimmich was assigned as the Chief of Orthopedics at the Navy Medical Center in Bethesda. She reorganized their Reservist Department during Operation Desert Storm. In 1998, she was selected as the woman of the year in Puerto Rico.

Brigadier General Marta Carcana

In July 2015, Puerto Rico Governor Alejandro Garcia Padilla nominated Colonel Marta Carcana for the position of Adjutant General of the Puerto Rican National Guard, a position that she unofficially held since 2014.

On September 4, 2015, she was confirmed as the first Puerto Rican woman to lead the Puerto Rican National Guard and promoted to Major General.

<u>Irene M. Zoppi also known as "RAMBA", was deployed to Kuwait, Iraq, and Saudi Arabia</u> with the 3rd Armored Division as a Military Intelligence Officer. She was one of few Latino women, who served during Desert Shield/Storm War in a Tank Division.

In 2018, Zoppi became the first Puerto Rican woman to reach the rank of Brigadier General in the United States Army. She is currently the Deputy Commanding General – Support under the 200th Military

Police Command at Fort Meade, Maryland. Zoppi is a Bronze Star Medal recipient.

CHAPTER 12

The Ultimate Sacrifice

Puerto Rican servicewomen were among the 41,000 women who participated in Operation Desert Shield and Operation Desert Storm.

As of July 2007, five Puerto Rican female soldiers have died while serving in the armed forces of the United States. Four deaths were combat-related, and one was during a training exercise.

They also served in the battlefields of Afghanistan and Iraq...

The Puerto Rican women who made the ultimate sacrifice in combat are the following:

SPC Frances M. Vega, September 2, 1983 – November 2, 2003, was born in San Francisco, California. She graduated from Antilles High School. Her grandfather, father and uncle also served in the U.S. military.

Vega was deployed to Iraq in what is known as the War on Terrorism. She became the first female soldier of Puerto Rican descent to die in a combat zone when on November 2, 2003. A surface-to-air missile was fired by protestors in Al Fallujah and hit the U.S. transport helicopter where she was in.

Vegas one of 16 soldiers who died in the Chinook crash. She was buried with full military honors and posthumously awarded a Bronze Star for bravery and a Purple Heart.

An Army Post Office in Iraq was named in her honor, and a sign from the post office was moved to the U.S. Army Adjutant General's Corps Museum in 2012.

One of the main gates at the Fort Buchanan military installation is also named in her honor.

It has a plaque that includes, "Specialist Frances M. Vega represents the character and patriotism of the countless American Soldiers who have answered the call to defend freedom.

SPC Aleina Ramirez Gonzalez 1972 – April 15, 2005 was born in the town of Hormigueros, Puerto Rico, died in Tikrit, Iraq, when a mortar struck her forward operating base.

SPC Lizbeth Robles, April 4, 1973 – March 1, 2005, born in Vega Baja, Puerto Rico, was the first female soldier born in Puerto Rico to die in the War on Terrorism. She was assigned to 360th Transportation Company, 68th Corps Support Battalion, 43rd Area Support Group.

SPC Robles volunteered for the 43rd Area Support Group, which rode in convoys to secure dangerous roadways for the delivery of fuel.

On February 28, 2005, SPC Robles and Sgt. Julio Negron sustained injuries after riding in a Humvee that flipped over by the town of Baiji, Iraq.

Sgt. Negron died on February 28, and SPC Robles died on March 1 at the 228th Combat Support Hospital in Tikrit due to her injuries.

Captain Maria Ines Ortiz, 1967 – July 10, 2007, born in Camden, New Jersey. She was the first Hispanic nurse, Puerto Rican descent, to die in combat and first Army nurse to die in Iraq.

She was killed by shrapnel from a mortar attack in the Baghdad Green Zone. She had volunteered for service in Iraq. Captain Maria Ines Ortiz was the first Army nurse to die in combat since the Viet Nam War.

The names of the four women are engraved in "El Monumento de la Recordación", The Monument of Remembrance, which is dedicated to Puerto Rico's fallen soldiers. This monument is situated in front of the Capitol Building in San Juan, Puerto Rico.

The first female soldier of Puerto Rican descent to die of a non-combat related accident was Spec. Hilda I. Ortiz Clayton.

Ortiz Clayton was an Army combat photographer who was killed in 2013 when a mortar exploded during an Afghan training exercise. She captured the explosion that killed her and four Afghan soldiers on a photo which she took.

Ortiz Clayton was the first combat documentation and production specialist to be killed in Afghanistan. She was assigned to the 55th Signal Company, Combat Camera, 21st Signal Brigade, Fort Meade, Maryland.

The 55th Signal Company named their annual competitive award for combat camera work "The Spc. Hilda I. Clayton Best Combat Camera (COMCAM) Competition" in her honor.

CHAPTER 13

Puerto Rico Calls in National Guard

I had to share this article from the Newspaper to show you that the National Guard is always around to help the citizens. I remember this day very clear.

By Matthew Hay Brown and Ray Quintanilla and Sentinel Staff Writers
Orlando Sentinel
Jul 20, 2004, at 12:00 am

SAN JUAN, Puerto Rico -- Facing a surge in killings and growing pressure for action, Gov. Sila Calderon has called in the National Guard to help patrol this U.S. territory.

In a mobilization that recalls the controversial "hard-handed" approach to crime of a decade ago, 500 troops with M-16s and body armor are set to join the embattled police forces in San Juan and three other cities as early as Thursday.

The open-ended deployment is intended to free officers to focus on the drug wars that have pushed the island body count toward new highs.

The move, which Calderon had resisted during weeks of public debate, comes after another bloody weekend here. At least five people, including the first police officer of the year, were gunned down Saturday and Sunday.

That brought to 445 the number killed on this island of 3.9 million since Jan. 1. That's 31 more than the same period last year, when the territory registered a homicide rate more than three times the national average.

National Guard Adj. Gen. Francisco Marquez called the shooting of police Officer Santos Silva Laboy on Saturday night the last straw. Police and National Guard commanders met Monday to work out details of the deployment.

Residents were reminded of the mano dura, the "hard-handed" approach employed by former Gov. Pedro Rossello, in the 1990s when he sent in the National Guard to occupy public-housing projects. Crime went down, but residents complained of civil-rights violations.

But those likeliest to be affected offered a mixed response. Nereida Machicote, 41, lives in the Luis Llorens Torres project, a notorious drug point in San Juan. She lost a 20-year-old son and an 18-year-old daughter in separate incidents there earlier this year.

"The National Guard probably wouldn't have changed anything," she said. "Both of them were killed by people they knew, and most of the people who die in the area are killed by people they know."

Hours after the mobilization was announced Sunday, three more people were gunned down in a drive-by shooting early Monday in San Juan.

It was the second triple homicide in the capital in a little more than a week. Three people were killed and five more wounded in a daylight gunbattle July 12 at the Lloren's Torres project.

And on Saturday night, Silva Laboy and a bystander were shot to death during an armed robbery in the capital. Police shot and killed a suspected gunmen at the scene.

Officials blame much of the violence on turf wars between gangs fighting for control of the lucrative drug trade. Hundreds of millions of dollars' worth of cocaine and heroin pass through this Connecticut-sized island annually on the way from South America to the U.S. mainland.

National Guard members were to be contacted today, briefed on rules of engagement Wednesday and possibly deployed Thursday, Army Maj. Millie Rosa said.

Plans call for troops from field artillery, infantry, and engineering units to patrol alongside police in San Juan, the suburbs of Bayamon and Carolina and the southern city of Ponce, and to help with security at large public events, she said. The soldiers will not carry handcuffs or be empowered to make arrests.

"We will not be the lead agency," Rosa said. "Our role in this mission will be to support the police."

That mission could expand to include troops occupying public-housing projects.

The mounting violence has emerged as a major issue in the current election campaign. Rossello, now running for governor against Calderon's protege, Anibal Acevedo Vila, had promised to revive the policy.

Manuel Feliciano, who has lived at Loren's Torres since the 1950s, said he would welcome the return of troops to the project.

"There's a lot of elderly who have been victimized," said Feliciano, 78, as two teenagers with walkie-talkies paced on a sidewalk nearby. "A lot of people just don't hear about it. If you're old, you can't go in some areas of this place. You always have to look out for people coming up behind you."

But Angel Gonzalez, 23 and unemployed, called troops "the wrong approach."

"The police won't let you go anywhere," he said. "It's like they want everyone to stay in the house, and when the National Guard gets here it's going to be worse."

What's needed, he said, is "police to arrest people who commit crimes, not those who they think are going to commit crimes."

Machicote remembered the mano dura. It did help crime go down, she said, but sometimes the troops would harass people who had done nothing wrong.

"They would stop you and ask a lot of questions about where you were going and why," she said. "It bothered a lot of people.

"Looking at how bad things are now, maybe that wasn't so bad."

I believe that the National Guard did an outstanding job, however, the residents of that housing project were criticizing them....

CHAPTER 14

The Borinqueneers

Are the Borinqueneers Forgotten Heroes?...........

The 65th Infantry originated as Puerto Rican outfit in the form of the Battalion of Porto Rican Volunteers on May 20, 1899. This happened in the aftermath of the Spanish-American War of 1898.

They were regarded as colonial troops, part of the first "American Colonial Army."

In 1908, and by then a regiment, the unit officially became part of the U.S. Army. It came to be known as the Porto Rican Regiment.

During WWI the regiment was sent to the Canal Zone in Panama- far from the European battlefields. In 1920, the unit's name changed from the Porto Rican Regiment to the 65th Infantry Regiment, United States Army.

While African American troops saw their role extended during WWII, greatly in part to Black leaders' involvement in demanding access to combat positions and officers commissions, Puerto Rican units were kept from any assignment that may involve combat.

The 65th served in North Africa and Europe during World War II, but not as first-line troops. Military authorities, reflecting the racial prejudice of the time, kept the regiment far from the front. The military followed a policy of racial segregation in which combat roles, with a few exceptions, were reserved for White troops. The military's institutional racism had unintended consequences.

Since the 65th was kept from combat, it experienced all kinds of training and its men and officers dutifully prepared for war. Non-combat assignments meant that the Borinqueneers suffered very few casualties throughout the war.

By WWII's end the 65th was a superbly trained and well-disciplined combat regiment.

The "Rum & Coke"

The story of the 65th could've ended right after WWII as the U.S. military rapidly demobilized the 12 million Americans in uniform. There was no reason to keep the "Rum & Coke" outfit around. This is how the 65th was referred to in mockery.

The unit was being gradually demobilized. However, on June 24, 1950, war broke out in Korea. We know what happened next. An unprepared U.S. military had to scrap the bottom of the barrel to find men and units ready for combat.

In Puerto Rico, the National Guard was activated, and the 65th was mobilized and ordered to Korea. The Borinqueneers were going to war as first-line combat troops, as part of the Army's 3rd Infantry Division.

On October 12, 1950, Puerto Ricans learned that the 65th was fighting in Korea. The island's newspapers were full of stories and pictures of the soldiers. There were plenty of ceremonies held before their departure. Island-wide, the people of Puerto Rico joined to support the 65th throughout the war.

Governor Luis Muñoz Marín often referred to the men of the 65th in his speeches. The crest of the 65th was displayed in public buses and train cars. Plazas and avenues were named to honor the regiment.

Returning soldiers, especially the wounded, were received as heroes and treated to public receptions by government officials. Muñoz Marín himself attended the burials of the fallen and sent his recorded speeches to the troops in Korea.

In those early days of the war, there was not a day in which the island's press failed to write about the Puerto Rican soldiers—and what their actions meant for Puerto Rico.

During the war, the 65th became a national icon on the island and among the growing Puerto Rican communities in the mainland. The island-based press and elected officials linked fighting in Korea with decolonization and the commonwealth formula.

Moreover, lengthy press editorials and the governor referred to the 65th as a method for achieving full manhood, forging a modern Puerto Rican, and a modern Puerto Rico.

Among the growing Puerto Rican colonial in New York, the actions of the Borinqueneers and Puerto Ricans were used in what we call nowadays "policies of respectability."

At a time in which mainstream media and social sciences talked openly about the "Puerto Rican problem" as more and more Puerto Ricans migrated to the continental U.S., local publications highlighted the Borinqueneers' heroics to deal with the community's critics.

The majority of the 61,000 Puerto Ricans who fought in the Korean War came from the island. Many served with the 65th. The vast majority were volunteers who several times completed the island's monthly recruiting quota. The chance that they may be sent to the 65th motivated thousands of Puerto Ricans to volunteer for service both in the mainland and on the island.

Throughout the conflict 3,540 Puerto Ricans became casualties of war, of whom 747 were killed in action.

The journey of these men helped established a bridge, and air route between New York and the island. It helped to guarantee the survival of Puerto Rican communities in the eastern seaboard.

Recruits and volunteers came mostly from the island. They were transported in cargo ships from Puerto Rico through the Panama Canal and from there to Korea, sometimes stopping in Hawaii and Japan before landing in Korea.

Their return was different, especially for the wounded and repatriated prisoners of war.

As any other American soldiers, gravely wounded Puerto Rican would be evacuated from Korea and find their way to the continental United States.

After a stay in Walter Reed Medical Hospital, most of these men would be returned to Puerto Rico. Their voyage was one that millions of Puerto Ricans after them would begin.

They would fly from Baltimore to LaGuardia Airport in New York where they would stay for a day or two.

Once in New York, the returning soldiers would participate in parades in "El Bronx and in Harlem".

The city's mayor would usually meet them along with city and community leaders and offer the key to the city to them. Their heroics were highlighted in articles next to news on the persecution of Puerto Ricans from Brooklyn to the Bronx.

Moreover, they would return to the island aboard recently renovated Eastern Airlines planes. This firm flew many soldiers, free of charge, to the island. The airline's advertisement for the new non-stop flights from San Juan to New York dotted the Puerto Rican and Latino press in the city.

The actions of the Borinqueneers during the first half of the war elevated them to iconic status. They were the living proof of what Puerto Ricans could do when given the opportunity. They were showing that they were second to none.

The chance to go to war also prove that the Boricuas were inferior to no one.

Then, tragedy struck. The replacement of highly-trained, combat-hardened troops with poorly trained—yet enthusiastic recruits spoke little English.

There was a lack of bilingual sergeants, the backbone of the American military. The new Continental officers that did not speak Spanish. They openly showed their hate for Puerto Rican soldiers.

They led them to tragic events during the battles of Outpost Kelly and Jackson Heights in the autumn of 1952. The back-to-back debacles were followed by a series of mass court martial in which eighty-seven enlisted men.

One Puerto Rican officer received sentences ranging from six months to ten years. It was a large total punishment of wages. Also, they were treating them like criminals.

Many had dishonorable discharges for charges varying from willful disobedience of a superior officer to cowardice before the enemy.

In 1953, the Secretary of the Army reviewed the cases and paid the unexecuted portions of the sentences of all but four of the accused. The soldiers who had their sentences remitted were returned to duty.

On March 4, 1953, an Army spokesman announced that the Army had decided to integrate the 65th Infantry with Continental troops, and to redistribute to other units the excess Puerto Rican troops.

The 65th would no longer be a Puerto Rican unit. Despite the soldiers' objections the regiment was quickly integrated as planned.

In 1954, the 65th Infantry returned to Puerto Rico and was reconstituted as an all-Puerto Rican formation. The island had its regiment back, but not for long. It was deactivated in 1956.

Colonel César Cordero, who had led the 65th during the tragic battle for Outpost Kelly, led a campaign that culminated with the reactivation and transfer of the 65th from the Army to the Puerto Rico National Guard in 1959.

Unlike its participation during the war, this event received scant publicity and soon the Borinqueneers and their epic ordeal faded into a distant and twisted memory.

Now, they are the forgotten heroes of a forgotten war....

On June 13, 2016 "El Sesenta y Cinco "was awarded the highest award Congress can grant. The Borinqueneers went from forgotten soldiers who had to face both the enemy and discrimination, to heroes earning praise from the leaders of Congress and the military.

The U.S. Army's 65th Infantry Regiment, the only all-Hispanic unit that hailed mostly from Puerto Rico, inspires pride for their dogged combat in the Korean War in the early 1950s.

These soldiers also spent decades trying to clear their name...

The segregated regiment, which took the nickname the Borinqueneers, honoring the Indigenous Taíno name for their homeland. They went from being published by General Douglas MacArthur for battlefield bravery to having 91 soldiers court martialed and jailed in 1952.

After intense public pressure, the Army quickly pardoned them, later blaming incompetent Army leadership, poor military tactics, racism and organizational prejudice for the events that landed the soldiers in the brig.

The findings of an internal Army investigation provided some proof for the soldiers, their families and for Puerto Rico's pride. Many died waiting for the broader pardon that would truly clear their names in the history books…

"It's a proud day for all those whose lives they saved and whose freedom they defended," said President Barack Obama at the 2014 White House ceremony awarding the once-vilified regiment the Congressional Gold Medal, the nation's top honor. "You've earned a hallowed place in our history."

Those words from the president, and that redemption from the top, took more than 60 years.…

CHAPTER 15

The Borinqueneers' Beginnings

LET ME TAKE YOU BACK HALF CENTURY

The Borinqueneers are best known for their fighting in the Korean War, 1950-53. This regiment of Puerto Ricans existed half a century before the Korean War....

After losing the Spanish American War in 1898, Spain ceded Puerto Rico, Cuba, and the Philippines to America.

A year later, Congress authorized the U.S. military to form the Puerto Rico Battalion of Volunteer Infantry, comprised mainly of men from its newly acquired territory.

It was incorporated into the regular U.S. Army in 1908. Look at what happened in 1920....

Two years after serving in World War I, it became the 65th Infantry Regiment.

During WWII, its soldiers earned a Distinguished Service Cross, two Silver Stars and 900 Purple Hearts for combat in Europe...

It was their impressive maneuvers in an Atlantic Fleet joint training exercise for the Army, Navy, Marines and Air Force, back home in Puerto Rico after the war, that propelled the 65th to Korea's front lines.

On the way, the soldiers took the nickname Borinqueneers.

Korean War Distinguished Service Earns MacArthur's Praise

Soon after arriving in Pusan, South Korea in September 1950, the 65th Infantry became known as a "well led, well trained and highly motivated" unit in various battles in the muddy hills and brush during Korea's harsh winter.

Most notably, the 65th fought off the Chinese People's Liberation Army in the Chosin Reservoir to safely evacuate the trapped U.S. Army's First Battalion. Officials who initially mocked at having to command the "rum and coke" platoon quickly changed their tune.

By the end of the 65th's first year in Korea, it had suffered 1,510 casualties while killing 15,787 enemy troops and taking 2,169 prisoners, according to the Historic Review on the 65th Court-martial: Report by the Department of Army's Center of Military History.

United Nations General Douglas MacArthur, who commanded the U.S.-led United Nations forces early in the war, wrote in 1951 that the 65th 's soldiers showed "magnificent ability and courage in field operations. They are a credit to Puerto Rico, and I am proud to have them in my command."

Humiliating and Mass Court Martials for the 65th regimen.......

In the fall of 1952, the unit's fortunes changed. Chinese troops launched major offensives against two U.S.-held outposts defended, in part, by the 65th.

Outpost Kelly in September and Jackson Heights a month later. The Borinqueneers suffered heavy casualties. Dismal troop morale sank further.

You know my dad, CSM Juan Jose Pagan Rodriguez, a Korea and Vietnam veteran, told me that Kelly Hill and Jackson Heights were just rocks. It was impossible for anyone to climb up there at all. They only had a tiny shovel to dig. It would have been nice to have a drill or something similar......

After the massacre at Outpost Kelly, unit commanders cut the Puerto Ricans' rice and beans rations, stripped the Borinqueneers nickname off the unit's vehicles. They also ordered the men to shave their mustaches until they could prove they were "real men" in battle.

Deeply insulted and facing what most thought was a suicide mission, dozens of soldiers refused orders to retake the Jackson Heights outpost.

The Army quickly courts martialed and convicted 91 of them for desertion and disobeying orders in December. All were dishonorably discharged. Sentences ranged from one to 16 years of confinement at hard labor.

"They treated us...like we were worth nothing," Raúl Reyes Castañeira, the youngest of four brothers who followed their father's footsteps into the 65th Infantry, told Univision's Aquí y Ahora newsmagazine show. "And we were giving our lives. So many young men there just dying. It was terrible."

"They treated us...like we were worth nothing," said Raúl Reyes Castañeira of the 65th Infantry. "And we were giving our lives."

CHAPTER 16

Internal Investigation

The Army tried to keep the court martials quiet, but soldiers' homebound letters and the local press blew the story open in January 1953. Puerto Rico's government, Congress, and the public demanded answers.

Army officials told Congress that the rotation of new, inexperienced soldiers and officers into the regiment the 65th were inexperience. The Puerto Rican didn't understand English and the officers no Spanish.

They were led to the failures and court martials. Secretary of the Army Robert Stevens used the point about the language barrier to justify pardoning all those convicted, overturning their sentences, and reinstating them in the Army.

A subsequent internal investigation listed many other problems, including inept leadership, a severe ammunition shortage and military tactics that needlessly increased casualties.

The 65th suffered 806 casualties in just those two months defending and attempting to retake the strategically questionable Kelly and Jackson Heights outposts.

The investigation also blamed "a command environment guilty of ethnic and organizational prejudice," both on and off the battlefield.

An Insult to Puerto Ricans

Investigators pointed out that the commanders who had court martialed the Puerto Rican soldiers had on other occasions opted not to prosecute white soldiers for abandoning the battlefield. Rather than use the moment to reform the 65th or fix certain practices, commanders chose to punish the battalion.

The probe also highlighted a double standard in how commanders treated and evaluated Puerto Rican officers and white officers and other instances of ethnic or racial prejudice in the Army's command structure.

For cultural historian Silvia Alvarez Curbelo, the court martials that tarnished the 65th's reputation were not seen on the island as isolated cases of discrimination. Rather, they posed an affront to Puerto Rican identity as U.S. citizens at a time when the island was ascendant, having elected its first governor four years earlier, had just ratified its constitution that year, and was close to ending a five-year wave of mass migration to the U.S.

"The Puerto Rican soldier performance was also an affair of dignity…a mixture of pride, courage, bravery, self-respect and patriotism," says Alvarez Curbelo, a professor of communications at the University of Puerto Rico.

That's why soldiers still alive today say that true salvation is important not just to clear their own names, but for Puerto Ricans to collectively remember the sacrifices made.

During the Korean War, also known as the "Forgotten War," some 61,000 Puerto Ricans served in the U.S. Army, 48,000 of them recruited on the island, according to the Army's Historic Review on the 65th Court-martial.

There were more than 700 dead and more than 2,000 wounded, Puerto Rico suffered one casualty for every 660 inhabitants, more than double the rate for the continental U.S.

CHAPTER 17

Father and Son fighting for the Same Cause

The following four stories are about my father and grandfather. They were American Soldiers serving our nation with pride.

In the early spring, in 1950, The Puerto Rico Army National Guard was training every soldier harder than ever. Everyone knew that soon the National Guard would be mobilized.

My mother and grandmother were sad during those days because they knew that every member in my family will be deployed to Korea.

Since my mother was pregnant with her second child, she was too big to work around the house. My grandmother, Guadalupe, let her rest because my mother was due soon. This time, both my grandmother Guadalupe and my great-grandmother had a bad feeling about this child.

My mother was always too tired and didn't want to eat. I guess my mom was always sick because she didn't see my father often enough.

On October 20, 1950, my mother went into labor for more hours than expected. She gave birth to another baby girl, my sister, Adelin.

My grandmother Lupe and great grandma Dolores were happy because the baby was small, but healthy.

Digna, my mother, wanted to know if my father was around. My father and grandfather were doing drill at Losey Field base known today as Fort Allen in Juana Diaz, Puerto Rico.

Both my father and grandfather were happy because the new baby was doing well. They wanted to go home, but all passes were denied.

Juan Jose Pagan Rodriguez, my dad, got very angry when he was told that he couldn't go to Ponce to see his family. He just wanted an hour pass to see his wife and daughter. The answer from the commander was no....

My father decided to jump the fence...

So, when his unit went on break, he started walking very fast. There were sugar cane fields before reaching the main road.

As soon as he reached the main street, a car stopped and to my father's surprise, it was his commander. The commander looked at him and told him to get in the car. The young Sergeant was surprised because he was escorted to Ponce to see his family.

The commander told him to stay the rest of the evening, but to return to the base the following day. My mother was very happy to see him. Adelin and I were beside my mom when my dad arrived. The whole family had a wonderful night together.

During the months that followed, things were very rough. Lots of soldiers were sent to Korea. My grandfather and my father were waiting for their orders...

Our nation was facing one of the worst times of that era. Puerto Rico was waiting and willing to fight in Korea.

I am proud to say, that my father, CSM Juan José Pagán Rodriguez, of the Puerto Rico Army National Guard and my grandfather, Staff Sergeant Julio Pagán Torres, now both deceased, were among those brave soldiers fighting for our country in one of the bloodiest conflicts.

CHAPTER 18

Getting Deployed

To understand the commotion that was going on in the states and Puerto Rico, I will give you some facts of what our soldiers were facing during that period....

On July 1, 1950, the Army's 24th Infantry Division became the first U.S. troop to arrive in Korea. They were transferred from Japan passing through the Port of Pusan. The troops took up Positions in Taejon, about 75 miles south of Seoul.

A couple of days later July 19, 1950, the 25th Infantry arrived followed by the 1st Marine Brigade and the 2nd Infantry Division in late July.

Things were getting worse in Korea that on July 20, 1950, the casualties were increasing. More than 2,400 men or 30% were reported dead. Taejon fell under the arms of the enemy.

All Americans and the rest of world were alarmed. This meant that many were going to be called to serve their country. The Reserves and the National Guard will be mobilized.

Puerto Rico, a beautiful island located in the Caribbean, and a Commonwealth of the United States, was getting ready.

There was no cultural or language barrier holding those brave men. Those "Boricuas" were well trained. I am proud to say that three members of my family were in the National Army Guard.

They knew that it won't be long for the guard to be call for active duty. All three were ready to serve their nation. They were <u>Staff Sgt. Julio</u>

Pagan Torres, my grandfather, as signed to 65th Infantry 4 machine gun 30 calibers, Sgt. Juan J. Pagan Rodriguez, my father, assigned to 65th Infantry Heavy Mortal Co. and the youngest, my uncle, Cpl. Julio Pagan Rodríguez was assigned to Artillery.

By early September, the new troops were combat ready in hardened fighting units. The Puerto Rican National Guard was mobilized on September 10, 1950. Every "Boricua's" family was worried because their loved ones will leave to an unknown land. Many have never been abroad. Now, they must face a lot of hardships.

It didn't take long for a humble family in Ponce to hear the worst news ever. Their sons and husbands must report for duty. This was awful because all three soldiers were assigned to infantry or artillery. The women were devastated when they heard the news on the radio.

Staff Sgt. Julio Pagan Torres and Sgt. Juan J. Pagan Rodriguez received their orders. Their unit, the 65th Infantry was being mobilized.

Cpl. Julio Pagan Rodriguez wasn't called at this time.

The 65th Infantry was now divided. That meant father and son were separated. The 296 Infantry was sent to Tortuguero. They were di-vided into three groups, 2nd to Juana Diaz and the 3rd to Cayey.

WAITING FOR THE WORST

Everything was moving too fast. The Puerto Rico Army National Guard was giving orders left and right. There was no question asked. It didn't matter if there were one sole survivor in a family. Men were needed to go abroad and fight for their country.

Sgt. Juan J. Pagán Rodriguez was ready to fight; however, he had a young wife and two young children. Sgt. Julio Pagán Torres had also young ones. They had a big problem. There was also a possibility that Cpl. Julio Pagán Rodriguez might be call for active duty. They wanted to serve, but they had a family.

The following day, both father and son decided to speak to their commander. The commander found it quite unusual for members of the same family to be called for active duty. He listened to their petition and wrote all the information given by my father and grandfather. He told

Sgt. Juan Pagán Rodriguez that he was the one chosen to go to Korea and that Sgt. Julio Pagán Torres will stay in Puerto Rico.

What follows, will not only put you in tears, but will make you wonder…

In November 1950, Sgt. Juan J. Pagán Rodriguez said goodbye to his beloved wife and family. He was only 22 years old but was fully aware of his commitment. His father promised him that he would take care of the whole family. Sgt. Juan J. Pagán Rodriguez just said, "Bendición Papito" and got on the bus…

Many "Boricuas" were also leaving Puerto Rico. This was the saddest day for the whole island. Saying goodbye was very hard. The 65th Infantry had already sent soldiers to Korea. Those first infantry soldiers made history throughout the nation. They were known as "The Borinqueneers" The 65th Infantry Regiment started the assault on January 31, 1951.

NO WORD FROM SGT JUAN PAGAN RODRIGUEZ

The Pagán family was very confused during this crisis because right after Sgt. Juan J. Pagán Rodriguez left Puerto Rico, his father Staff Sgt. Julio Pagán received new orders. These orders stated that he was leaving for Korea in December 1950.

This was the worst Christmas gift that anyone could receive.

Now, Staff Sgt. Julio Pagán Torres was also leaving his family. He told his wife, Guadalupe, "No te apures, todo va a salir bien". He couldn't face his daughter in law, Digna. She was holding her youngest daughter Adelin.

Digna was too upset to say goodbye. Sgt. Juan J. Pagán Rodriguez left the island months before and no one knew his whereabouts. The so many visits to the Red Cross were made in vain.

Sgt. Julio Pagán Torres even went to his commander for an answer of his previous visit. The commander apologized for the awful mess and stated that he was sorry. He told Sgt. Pagán Torres those orders were revoked because they got to Washington too late. Communication was very slow in those days…….

ILL FEELINGS IN THE FRONT LINES

Sgt. Juan J. Pagán Rodriguez was already fighting in the front lines. He got to Korea in January 1951 and at this point he was uneasy. He had been away from his family for nearly two months and no news was received.

It was hard to get anything where he was stationed. His new acquired family was his buddies, fellow "BORICUAS". All of them were waiting for any kind of news from Puerto Rico.

In Ponce, Puerto Rico, things weren't that great. With the breadwinner gone, it wasn't easy to raise all those children. Guadalupe and Digna had to go to the Red Cross. They wanted to hear news from their husbands.

The Red Cross assured them that both father and son were fine. Food and emergency money were provided. Digna was worried because the youngest daughter was very ill. Adelin was a very fragile child and needed medical attention.

When the Red Cross saw the baby, they referred her to the best doctors. The child was well taken cared and recovered within months.

By the end of February, troops were sent to the front lines once again....

CHAPTER 19

In Korea Sgt. Juan J. Pagan Rodriguez

One morning, <u>Sgt. Juan Jose Pagán Rodriguez</u> was ordered to take a couple of guys to a designated area. <u>Sgt. Pagán Rodriguez</u> briefed his men and started walking.

It was a cold bitter day and a lot of snow on the ground. The young soldiers were still trying to get used to that weather. They were all melancholy because they missed their sunny and warm Puerto Rico. Many had suffered from frost bites. It wasn't easy keeping those soldiers motivated. They haven't heard anything from their families in months.

As they were walking, <u>Sgt. Pagán Rodriguez</u> started telling funny stories. The soldiers felt at ease. They reached their destination point. There were many wounded and others were suffering from the cold. <u>Sgt. Pagán Rodriguez</u> and his Troop relieved those men.

The fire never seized. <u>Sgt. Pagán Rodriguez</u> has been on his post for nearly a week. He was hungry and so were his men. They needed clean uniforms and chow.

<u>Sgt. Juan J. Pagán Rodriguez</u> kept fighting even though he didn't receive any news from Puerto Rico.

Suddenly, he received a message. He was ordered to report to his Commander. The young sergeant was surprised, but at the same time was happy to take a shower and change his uniform. He was escorted to his superior and to his surprise, there was <u>Staff Sergeant Julio Pagán Torres</u> waiting for him.

Words couldn't describe the emotion that those two human beings were feeling. Tears of joy were rolling down their faces. Sgt. Pagán Rodriguez asked his father about the family. He was also puzzled and questioning his father's arrival…both….in Korea…

The Commander of the 65th Infantry told both father and son that they would have to wait for new orders. He also told them that they will leave for Puerto Rico soon….

Those orders never came. Sgt. Juan J. Pagán Rodriguez was once again separated from his father……

A couple of days have gone by….

Sgt. Juan J. Pagán Rodriguez and his men were going to another camp site.

They had a couple of jeeps with plenty of supply. Sgt. Pagán Rodriguez saw a troop right in front of him. They were going to the same unit.

At that point, Sgt. Juan Pagán Rodriguez got the surprise of his life. His father, Staff Sgt. Julio Pagán Torres was among those men! He called his father, and both rode on the same jeep.

Once they arrived at their designated area, their new commandant called them. This time he gave them written orders. That was the best news Sgt. Pagán Rodriguez has received. He was going home, and his father was going with him safe and sound.

Sgt. Pagán Rodriguez and Staff Sgt. Julio Pagán Torres didn't want to be part of the big reception that was waiting for them in Puerto Rico…..

They were the first father and son wearing the same uniform and fighting for the same cause, but they just wanted to see their family.

They went to Ponce without being noticed. A taxi driver was the only witness when they reached home. There were a few gathered in front of the house. None of them were aware that a taxi had stopped there.

The two sergeants got off the taxi very quietly and opened the gate. Digna and Guadalupe started running once they saw them. It was a great day for the Pagán Family.

The Korean War brought Puerto Rican soldiers their greatest visibility, highest awards, and most punishing losses. There were 43, 434 Puerto Ricans in this war and 39, 591 of them were volunteers.

The 65th Infantry was chosen to guard the nation. They received awards for their bravery. It was also the last group of soldiers to leave the combat zone. Some bullets were whizzing by them as they boarded the ship to evacuate.......

FOR THEIR SERVICE, I SALUTE OUR "BORICUA" Korean's Heroes. We will never forget them.

Staff Sergeant Julio Pagán Torres and Sergeant Juan J. Pagán Rodríguez were the first father and son to serve the nation. They were in combat together and together returned to Ponce, Puerto Rico.

CSM Juan J. Pagán Rodriguez, my father, was very proud of being a soldier during the Korean Conflict. He told me how each soldier was being verbally abused.

Also, let me remain you, that when the first group went to Korea, they were not given the proper winter uniforms. They still fought without any complaint....

CSM JUAN J. PAGAN RODRIGUEZ
This poem is dedicated to my dad
Born 01/29/1929 Died 03/28/2020
MY HERO
In choosing of becoming an NCO…
You accepted many responsibilities
In choosing of becoming a father…
You accepted many responsibilities
You are a role model, a trainer, and a loving father…
My hero…
As I sit here, thoughts of yesteryears come to mind…
You my father and a soldier…
Dealing with your family
Dealing with your troop…
Both tasks closely related and hard
An Army Non-Commissioned Officer and a father
Of four…
Your wisdom of many years made you a great leader…
Your wisdom of many years made you the father you are…
I salute you dear father…
I salute you for all the years
You devoted to us and to our nation

CHAPTER 20

North Vietnam and South Vietnam

The Vietnam War was fought between communist North Vietnam, supported by its communist allies, and the government of South Vietnam, supported by the United States and other nations.

The United States entered the war to prevent a communist takeover of South Vietnam as part of their wider strategy of containment.

The Military advisors arrived at beginning of 1950. U.S. involvement escalated in the early 1960s and combat units were deployed beginning in 1965. Involvement peaked in 1968 at the time of the Tet Offensive.

During the Vietnam War, an estimated 48,000 Puerto Ricans served in the four branches of the armed forces. Amongst the highest-ranking Puerto Ricans who served in the United States Navy and had distinguished military careers were Admiral Horacio Rivero, Jr. and Vice Admiral Diego E. Hernández.

Admiral Horacio Rivero, Jr.

Admiral Horacio Rivero, Jr., the first Puerto Rican four-star Admiral in the United States Navy, oversaw the day-to-day work of the Navy as the Vice Chief of Naval Operations. He was a stern supporter of a "brown-water navy," or riverine force, on the rivers of South Vietnam.

Lieutenant Diego E. Hernández, who retired from the Navy with the rank of Vice Admiral, flew two combat tours in Vietnam during the war. He also served as Aide and Flag Lieutenant to Commander, Carrier Division 14.

At sea, he was the commander of a fighter squadron, a carrier air wing, and a fleet oiler, the USS Truckee. Hernández later became the first Hispanic to be named Vice Commander, North American Aerospace Defense Command, NORAD.

Amongst the Puerto Ricans who served in the United States Air Force and had distinguished military careers were:

Major General Salvador E. Felices, Brigadier General Antonio Maldonado, Brigadier General Antonio J. Ramos, Brigadier General José M. Portela, Brigadier General Ruben A. Cubero and Colonel Héctor Andrés Negroni.

Major General Salvador E. Felices held various positions within the military. In June 1968, he was named commander of the 306th Bombardment Wing. He flew 39 combat bombing missions over North Vietnam during the Vietnam War in a B-52 aircraft.

In 1969, he became the commander of the 823rd Air Division which covered the regions of Florida, Puerto Rico, North Carolina, and Georgia.

In May 1970, Felices was named Assistant Deputy Chief of Staff at the Headquarters of Strategic Air Command, SAC. He was responsible for SAC's intercontinental ballistic missile, ICBM operational testing programs."

Brigadier General Antonio Maldonado, who in 1967 became the youngest pilot and Aircraft Commander of a B-52 Stratofortress nuclear bomber, was assigned in January 1971 to the 432nd Tactical Fighter Reconnaissance Wing, Udon Royal Thai Air Force Base in Thailand.

His active participation in the war included 183 air combat missions over North and South Vietnam, Laos and Cambodia, logging more than 400 combat flying hours in the F-4C Phantom.

Brigadier General Antonio J. Ramos, the first Hispanic to serve as commander, Air Force Security Assistance Center, Air Force Materiel Command, and dual hatted as Assistant to the Commander for International Affairs, Headquarters Air Force Materiel Command, also served in Vietnam.

In November 1971, Ramos who was then a Lieutenant, was assigned to the 310th Tactical Airlift Squadron, Phan Rang Air Base and Tan Son Nhut Air Base, South Vietnam.

In August 1972, he was transferred to U-Tapao Royal Thai Naval Airfield in Thailand where he was the Base Operations Officer until November 1972.

Brigadier General José M. Portela, as a First Lieutenant, was sent to the Republic of Vietnam during the war and participated in numerous combat missions.

On June 8, 1972, he was promoted to Captain and on September 1972, was reassigned to the 3rd Military Airlift Squadron at Charleston Air Force Base, South Carolina as a C-5 pilot. During his stint there he was assigned to the C-141s and in 1972 became the youngest C-141 Starlifter aircraft commander and captain at the age of 22.

He served at CAF until July 1973, when he joined the Air Force Reserve as a C-5A Initial Cadre at the 312th Airlift Squadron at Travis Air Force Base in California.

Brigadier General Ruben A. Cubero was a Captain when sent to the Republic of Vietnam on May 1969. He was assigned to the 1st Brigade, 25th Infantry Division, 19th Tactical Air Support Squadron, Tay Ninh West where he flew an OV-10 and served as a forward air controller.

In November 1969, he was reassigned to the 19th Tactical Air Support Squadron, at Bien Hoa Air Base. Cubero later became the first Hispanic graduate of the United States Air Force Academy, to be named Dean of the Faculty of the academy.

Colonel Héctor Andrés Negroni, the first Puerto Rican graduate of the United States Air Force Academy, was a Captain when he participated in combat missions during the war and accumulated over 600 combat hours.

During his tour he served in the 553rd Reconnaissance Squadron stationed in Korat, Thailand and as Chief of Combat Operation in the 7th Airborne Command and Control Squadron in Udon, Thailand.

CHAPTER 21

The Medal of Honor

Puerto Rican recipients of the Medal of Honor

Four Puerto Ricans were awarded the Medal of Honor, the highest United States military decoration for heroism.

They were Captain Humbert Roque Versace, Captain Eurípides Rubio, PFC Carlos James Lozada and Specialist Four Hector Santiago-Colon.

All four were members of the United States Army and all four awards were posthumous.

Captain Humbert Roque "Rocky" Versace

Captain Humbert Roque "Rocky" Versace was a United States Army officer of Puerto Rican–Italian descent began his first tour of duty in the Republic of Vietnam as an intelligence advisor.

Versace was captured during his second tour and taken to a prison deep in the jungle along with two other Americans, Lieutenant Nick Rowe, and Sergeant Dan Pitzer.

He tried to escape four times but failed in his attempts. The Viet Cong separated Versace from the other prisoners. The last time the prisoners heard his voice, he was loudly singing "God Bless America".

On September 26, 1965, North Vietnam's "Liberation Radio" announced the execution of Captain Humbert Roque Versace. Versace's remains have never been recovered.

On July 8, 2002, in a ceremony in the White House East Room, Versace was posthumously awarded the Medal of Honor by President George W. Bush for his heroism, the first time an Army POW had been awarded the nation's highest honor for actions in captivity.

Captain Eurípides Rubio

He was a member of H&H Co., 1st Battalion, 28th Infantry, 1st Infantry Division, RVN.

On November 8, 1966, Rubio's company came under attack from the North Vietnamese Army. He left the safety of his post and received two serious wounds. He faced the intense enemy fire to distribute ammunition, re-establish positions and provided aid to the wounded.

Despite his pain, Capt. Rubio accepted full command when a rifle company commander was medically evacuated. He was then wounded a third time as he tried to move amongst his men to encourage them to fight with renewed effort.

While aiding the evacuation of wounded personnel, he noted that a U.S. smoke grenade, which was intended to mark the Viet Cong's position for an air strike, had fallen dangerously close to friendly lines. He ran to move the grenade but was immediately struck to his knees by enemy fire.

Despite of his wounds, Rubio managed to collect the grenade and run through enemy fire to within 20 meters of the enemy position and threw the by then already smoking grenade into the enemy before he fell for the final time.

Using the now repositioned grenade as a marker, friendly air strikes were directed to destroy the hostile positions.

He was assigned to Co. A 2nd Battalion, 503 Infantry, 173rd Airborne Brigade.

PFC Carlos James Lozada

On November 20, 1967, at Dak To, Lozada spotted a North Vietnamese Army company rapidly approaching his outpost. He alerted his comrades and opened fire with a machine gun, killing at least twenty enemy soldiers and disrupting their initial attack.

He realized that if he abandoned his position there would be nothing to hold back the surging North Vietnamese soldiers and that his entire company withdrawal would be jeopardized.

As a result, he told his comrades to move to the back. He also informed them that he would supply cover for them. He continued to deliver a heavy and accurate volume of suppressive fire against the enemy until he was mortally wounded.

PFC Lozada was carried during the withdrawal....

Specialist Four Héctor Santiago Colón

On June 28, 1968, members of Santiago-Colon's Company B of the 5th Battalion, 7th Cavalry, 1st Cavalry Division were engaged in combat at Quảng Trị Province.

An enemy, North Vietnamese, soldier tossed a hand grenade into Santiago Colon's foxhole.

When Santiago Colon realized that the hand grenade was in the foxhole, there was no time to throw get out.

He tucked it in to his stomach and then turned away from his comrades. Santiago Colon absorbed the full impact of the blast. He sacrificed his life to save his fellow soldiers from death.

CHAPTER 22

The Navy Cross

Puerto Rican recipients of the Navy Cross

Two Puerto Ricans were awarded the Navy Cross, the second highest medal that can be awarded by the U.S. Navy and are awarded to members of the U.S. Navy or U.S. Marine Corps for heroism or distinguished service.

They were <u>Sergeant Angel Mendez</u> and <u>Corporal Miguel Rivera-Sotomayor</u>. Both men were members of the United States Marine Corps.

<u>Sgt. Angel Mendez</u>
<u>1946–1967</u>

Corporal Angel Mendez was among the many men who volunteered to join the Marine Corps right after graduating from high school. He was assigned to Company F, 2nd Battalion, 7th Marines, 1st Marine Division on March 16, 1967, and conducting a search and destroy mission with his company when his company came under attack from a Viet Cong battalion.

Half of a platoon was pinned down under enemy fire. Mendez, volunteered to lead a squad to assist the pinned-down Marines in returning to friendly lines with two dead and two seriously wounded. Mendez exposed himself and opened fire on the enemy. His Platoon

Commander, Lieutenant Ronald D. Castille was seriously wounded, and he fell, unable to move.

Mendez shielded him with his body as he applied a dressing to the wound. He picked up the Lieutenant and started to carry him to friendly lines, which were more than seventy-five meters away.

Mendez was hit in the shoulder, yet he chose to act as rear man. He continued to shield his Lieutenant with his own body until he was mortally wounded.

Mendez was posthumously awarded the Navy Cross and promoted to Sergeant.

For saving the life of his platoon commander, Lieutenant Castille, now one of the seven justices of the Supreme Court of Pennsylvania U.S. Senator Charles Schumer has recommended that Mendez' award be upgraded to Medal of Honor.

Corporal Miguel Rivera Sotomayor

He was born in Philadelphia, Pa. to Puerto Rican parents.

Rivera Sotomayor belonged to Company F, 2nd Battalion, 9th Marines, 3rd Marine Division. He silenced enemy machine guns and allowed his platoon to move from its pinned down position to establish an effective base of fire against the enemy.

CHAPTER 23

The Distinguished Service Cross

Puerto Rican recipients of the Distinguished Service Cross

Five Puerto Ricans were awarded the Distinguished Service Cross, DSC, the second highest military decoration of the United States Army.

Actions which merit the Distinguished Service Cross must be of such a high degree to be above those required for all other U.S. combat decorations but not meeting the criteria for the Medal of Honor.

They were Staff Sergeant Efraín Figueroa-Meléndez, Spc4 Fruto James Oquendo, Sergeant First Class Wilfredo Pagan-Lozada, First Sergeant Ramiro Ramirez and Private First-Class Reinaldo Rodriguez. Four of the awards were posthumous.

Spc4 Fruto James Oquendo

Spc4 Fruto James Oquendo, died May 6, 1969, of Puerto Rican descent, was born in New York City. Oquendo was a member of the US Army and in Vietnam served with Company C, 2d Battalion, 8th Cavalry Regiment, 1st Brigade of the 1st Cavalry Division. He was mortally wounded while defending his area during a hand-to-hand struggle.

Sergeant First Class Wilfredo Pagán-Lozada

Sergeant First Class Wilfredo Pagan-Lozada, died February 9, 1967.

He born in New York City to Puerto Rican parents. Pagan-Lozada was a member of the US Army and served in Vietnam with Company D, 2d Battalion, 5th Cavalry Regiment, 1st Cavalry Division.

At the cost of his life, Sgt. Pagan-Lozada, charged into a through a hail of bullets to save an officer's life.

First Sergeant Ramiro Ramirez

First Sergeant Ramiro Ramirez was a member of Company C, 1st Battalion, 18th Infantry Regiment, 2d Brigade, 1st Infantry Division.

First Sergeant Ramirez despite being wounded pulled one of his men to the safety of a bomb crater and refused aid until all others had been treated.

After receiving word that another man had been severely wounded, Sergeant Ramirez volunteered to rescue him. He was hit on the arm and chest as he left the crater.

PFC Reinaldo Rodríguez

Private First-Class Reinaldo Rodríguez died on January 15, 1971. He was born in Guanica, Puerto Rico.

He belonged to Company C, 1st Battalion, 27th Infantry Regiment, 2d Brigade, 25th Infantry Division. Private Rodriguez provided cover fire for his comrades maintaining suppressive fire upon the adversary until he was wounded a third time.

Although evacuated Pvt. Rodriguez was immediately rescued to the rear medical facilities. Rodriguez died due to his wounds.

CHAPTER 24

The Most Decorated Hispanic American soldier

SFC Jorge Otero Barreto

Sergeant First Class Jorge Otero Barreto from the town of Vega Baja, Puerto Rico, with 38 decorations, which included 3 Silver Star Medals, 5 Bronze Star Medals with Valor, 4 Army Commendation Medals, 5 Purple Heart Medals and 5 Air Medals, has been called the most decorated U.S. soldier of the Vietnam War.

Otero Barreto was a member of the U.S. Army from 1961 to 1970. He served in five tours in Southeast Asia, starting as an advisor who helped train Vietnamese troops.

Otero-Barreto participated in 200 combat missions and was awarded 38 military decorations. This made him the most decorated soldier in the United States Armed Forces, for his service during the Vietnam war.

Among his many decorations are 3 Silver Stars, 5 Bronze Stars with Valor, 5 Purple Hearts and 5 Air Medals.

CHAPTER 25

Puerto Ricans Missing in Action

A total of 18 Puerto Ricans were listed as Missing in Action, MIA. This number does not include those who resided in the United States mainland. These numbers only include those who resided in Puerto Rico.

They were all members of the Army with the exceptions of First Lieutenant Jose Hector Ortiz who was a member of the United States Air Force and PFC. Jose Ramon Sanchez a U.S. Marine.

PFC. Humberto Acosta-Rosario is the only one whose body has never been recovered and is currently still listed as MIA.

PFC Humberto Acosta-Rosario

PFC Humberto Acosta-Rosario was a member of Company B, 1st Battalion, 5th Infantry, Mechanized; 25th Infantry Division, United States Army.

On August 22, 1968, Acosta-Rosario accompanied some members of his unit during a scouting mission. His unit was attacked by North Vietnamese Army.

They were regulars in the vicinity of Ben Cui Rubber Plantation, east of Tay Ninh City, Tay Ninh Province. Acosta-Rosario's, Company B, was forced to withdraw from the battlefield under heavy enemy attack.

The unit regrouped and discovered that PFC Acosta-Rosario and another machine gunner, PFC Philip T. DeLorenzo, were reported missing.

NORMA IRIS PAGAN MORALES

An extensive ground search was conducted by members of Company B for the two missing soldiers. The only body recovered was that of PFC DeLorenzo's, along with the two M-60 machine guns.

A search by two battalions who were brought in to sweep the area of only enemy activity did not produce Acosta-Rosario's body. He was officially listed as Missing in Action.

In March 1978, Acosta-Rosario was declared dead, however, the body was never found.

PFC Jose Ramon Sanchez

PFC. Jose Ramon Sanchez was assigned to Company D, 1st Battalion, 4th Marines, 3rd Marine Division...

On June 6, 1968, he was among a group of fellow Marines who comprised a patrol operating in the rugged jungle covered mountains southwest of Khe Sanh, Quảng Trị Province, South Vietnam. Their mission was to block NVA troops and supplies from infiltrating toward Khe Sanh. The Marines engaged a communist force of unknown size in heavy combat.

As the fierce firefight raged around them, the Marines, who were outnumbered and rapidly running low on ammunition, requested an emergency extraction.

A CH46A Sea Knight helicopter was sent for Sanchez and the rest of the patrol who were on Hill 672.'...

As the helicopter gained altitude, it was immediately struck by intense and accurate enemy ground fire causing it to enter a nose-low attitude and crash onto an east/west mountain ridgeline, roll down to the bottom of the hill and burst into flames.

Within an hour and a half, a search and recovery, SAR, team was inserted into the crash site. The team members pulled the charred bodies of the aircrew and passengers from what was left of the burned-out helicopter and placed them in body bags.

Of the 12 of the 23 Marines aboard who were killed, 4 were reported as MISSING IN ACTIO/KILLED IN ACTION, besides Sanchez the other three were Cpl. Palacios and Cpl. Harper.

Various attempts were made to recover the bodies of the four....

In 2006, a team began excavating the site and recovered human remains and non-biological material evidence including La Plant's identification tag.

While at the site, a Vietnamese citizen turned over to the team human remains that he claimed to have found amid the wreckage.

In 2007, another team completed the excavation and recovered additional human remains, life support material and aircraft wreckage.

On November 5, 2008, The Department of Defense POW/Missing Personnel Office, DPMO, announced that the remains of four U.S. servicemen, including Sanchez, were identified.

The remains of the four men share a single casket along with a box engraved with their names which was buried with full military honors at Arlington National Cemetery.

CHAPTER 26

Racial Tensions of the 1960's

The Vietnam War coincided with the protests of the Civil Rights Movement during the 1960's in the United States.

Minority groups, such as Hispanics, were discriminated at home and within the U.S. armed forces.

According to a study made in 1990, by the Department of Psychiatry, Columbia University, Department of Epidemiology, Mailman School of Public Health, Columbia University, and New York State Psychiatric Institute; called the National Survey of the Vietnam Generation (NSVG), Hispanics, among them Puerto Ricans, were younger than both Black and White majority veterans when they went to Vietnam.

Hispanics experienced more prejudice and discrimination in Vietnam than Blacks.

Minority groups would often band together with those of their own racial or ethnic backgrounds. One such group was "Puerto Rican Power in Unity" which eventually became "Latin Power in Unity."

The objective of this group was to unite all the Hispanic Marines regardless of their national background, as a brotherhood. Together they shared their cultures and demanded to be treated equally as their Black and White counterparts in the military.

On April 23, 1975, President Gerald Ford gave a televised speech declaring an end to the Vietnam War. Some sources state that a total of 345 Puerto Ricans who resided in the island died in combat. That wasn't true.

According to a report by the Department of Defense, titled "Number of Puerto Ricans serving in the U.S. Armed Forces during National Emergencies" was more. Total of Puerto Rican soldiers that died was 455 and that were wounded was 3,775.

Because of lack of separate documentation, the total number of Puerto Ricans who lived in the mainland United States and died is unknown.

At the time, Puerto Ricans were not tabulated separately, but were generally included in the general white population census count. Separate statistics were kept for African Americans and Asian Americans.

The names of those who died are inscribed in both the Vietnam Veterans Memorial located in Washington, D.C. and in El Monumento de la Recordación, The Wall of Remembrance, located in San Juan, Puerto Rico.

According to a study made by the Department of Epidemiology and Public Health and the Department of Psychiatry, Yale University, Puerto Rican Vietnam veterans, have a higher risk for posttraumatic stress disorder, PTSD, and experience more severe PTSD symptoms than non-Hispanic white Vietnam veterans, however, despite the hardships suffered by the experiences of war, many went on to live normal everyday lives.

Among the Puerto Ricans who served in Vietnam and held important presidential administrative positions in the Administration of President George W. Bush were Major General William A. Navas Jr., who was awarded the Bronze Star Medal and was named Assistant Secretary of the Navy on June 6, 2001.

Dr. Richard Carmona, a former Green Beret who was awarded two Purple Hearts. He was appointed Surgeon General in March 2002.

World War I, WWI or WW1, also known as the First World War, was a global war centered in Europe that began on 28 July 1914 and lasted until 11 November 1918.

From the time of its occurrence until the approach of World War II in 1939, it was called simply the World War or the Great War, and thereafter the First World War or World War I.

In America, it was initially called the European War...

More than 9 million combatants were killed. It was a scale of death impacted by industrial advancements, geographic stalemate and reliance on human wave attacks.

It was also the fifth-deadliest conflict in world history, paving the way for major political changes, including revolutions in many of the nations involved.

The war drew in all the world's economic great powers, which were assembled in two opposing alliances. They were the Allies, based on the Triple Entente of the United Kingdom, France and the Russian Empire and the Central Powers of Germany and Austria-Hungary.

Although Italy had also been a member of the Triple Alliance alongside Germany and Austria-Hungary, it did not join the Central Powers. Austria-Hungary had taken the offensive against the terms of the alliance.

These alliances were both reorganized and expanded as more nations entered the war:

Italy, Japan, and the United States joined the Allies, and the Ottoman Empire and Bulgaria the Central Powers.

Ultimately, more than 70 million military personnel, including 60 million Europeans, were mobilized in one of the largest wars in history.

Although a rebirth of imperialism was an underlying cause, the immediate trigger for war was the 28 June 1914 assassination of Archduke Franz Ferdinand of Austria, heir to the throne of Austria-Hungary, by Yugoslav nationalist Gavrilo Princip in Sarajevo.

This set off a diplomatic crisis when Austria-Hungary delivered an ultimatum to the Kingdom of Serbia, and international alliances formed over the previous decades were invoked.

Within weeks, the major powers were at war and the conflict soon spread around the world...

On 28 July 1914, the Austro-Hungarians fired the first shots in preparation for the invasion of Serbia.

As Russia mobilized, Germany invaded neutral Belgium and Luxembourg before moving towards France, leading Britain to declare war on Germany.

After the German march on Paris was brought to a halt, what became known as the Western Front settled into a battle of attrition, with a trench line that would change little until 1917.

Meanwhile, on the Eastern Front, the Russian army was successful against the Austro-Hungarians, but was stopped in its invasion of East Prussia by the Germans.

In November 1914, the Ottoman Empire joined the war, opening fronts in the Caucasus, Mesopotamia, and the Sinai. Italy and Bulgaria went to war in 1915 and Romania in 1916.

The war approached a resolution after the Russian Tsar's government collapsed in March 1917 and a subsequent revolution in November brought the Russians to terms with the Central Powers.

After a 1918 German offensive along the western front, the Allies drove back the Germans in a series of successful offensives and American forces began entering the trenches. Germany, which had its own trouble with revolutionaries, agreed to an armistice on 11 November 1918, ending the war in victory for the Allies.

By the end of the war, four major imperial powers. They were the German, Russian, Austro-Hungarian and Ottoman empires. They ceased to exist.

The successor states of the former two lost substantial territory, while the latter two were dismantle. The map of Europe was redrawn, with several independent nations restored or created.

The League of Nations formed with the aim of preventing any repetition of such an appalling conflict. This aim failed, with weakened states, renewed European nationalism and the humiliation of Germany contributing to the rise of fascism and the conditions for World War.

CHAPTER 27

Two Puerto Rican Soldiers Killed in Iraq

The heroic and sad journey of two Puerto Rican soldiers from San Juan and Vega Alta to Taji, Iraq, to the Dover Air Force Base, and finally back home to the Caribbean Island is nearly complete.

Sgt. José M. Cintrón Rosado, 38, and Spc. José Delgado Arroyo, 41, who were killed Jan. 2 when an improvised explosive device detonated in the path of their convoy, are scheduled to be flown to their native Puerto Rico.

The deportation of their bodies – dressed in proper ranks and resting in American-flag-draped caskets – will be welcomed home ceremoniously with an honor guard, the Puerto Rico National Guard said.

"Any loss is tragic and tough," said Major Paul Dahlen of the Puerto Rico National Guard, where the soldiers were assigned. "We're a pretty close group. We consider ourselves a family."

The deaths of Cintrón Rosado and Delgado Arroyo, the third and fourth soldiers from the Puerto Rico National Guard killed since Sept. 11, 2001, are a sad reminder of the sacrifice Puerto Ricans and Latinos have made to the wars in Iraq and Afghanistan.

In all, 593 Latino members of the military have been killed since Oct. 7, 2001, when U.S. soldiers and Marines first landed in Afghanistan, according to the Department of Defense.

That number doesn't include casualties who have committed suicide after returning from their tours.

The most recent example of that ultimate sacrifice is embodied in Cintrón Rosado and Delgado Arroyo. Best friends, the soldiers, part of an engineering unit responsible for clearing roadways of so-called IEDs, were deployed together in April.

"It's a tough job, a dangerous job," said Dahlen. "They're the ones looking to...ensure roadways, so that everyone can continue their jobs and peace in the area."

The soldiers were in the lead vehicle of a convoy of about half a dozen vehicles when, at 8:30 p.m. Iraqi time, the IED exploded. They were the only casualties.

"My husband adored the military," said Cintrón Rosado's widow, María Robles, during a press conference, a portion of which was aired on Primera Hora's Web site. "It was his life, his passion. He was committed to do it for his country."

In addition to his wife, Cintrón Rosado is survived by his sons, Kevin, and Carlos, who are 12 and 14 years old, respectively; Delgado Arroyo leaves behind his wife, Zugeily Colón del Valle, a daughter, and a son.

The soldiers were posthumously promoted: Cintrón Rosado to staff sergeant, Delgado Arroyo to sergeant.

Their bodies will be viewed on Saturday and will be buried shortly thereafter in the Puerto Rico National Cemetery in Bayamón.

Their loss underscores the commitment Puerto Rican soldiers have demonstrated in the military efforts in Iraq, Afghanistan, and other parts of the world where the United States has a presence.

Before Cintrón Rosado and Delgado Arroyo, two Puerto Rican National Guardsmen died in Iraq in 2003 and in 2007. There are still 100 soldiers based there, Dahlen said.

There are only a handful of Puerto Rico National Guard soldiers in Afghanistan, but approximately 1,000 members at different posts worldwide, he added.

"Soldiers from the Puerto Rican National Guard have played a major role in every conflict and military operation for the past 100 years," Dahlen said. "From World War II to Vietnam to the current wars, we have been very much involved, and very proud to do so."

CHAPTER 28

Recorded Military history of Puerto Rico

Puerto Rico's military legacy covers the period from the 16th century until the present engagement of Puerto Ricans soldiers in the United States Armed Forces.

Puerto Rico was part of the Spanish Empire for four centuries. Puerto Rican defended themselves against invasions from the British, French, and Dutch. During that time, Puerto Rico was really the melting pot of the Caribbean.

Puerto Ricans fought alongside General Bernardo de Gálvez during the American Revolutionary War in the battles of Baton Rouge, Mobile, Pensacola and St. Louis. During the mid-19th century, Puerto Ricans residing in the United States fought in the American Civil War.

In the 1800s, the mission for Latin American independence from Spain spread to Puerto Rico, in the short-lived revolution known as the "Grito de Lares". It ended with the "Intento de Yauco".

The island was invaded by the United States during the Spanish American War. After the war ended, Spain officially ceded the island to the United States under the terms established in the Treaty of Paris of 1898.

Puerto Rico became a United States territory, and the "Porto Rico Regiment" Puerto Rico's name was changed to Porto Rico was established on the island.

Upon the outbreak of World War I, the U.S. Congress approved the Jones–Shafroth Act, which extended United States citizenship, the

Puerto Rican House of Delegates rejected US citizenship with limitations upon Puerto Ricans.

By becoming citizens, it made them eligible for the military draft. Since then, as citizens of the United States, Puerto Ricans have participated in every major United States military engagement.

During World War II, Puerto Ricans participated in the Pacific and Atlantic. This was not only as soldiers but also for commanders.

It was during the WW II conflict that Puerto Rican nurses were allowed to participate as members of the WAACs. Four Puerto Ricans were awarded the Medal of Honor.

The highest military honor in the United States, for their actions during the Korean War. The members of Puerto Rico's 65th Infantry Regiment distinguished themselves in combat in the Korean War and were honored with the Congressional Gold Medal.

During the Vietnam War five Puerto Ricans were awarded the Medal of Honor. Presently, Puerto Ricans continue to serve in the military of the United States.

CHAPTER 29

17th century

The Dutch Republic World Military and Commercial Power

The Dutch Republic was a world military and commercial power by 1625, competing in the Caribbean with the English.

The Dutch wanted to establish a military stronghold in the area, and dispatched Captain Boudewijn Hendricksz also known as Boudoyno Henrico or Balduino Enrico to capture Puerto Rico.

On September 24, 1625, Enrico arrived at the coast of San Juan with 17 ships and 2,000 men. Enrico sent a message to the governor of Puerto Rico, Juan de Haro, ordering him to surrender the island.

De Haro refused; he was an experienced military man and expected an attack in the section known as Boquerón. He therefore had that area fortified. However, the Dutch took another route and landed in La Puntilla.

De Haro realized that an invasion was inevitable and ordered Captain Juan de Amézqueta and 300 men to defend the island from El Morro Castle and then had the city of San Juan evacuated. He also had former governor Juan de Vargas organize an armed resistance in the interior of the island.

On September 25, 1625, Hendricksz attacked San Juan, besieging El Morro Castle and La Fortaleza, the Governor's Mansion. He invaded the capital city and set up his headquarters in La Fortaleza.

The Dutch were counterattacked by the civilian militia on land and by the cannons of the Spanish troops in El Morro Castle. The land battle left 60 Dutch soldiers dead and Hendricksz with a sword wound to his neck which he received from the hands of Amézqueta.

The Dutch ships at sea were boarded by Puerto Ricans, who defeated those aboard. After a long battle, the Spanish soldiers and volunteers of the city's militia were able to defend the city from the attack and save the island from an invasion.

On October 21, 1625, Hendricksz set La Fortaleza and the city ablaze. Captains Amézqueta and Andrés Botello decided to put a stop to the destruction and led 200 men in an attack against the enemy's front and rear guard.

They drove Hendricksz and his men from their trenches and into the ocean in haste to reach their ships.

Hendricksz upon his retreat left behind him one of his largest ships, stranded, and over 400 dead.

He then tried to invade the island by attacking the town of Agueda. He was again defeated by the local militia and abandoned the idea of invading Puerto Rico.

In 1693, the Milicias Urbanas de Puerto Rico were organized in almost every town. Every native male, aged between 16 and 60, was obligated to serve in these companies, unless he had an official exemption on account of physical disability or family hardship.

CHAPTER 30

Captain Miguel Henriquez

While Spain and England were in a power struggle in the New World, Puerto Rican privateering of English ships was encouraged by the Spanish Crown. <u>Captain Miguel Enríquez</u> and <u>Captain Roberto Cofresí.</u>

In the 19th century, were two of the most famous Puerto Rican privateers. In the first half of the 18th century, Henriquez, a shoemaker by occupation, decided to try his luck as a privateer.

He showed great valor in intercepting English merchant ships and other ships dedicated to contraband that were infesting the seas of Puerto Rico and the Atlantic Ocean in general.

Henriquez organized an expeditionary force which fought and defeated the English in the island of Vieques. He was received as a national hero when he returned the island of Vieques to the Spanish Empire and to the governorship of Puerto Rico.

In recognition of his service, the Spanish Crown awarded Henriquez the Medalla de Oro de la Real Efigie "The Gold Medal of the Royal Effigy", named him "Captain of the Seas and War", and gave him a letter of marque and reprisal, thus granting him the privileges of privateer.

<u>18th century</u>
<u>Armed conflicts with the British</u>

The English continued their attacks against Spanish colonies in the Caribbean, taking minor islands including Vieques east of Puerto Rico.

On August 5, 1702, the city of Arecibo, on Puerto Rico's northern coast, was invaded by the British. Armed only with spears and machetes, under the command of Captain Antonio de los Reyes Correa, 30 militia members defended the city from the English, who were armed with muskets and swords.

The British were defeated, suffering 22 losses on land and 8 at sea. Reyes Correa was declared a national hero and was awarded the Medalla de Oro de la Real Efigie,"Gold Medal of the Royal Image" and the title of "Captain of Infantry" by King Philip V.

Native-born Puerto Rican "los Criollos" had petitioned the Spanish Crown to serve in the regular Spanish army, resulting in the 1741 organization of the Regiment Fijo de Puerto Rico.

The Fijo served in the defense of Puerto Rico and other Spanish overseas possessions, performing in battles in Santo Domingo, other islands in the Caribbean, and South America, most notably in Venezuela.

However, Puerto Rican complaints that the Fijo was being used to control the revolution in Venezuela caused the Crown to bring the Fijo home and in 1815 it was mustered out of service.

In 1765, the Spanish Crown sent Field Marshal Alejandro O'Reilly to Puerto Rico to form an organized militia.

O'Reilly, known as the "Father of the Puerto Rican Militia", oversaw training to bring fame and glory to the militia in future military engagements, nicknaming the civilian militia the "Disciplined Militia." O'Reilly was later appointed governor of colonial Louisiana in 1769 and became known as "Bloody O'Reilly."

CHAPTER 31

American Revolutionary War

<u>Brigadier General Ramón de Castro</u>

During the American Revolutionary War, Spain lent the rebelling colonists the use of its ports in Puerto Rico, through which flowed financial aid and arms for their cause.

An incident occurred in the coast of Mayagüez, in 1777, between two Continental Navy ships, the Eudawook and the Henry, and a Royal Navy warship, HMS Glasgow. Both American ships were chased by the larger and more powerful Glasgow.

The American colonial ships were close to the coast of Mayagüez; members of the Puerto Rican militia of that town, realizing that something was wrong, signaled for the ships to dock at the town's bay.

After the ships docked, the crews of both ships got off and some Mayagüezanos boarded and raised the Spanish flag on both ships. The commander of the Glasgow became aware of the situation and asked the island's governor, Jose Dufresne to turn over the ships.

Dufresne refused and ordered the British warship out of the Puerto Rican dock.

The governor of Louisiana, Bernardo de Gálvez, was named field marshal of the Spanish colonial army in North America.

In 1779, Galvez and his troops, composed of Puerto Ricans and people from other Spanish colonies, distracted the British from the revolution by capturing Pensacola, the capital of the British colony of West Florida and the cities of Baton Rouge, St. Louis and Mobile.

The Puerto Rican troops, under the leadership of Brigadier General Ramón de Castro, helped defeat the British and Indian army of 2,500 soldiers and British warships in Pensacola.

Galvez and his multinational army also provided the Continental Army with guns, cloth, gunpowder, and medicine shipped from Cuba up the Mississippi River.

General Ramón de Castro, who was Galvez's Aide-de-camp in the Mobile and Pensacola campaigns, became the appointed governor of Puerto Rico in 1795.

CHAPTER 32

British attack Puerto Rico

Anglo-Spanish War 1796–1808
&
Battle of San Juan 1797

Uniform used by the Freed Black Militia of Puerto Rico

On February 17, 1797, the governor of Puerto Rico Brigadier General Ramón de Castro, received news that Great Britain had invaded the island of Trinidad. Believing that Puerto Rico would be the next British goal, he decided to put the local militia on alert and to prepare the island's forts against any military action.

On April 17, 1797, British ships under the command of Sir Ralph Abercromby approached the coastal town of Loíza, to the east of San Juan. On April 18, British and Hessian troops landed on Loíza's beach.

Under the command of de Castro, British ships were shot at by artillery from both El Morro and the San Gerónimo fortresses but were beyond reach.

After the invaders disembarked. practically all fighting was land based with many skirmishes, field artillery and mortar fire exchanges between the San Gerónimo and San Antonio Bridge fortress and British positions in El Condado to the East and El Olimpo hill in Miramar to the South.

The British tried to take the San Antonio, a key passage to the San Juan Isle, and repeatedly bombarded the nearby San Gerónimo almost demolishing it.

At the Martín Peña Bridge, they were met by the likes of <u>Sergeants José and Francisco Díaz</u> and <u>Colonel Rafael Conti</u> who together with <u>Lieutenant Lucas de Fuentes</u> attacked the enemy with two cannons.

After fierce fighting by the Spanish forces and local militia, they were defeated in all attempts to advance into San Juan.

The invasion failed because Puerto Rican volunteers and Spanish troops fought back and defended the island in a manner described by a British lieutenant as of "astonishing bravery".

CHAPTER 33

"La Rogativa" folklore

The defense of San Juan served as the base for the legend of "La Rogativa".

According to the popular Puerto Rican legend, on the night of April 30, 1797, the townswomen, led by a bishop, formed a rogativa, prayer procession.

They marched throughout the streets of the city singing hymns and carrying torches while at the same time praying for the deliverance of the city.

Outside the walls, the invaders mistook the torch-lit movement for the arrival of Spanish reinforcements...

When morning came, the enemy was gone from the island. The city was saved from a possible invasion.

Four statues, sculptured by Lindsay Daen in the Plazuela de la Rogativa, Rogativa Plaza, in Old San Juan, pay tribute to the bishop and townswomen who participated in La Rogativa.

CHAPTER 34

Attack of Aguadilla

The British also attacked Aguadilla and Punta Salinas. They were defeated by Colonel Conti and the members of the militia in Aguadilla, and the British troops that had landed on the island were taken prisoner.

The British retreated on April 30, 1797, to their ships. Then on May 2, 1797, they sailed northward.

Since the defeat given to the British forces, Governor Ramon de Castro petitioned Spanish King Charles IV for recognition for the victors; he was promoted to field marshal and several others were promoted and given pay raises.

In December 1797, the British persisted in invading Puerto Rico, after Abercromby's defeat, with unsuccessful skirmishes on the coastal towns of Aguadilla, Ponce, Cabo Rojo, and Mayagüez.

This continued to occur until 1802 when the Treaty of Amiens ended the War of the Second Coalition between European powers and Revolutionary France.

CHAPTER 35

19th century
Field Marshal Demetrio O'Daly

France had threatened to invade the Spanish colony of Santo Domingo...

In 1808, the Spanish Crown sent their Navy, under the command of Puerto Rican <u>Captain Ramón Power y Giralt</u>, to prevent the invasion of Santo Domingo by the French by enforcing a blockade.

<u>Col. Rafael Conti</u> organized a military expedition with the intention of defending the Dominican Republic. They were successful and were proclaimed as heroes by the Spanish Government.

San Juan native <u>Demetrio O'Daly</u> was a Sergeant Major in the Spanish Army when he participated in the 1809 Peninsular War. This event was also known as the Spanish War of Independence. It happened right after the Napoleonic Invasion of 1808.

All those mentioned conflicts were due to the kidnapping of both King Charles IV and Prince Ferdinand later known as King Ferdinand VII.

When King Ferdinand returned from exile and kidnapping, he repealed the Constitution of 1812. King Ferdinand felt that Napoleonic maneuver weaken the countries.

<u>O'Daly</u> was a defender of the Spanish Constitution of 1812 and was considered a rebel and exiled from Spain by King Fernando VII in 1814.

In 1820 O'Daly, a liberal constitutionalist, together with fellow rebel Col. Rafael Riego organized and led the Revolt of the Colonels.

It was not a revolt against the king, but a revolt to force him reinstate the constitution which was successful.

This was called the Trienio Liberal/Liberal Three years from 1820until 1823.

During this process O'Daly was promoted to field marshal and awarded the Cruz Laureada de San Fernando, Laureate Cross of Saint Ferdinand, the highest military decoration awarded by the Spanish government.

CHAPTER 36

American Civil War

Lieutenant Augusto Rodríguez

Lieutenant Augusto Rodríguez was born in 1841 and died on March 22, 1880. He was a Puerto Rican who served as an officer in the Union Army during the American Civil War. Rodríguez served in the defenses of Washington, D.C., and led his men in the Battles of Fredericksburg and Wyse Fork.

Augusto Rodríguez was born in San Juan, Puerto Rico, when the island was a Spanish province. He emigrated with his family to the United States in the 1850s.

The 1860 census of New Haven, Connecticut, shows there were 10 Puerto Ricans living there, amongst them Augusto Rodríguez, who resided in Columbus Ave.

On August 20, 1862, Rodríguez, whose name was misspelled as Rodreques, married Miss. Eliza Hickox in New Haven. They had a daughter name Clara.

During the 19th century, commerce existed between the ports of the eastern coast of the United States and Puerto Rico. Ship records show that many Puerto Ricans traveled on ships that sailed from and to the U.S. and Puerto Rico. Many of them settled in places such as New York, Connecticut, and Massachusetts.

Upon the outbreak of the American Civil War, many Puerto Ricans joined the ranks of the military armed forces. However, since Puerto Ricans were still Spanish subjects, they were inscribed as Spaniards.

On July 23, 1862, Rodríguez volunteered and joined the 15th Connecticut Volunteer Infantry. For unknown reasons his name was misspelled and listed as "Augustus Rodereques".

He originally held the rank of First Sergeant of Company I. He was promoted to 2nd Lieutenant on April 12, 1864.

The 15th Connecticut was organized on August 25, 1862, in New Haven, and was also known as the "Lyon Regiment" in honor of Nathaniel Lyon, the first general officer killed in the U.S. Civil War.

The Regiment left Connecticut for Washington, D.C., on August 28, and was attached to Casey's Provisional Brigade, Military District of Washington, serving in the defenses of Washington until September 17, 1862.

On December 1 through 6, 1862, the 15th Connecticut Infantry marched to Fredericksburg, Virginia, and was assigned to the 2nd Brigade, 3rd Division, IX Corps, Army of the Potomac commanded by Maj. Gen. Ambrose E. Burnside.

Lieutenant Rodríguez led his men in the Battle of Fredericksburg which was fought against General Robert E. Lee's Confederate Army of Northern Virginia from December 12 thru 15.

The battle resulted in a disastrous defeat for General Burnside and the Union Army. Burnside attempted to make an offensive movement on January 20, 1863, in which Lt. Rodríguez and the men of the 15th Connecticut Regiment were involved. However, the offensive, which became known as the Mud March, was aborted because of constant rain.

In March 1865, Rodríguez and the 15th Connecticut were assigned to the 2nd Brigade, 2nd Division, District of Beaufort, North Carolina, Department of North Carolina.

From March 8 thru 10, Rodríguez once more led his men in combat in the Battle of Wyse Fork, a confrontation against a Confederate army being gathered under Confederate General Joseph E. Johnston and Union troops under the command of Maj. Gen. John M. Schofield.

On the first day of the battle, Lieutenant Rodriguez, along with most of the 15th Connecticut, was surrounded and compelled to surrender.

Rodriguez and his comrades were paroled on March 26. The outcome of the battle resulted in a Union victory.

In the closing months of the war, the 15th Connecticut Infantry was assigned to head duty as part of the garrison upon the occupation of Kinston, North Carolina, by Union forces.

The regiment remained at Kinston until June 6, 1865, when it was ordered to New Bern, North Carolina, to prepare for leave.

The regiment was marshalled out on June 27, 1865, and Rodríguez was discharged in New Haven on July 12, 1865.

After the war Rodríguez became the proprietor of a cigar store, a bartender and saloon keeper. He was also a firefighter in New Haven.

On July 3, 1873, Rodríguez applied for a disability service-connected pension. According to Rodríguez, he claimed to have developed Rheumatoid arthritis during his service in the U.S. Army. He was awarded a pension of $2.00, two dollars, a month.

He died in his home in New Haven on March 22, 1880, and was buried under the name of "Gustave Rodrique" in grave #2 in the Firefighters Pantheon at the Evergreen Cemetery in New Haven.

On Veterans Day, November 11, 2013, Rafael Cruz Miller, and a group representing the Puerto Rican community in Connecticut placed a floral arrangement in a ceremony which recognized Rodriguez as Puerto Rico's first known U.S. Armed Forces veteran.

On August 14 of 2019, Lt. Augusto Rodríguez earthly remains were exhumed from his gravesite at Firefighters Pantheon at the Evergreen Cemetery in New Haven, Connecticut.

On August 15, 2019, at one o clock in the afternoon, his earthly remains where honored with full military honor by the Puerto Rico National Guard and interred at The Puerto Rico National Cemetery. The remains where entombed in a special section of the cemetery.

A New Haven notable mural of Lt. Augusto Rodríguez could be found on Park Street, New Haven.

CHAPTER 37

Slave revolts

Slavery was abolished in Puerto Rico in 1873, however, the wealth accumulated by many landowners in Puerto Rico through a plantation economy was generated by the exploitation of slaves.

According to one source, this reliance on slavery "generated its opposition, disobedience, uprisings and flights."

In Puerto Rico, there were many minor slave revolts in which the slaves clashed with the military establishment.

In July 1821, Marcos Xiorro, a slave, planned and organized a conspiracy against the slave masters and the colonial government of Puerto Rico.

According to his plot, which was to be carried out on July 27, 1821, during the festival celebrations for Santiago, St. James, several slaves were to escape from various plantations in Bayamón.

It included the haciendas of Angus McVean, C. Fortnight, Miguel Andino and Fernando Fernández. They were then to proceed to the sugarcane fields of Miguel Figueres and retrieve cutlasses and swords which were hidden in those fields.

Xiorro, together with a slave from the McBean plantation named Mario and another slave named Narciso, would lead the slaves from Bayamón and Toa Baja.

They would then capture the city of Bayamón. They would burn the city and kill those who were not black...

After this was done, they would all come together with slaves from the adjoining towns of Río Piedras, Guaynabo, and Palo Seco.

With this critical mass of slaves, all armed and heartened from a series of quick victories, they would then invade the capital city of San Juan, where they would then declare Xiorro as their king.

Unfortunately for the slave conspirators, the plot was revealed by a fellow slave to the authorities.

In response, the mayor of Bayamón mobilized 500 soldiers...

Marcos Xiorro and other slaves' ringleaders and their followers of the conspiracy were captured immediately. A total of 61 slaves were imprisoned in Bayamón and San Juan. The ringleaders were executed and the outcome of Xiorro remains a mystery...

There were other minor revolts up until the abolition of slavery in the island became official.

Revolt against Spain
South America

General Antonio Valero de Bernabé, the "Liberator from Puerto Rico"

In 1822, there was an attempt, known as the Ducoudray Holstein Expedition, conceived, carefully planned, and organized by General Henri La Fayette Villaume Ducoudray Holstein to invade Puerto Rico and declare it a republic.

This invasion was different from all its ancestors. All this happened because none before had intended to make Puerto Rico an independent nation.

No one even try to use the Taino name "Boricua" as the official name of the republic.

Puerto Rico intended more as a commercial venture than a patriotic effort. It was the first time an invasion intended to make the city of Mayagüez the capital of the island.

Plans of the invasion were soon disclosed to the Spanish authorities and the plot never occurred.

CHAPTER 38

The Liberator from Puerto Rico

Antonio Vicente Miguel Valero de Bernabé Pacheco was born on October 26, 1790, and died on June 7, 1863, at the age of 73. He was known as The Liberator from Puerto Rico.

The Liberator from Puerto Rico was a Puerto Rican military leader. Trained in Spain, he fought with the Spanish Army to expel the French leader, Napoleon, from Spain and was promoted to colonel during these years.

A variant of his name, Manuel Antonio Valero, has been adopted by some historians, but it is not present in official documentation, nor was it used by him.

Valero de Bernabé had recently graduated from the military academy when Napoleon convinced King Charles IV of Spain to permit the French leader to pass through Spain with his army to attack Portugal. When Napoleon later refused to leave Spanish soil, the government declared war.

Valero de Bernabé joined the Spanish Army and fought as an official of the Murcia Division of Spain and helped defeat Napoleon's army at the Siege of Saragossa, 1808, in the Peninsular War, also known as the Spanish War of Independence.

Valero de Bernabé was a direct descendant of the Aragonese aristocracy and a noble with the recognition of Infanzonería e Hidalguía as a birthright. His titles were traced to May 10, 1372, when Peter IV of Aragon granted the recognitions to Miguel de Bernabé, his siblings and descendants, for his actions during the War of the Two Peters, where he died incinerated at the castle of Báguena after refusing to surrender the fortification to the Castilian forces.

Numerous of his descendants would gather other noble titles, marrying into other aristocratic lineages, becoming counts or marquis.

Military tradition was also present and Aurelio Valero de Bernabé would become a Caballero de Malta.

Among them was also inquisitor Pedro de Arbués y Valero, who was canonized by the Catholic Church in 1867.

However, with time the confusing language of the recognition led to numerous legal proceedings, peaking with several taking place before the General Courts in 1678.

In response, king Phillip and the Fourth Arm of the General Courts elaborated a Ley y Fuero del Reino establishing that these noble titles were recognized to all descendants of Miguel de Bernabé and his sisters, regardless of the origin of their lineage, and that the descendants of the male members of the family would inherit them.

Among the beneficiaries of this infanzería was Juan Valero de Bernabé, father of Antonio Valero de Bernabé Ibañez, the great-grandfather of Valero de Bernabé Pacheco.

During this conflict, he was involved in the defense of the Arrabal, holding his post despite the French advance and being taken prisoner as a result.

After this action, Valero de Bernabé was awarded many decorations and promoted to the rank of colonel at the age of 19.

When Ferdinand VII assumed the throne of Spain in 1813, Valero de Bernabé became critical of the new king's policies towards the Spanish colonies in Latin America. He developed a keen hatred of the monarchy, resigned his commission in the army, and in 1821 emigrated to Mexico with his family.

There he joined the Army of the Three Guarantees headed by Agustín de Iturbide and was appointed as Chief of Staff. He successfully fought for Mexico's independence from Spain, achieved in 1821, after which the people proclaimed Iturbide the Emperor of Mexico, gaining the rank of Brigadier General.

Since Valero de Bernabé had developed anti-monarchist feelings following his experiences in Spain, he led an unsuccessful revolt against Iturbide. He fled the country but was captured by a Spanish pirate and handed over to the authorities in Cuba, where he was imprisoned. Valero de Bernabé escaped from jail with the help of a group of supporters of secessionists from South America.

He joined Simón Bolívar to fight for the independence of the Central and South American colonies from Spain. He also supported the independence of Puerto Rico and Cuba. Like Bolivar, he advocated forming a federation of Latin American nations.

After serving as the Chief of Operations against the faction led by Tadeo Piñago, who was defeated and killed in action, Valero de Bernabé was promoted to Brigadier General. He was named General in Chief of the armies in the provinces of Aragua, Caracas and Guarico, which involved actions at Boca Chica, Jengibre and San Francisco de Tiznado.

Valero de Bernabé led his division in the unsuccessful revolution organized by Falcón. From there he migrated to Colombia and reached Bogotá.

President Mosquera named him Commander in Chief of the 1st Division and Military Chief of the State of Boyacá.

Valero de Bernabé was both a founding father of Venezuela and of the Federal Party of Venezuela. Falsely accused of plotting against Bolívar, he was sent into exile with his family.

When Bolívar died in 1830, Valero de Bernabé was allowed to serve as an honor guard at his funeral. He remained politically active until his own death.

In a career that spanned six decades, taking place in Europe and throughout the Americas, Valero also served in several military and administrative posts.

He was the Commander in Chief of the 2nd Division of the Colombian Army that aided Bolívar at Peru. Bolívar named him Military Chief of the Department of the Panama isthmus.

Valero was also Chief of Staff of the Colombian Army, Military Commander of Valles de Aragua, Military Governor of Puerto Cabello, Minister of War and Navy of Venezuela, under José Tadeo Monagas and José Antonio Páez, Chief of Staff of Mexico, Chief of Operations in the successful campaign against Tamanaco and Güires, Commander of Arms of the province of Caracas.

In addition, Valero received several commendations including the cross of the Independence of Mexico, the Medalla del Libertad or and the Medal del Callao and the Bust of the Liberator of Venezuela.

CHAPTER 39

María de las Mercedes Barbudo

The Puerto Rican Independence movement meetings were held in St. Thomas. They were discovered by the Spanish authorities. The members of the movement were either imprisoned or exiled.

In a letter dated October 1, 1824, which Venezuelan rebel leader José María Rojas sent to María de las Mercedes Barbudo, stated that the Venezuelan rebels had lost their principal contact with the Puerto Rican Independence movement in the Danish Island of Saint Thomas.

Therefore, the secret communication which existed between the Venezuelan rebels and the leaders of the Puerto Rican independence movements was in danger of being discovered.

Mercedes Barbudo, also known as the "first Puerto Rican female freedom fighter", was a businesswoman who became a follower of the independence ideal for Puerto Rico.

Upon learning that Bolivar dreamed of eventually creating an American Revolution-style federation, Mercedes Barbudo got involved.

This new movement would be known as the United Provinces of New Granada, between all the newly independent republics. All with a government ideally set-up solely to recognize and uphold individual rights.

Since Mercedes was involved with the Puerto Rican Independence, she had ties with the Venezuelan rebels led by Simón Bolívar. He was against Spanish colonial rule in Puerto Rico.

Unknown to Mercedes Barbudo, the Spanish authorities in Puerto Rico under <u>Governor Miguel de la Torre</u>, were suspicious of the correspondence between her and the rebel factions of Venezuela.

Secret agents of the Spanish Government had retained some of her mail and delivered it to <u>Governor de la Torre</u>. He ordered an investigation and had her mail confiscated.

The Government believed that the correspondence served as propaganda of the Bolivian ideals and that it would also serve to motivate Puerto Ricans to seek their independence.

<u>Governor Miguel de la Torre</u> ordered Mercedes arrest on the charge that she planned to overthrow the Spanish Government in Puerto Rico.

Since Puerto Rico did not have a women's prison, she was held without bail at the Castillo San Cristóbal...

Among the evidence which the Spanish authorities presented against her was Rojas' letter. She was exiled to Cuba, where she was able to escape and made her way to Venezuela, where she spent her final days.

CHAPTER 40

Roberto Cofresí y Ramírez de Arellano

Roberto Cofresí was born on June 17, 1791, in Cabo Rojo, Puerto Rico and died on March 29, 1825, in San Juan Puerto Rico at the age of 33. He was known as the pirate from Puerto Rico.

Cofresí was born into a noble family, but the political and economic difficulties faced by the island as a colony of the Spanish Empire during the Latin American wars of independence meant that his household was poor.

Cofresí worked at sea from an early age which familiarized him with the region's geography, but it provided only a modest salary. He eventually decided to abandon the sailor's life and became a pirate. He had previous connections to land-based criminal activities.

The reason for Cofresí's change of vocation is unknown. Many historians speculate that he may have worked aboard El Scipión, a ship owned by one of his cousins.

At the height of his career, Cofresí evaded capture by vessels from Spain, Gran Colombia, the United Kingdom, Denmark, France, and the United States.

He commanded several small-draft vessels, the best known a fast six-gun sloop named Anne. He preferred speed and maneuverability over firepower. He operated them with small, rotating crews which most period documents numbered at 10 to 20.

Cofresi preferred to outrun his accusers, but his convoy engaged the West Indies Squadron twice, attacking their boats USS Grampus and USS Beagle.

Most of his crew members were recruited locally, although men occasionally joined them from the other Antilles, Central America, and Europe.

He never confessed to murder, but he reportedly bragged about his crimes, and 300 to 400 people died because of his looting, mostly foreigners.

Cofresí was too much for local authorities, who accepted international help to capture the pirate. Spain created an alliance with the West Indies Squadron and the Danish government of Saint Thomas.

On March 5, 1825, the alliance set a trap which forced Anne into a naval battle. After 45 minutes, Cofresí abandoned his ship and escaped overland. He was recognized by a resident who ambushed and injured him.

Cofresí was captured and imprisoned, making a last unsuccessful attempt to escape by trying to bribe an official with part of a hidden stash.

The pirates were sent to San Juan, Puerto Rico, where a brief military tribunal found them guilty and sentenced them to death.

On March 29, 1825, Cofresí and most of his crew were executed by firing squad.

He inspired stories and myths after his death, most emphasizing a Robin Hood-like "steal from the rich, give to the poor" philosophy which became associated with him.

This portrayal has grown into legend, commonly accepted as fact in Puerto Rico and throughout the West Indies. Some of these claim that Cofresí became part of the Puerto Rican independence movement and other secessionist initiatives, including Simón Bolívar's campaign against Spain.

Historical and mythical accounts of his life have inspired songs, poems, plays, books, and films.

In Puerto Rico, caves, beaches, and other alleged hideouts or locations of buried treasure have been named after Cofresí. A resort town is named for him near Puerto Plata in the Dominican Republic.

In 1945, historian Enrique Ramírez Brau speculated that Cofresí may have had Jewish ancestry.

A theory, held by David Cuesta and historian Ursula Acosta, a member of the Puerto Rican Genealogy Society, held that the name Kupferstein, "copper stone", may have been chosen by his family when the 18th-century European Jewish population adopted surnames.

The theory was later discarded when their research uncovered a complete family tree prepared by Cofresí's cousin, Luigi de Jenner, indicating that their name was spelled Kupferschein not Kupferstein.

Originally from Prague, Cofresí paternal father, Cristoforo Kupferschein, received a recognition and coat of arms from Ferdinand I from Austria in December 1549. Eventually, he moved to Trieste. His last name was probably adapted from the town of Kufstein.

After its arrival, the family became one of Trieste's early settlers. Cristoforo's son Felice was recognized as a noble in 1620, becoming Edler von Kupferschein.

The family gained prestige and became one of the city's wealthiest, with the next generation receiving the best possible education and marrying into other influential families.

Cofresí's grandfather, Giovanni Giuseppe Stanislas de Kupferschein, held several offices in the police, military, and municipal administration.

According to Acosta, Cofresí's father Francesco Giuseppe Fortunato von Kupferschein received an education and left at age 19 for Frankfurt, probably in search of a university or legal practice.

In Frankfurt he mingled with influential figures such as Johann Wolfgang von Goethe, returning to Trieste two years later.

As a cosmopolitan, mercantile city Trieste was a probable hub of illegal trade, and Francesco was forced to leave after he killed Josephus Steffani on July 31, 1778.

Although Steffani's death is commonly attributed to a duel, given their acquaintanceship, both worked at a criminal court, it may have been related to illegal activity.

Francesco's name and those of four sailors soon became connected to the murder. Convicted, the fugitive remained in touch with his family. Francesco went to Barcelona, reportedly learning Spanish there.

By 1784 he had settled in Cabo Rojo, Puerto Rico, a harbor town recently separated from the municipality of San Germán. There he was accepted by the local upper classes with the Spanish honorific Don, "of noble origin".

Francesco's name was Hispanicized to Francisco José Cofresí, his third given name was not, which was easier for his neighbors to pronounce.

Since he was related to illegal commerce in his homeland, he probably relocated to Cabo Rojo for strategic reasons. Its harbor was far from San Juan, the capital.

Francisco soon met María Germana Ramírez de Arellano y Segarra, and they got married. His wife was born to Clemente Ramírez de Arellano y del Toro y Quiñones Rivera. He was a noble and first cousin of town founder Nicolás Ramírez de Arellano y Martínez de Matos.

Her paternal family, descended from the Jimena royal dynasty of the Kingdom of Navarre and the first royal house of the Kingdom of Aragón said house was established by a Jimena prince, owned a significant amount of land in Cabo Rojo.

After their marriage, the couple settled in El Tujao or El Tujado near the coast.

Francisco's father, Giovanni died in 1789. A petition pardoning him for Steffani's murder a decade before was granted two years later enabling him to return to Trieste. There is no evidence that exists that Francisco ever returned to the city.

The Penniless Nobleman and Bandit

The Latin American wars of independence had repercussions in Puerto Rico. This was due to widespread privateering and other naval warfare, maritime commerce suffered heavily.

Cabo Rojo was among the municipalities affected most, with its ports at a virtual standstill. African slaves took to the sea in an attempt at freedom. The merchants were assessed higher taxes and harassed by foreigners.

Under these conditions, Cofresí was born to Francisco and María Germana. The youngest of four children, he had one sister Juana and two brothers Juan Francisco and Juan Ignacio.

Cofresí was baptized into the Catholic Church by José de Roxas, the first priest in Cabo Rojo, when he was fifteen days old. María died when Cofresí was four years old, and an aunt assumed his upbringing.

Francisco then began a relationship with María Sanabria, the mother of his last child Julián. A don by birth, Cofresí's education was above average.

Since there is no evidence of a school in Cabo Rojo at that time, Francisco may have educated his children or hired a tutor. Cofresí was raised in a multicultural environment. He probably knew Dutch and Italian.

In November 1814 Francisco died, leaving a modest estate. Roberto was probably homeless, with no income.

On January 14, 1815, three months after his father's death, Cofresí married Juana Creitoff in San Miguel Arcángel parish, Cabo Rojo.

Contemporary documents are unclear about her birthplace. it is believed and listed as Curaçao. She was probably born in Cabo Rojo to Dutch parents.

After their marriage, the couple moved to a residence bought for 50 pesos by Creitoff's father, Geraldo.

Months later Cofresí's father in-law lost his humble home in a fire, pushing the family into debt.

Three years after his marriage, Cofresí owned no property and lived with his mother-in-law, Anna Cordelia.

He established ties with residents of San Germán, including his brothers-in-laws. They were the wealthy merchants Don Jacobo Ufret and Don Manuel Ufret.

The couple struggled to begin a family of their own, conceiving two sons Juan and Francisco Matías who died soon after birth.

Although he belonged to a prestigious family, Cofresí was not wealthy...

In 1818 he paid 17 maravedís in taxes, spending most of his time at sea and earning a low wage.

According to historian Walter Cardona Bonet, Cofresí probably worked in several fishing corrals in Boquerón Bay. The corrals belonged to the aristocrat Cristóbal Pabón Dávila, a friend of municipal port captain José Mendoza.

This connection is believed to have later protected Cofresí, since Mendoza was godfather to several of his brother Juan Francisco's children.

The following year he first appeared on a government registry as a sailor, and there is no evidence connecting him to any other jobs in Cabo Rojo.

Although Cofresí's brothers were maritime merchants and sailed a boat, Avispa, he probably worked as an able fisherman.

On December 28, 1819, Cofresí was registered on Ramona, ferrying goods between the southern municipalities.

In addition, her frequent voyages to the Mona Passage and Cofresí's recognition by residents indicate that he occasionally accompanied Avispa. That year, Cofresí and Juana lived in Barrio del Pueblo and paid higher taxes than the previous year, five reales.

Political changes in Spain affected Puerto Rico's stability during the first two decades of the 19th century.

Europeans and refugees from the American colonies began arriving after the Royal Decree of Graces of 1815, changing the archipelago's economic and political environments.

With strategic acquisitions, the new arrivals triggered a rise in prices. Food distribution was inefficient, particularly in non-agricultural areas.

By 1816, Governor Salvador Meléndez Bruna shifted responsibility for law enforcement from the Captaincy General of Puerto Rico to the mayors.

Driven by hunger and unmotivated and desperate, the local population drifted toward crime poverty, highway robbers continued to roam southern and central Puerto Rico.

In 1817, the wealthy San Germán residents requested help with the criminals. They were invading houses and shops. The following year, Meléndez established a high-security prison at El Arsenal in San Juan.

During the next few years, the governor transferred repeat offenders to San Juan. Cabo Rojo, with its high crime rate, also dealt with civil strife, inefficient law enforcement and corrupt officials.

While he was still a don, Cofresí led a criminal gang in San Germán which stole cattle, food, and crops. He was associated to an organization operating near the Hormigueros since at least 1818 and to another nobleman, Juan Geraldo Bey.

Among Cofresí's associates were Juan de los Reyes, José Cartagena and Francisco Ramos, and the criminals continued to thrive in 1820.

The situation worsened with the arrival of unauthorized street vendors from nearby municipalities, who were soon robbed. A series of storms and droughts drove residents away from Cabo Rojo, worsening the already-poor economy. The authorities retrained the unemployed and underemployed as night watchmen.

The regional harvest was destroyed by a September 28, 1820, hurricane, triggering the region's largest crime wave to date.

Newly appointed Puerto Rican governor Gonzalo Aróstegui Herrera immediately ordered Lieutenant Antonio Ordóñez to round up as many criminals as possible.

On November 22, 1820, a group of fifteen men from Cabo Rojo participated in the highway robbery of Francisco de Rivera, Nicolás Valdés, and Francisco Lamboy on the outskirts of Yauco.

Cofresí is believed to have been involved in this incident because of its timing and the criminals' connection to an area headed by his friend, Cristóbal Pabón Dávila. The incident sparked an uproar in towns throughout the region and convinced the governor that the authorities were conspiring with the criminals.

Among measures taken by Aróstegui were a mayoral election in Cabo Rojo, Juan Evangelista Ramírez de Arellano, one of Cofresí's relatives, was elected.

The incoming mayor was ordered to control crime in the region, an unrealistic demand with the resources at his disposal. Bernardo Pabón Davila, a friend of Cofresí and relative of Cristóbal, was assigned to prosecute the Yauco incident.

Bernardo reportedly protected the accused and argued against pursuing the case, saying that according to "private confidences" they started fleeing to the United States.

Other initiatives to capture highway robbers in Cabo Rojo were more successful, resulting in over a dozen arrests; among them was the nobleman Bey, who was charged with murder. Known as "El Holandés", Bey testified that Cofresí led a criminal gang.

Cofresí's primary collaborators were the Ramírez de Arellano family, who prevented his capture as Cabo Rojo's founding family with high positions in politics and law enforcement.

The central government issued wanted posters for Cofresí, and in July 1821 he and the rest of his gang were captured. Bey escaped, becoming a fugitive.

Cofresí and his men were tried in San Germán's courthouse, where their connection to several crimes was proven.

On August 17, 1821, while Cofresí was in prison. Juana gave birth to their only daughter, Bernardina.

Due to his noble status, Cofresí probably received a pass for the birth and took the opportunity to escape. In alternative theories, he broke out or was released on parole.

While Cofresí was a fugitive, Bernardo Pabón Davila was Bernardina's godfather and Felícita Asencio her godmother.

On December 4, 1821, a wanted poster was circulated by San Germán mayor Pascacio Cardona. There is little documentation of Cofresí's whereabouts in 1822.

Historians have suggested that he exploited his upper-class connections to remain concealed. The Ramírez de Arellano family held most regional public offices, and their influence extended beyond the region.

Other wealthy families, including the Beys, had similarly protected their relatives and Cofresí may have hidden in plain sight due to the inactivity of Cabo Rojo authorities.

When he became a wanted man, he moved Juana and Anna to her brothers' houses and would visit in secret. Juana also visited him at his headquarters in the rural ward of Pedernales in Cabo Rojo.

It is unknown how far Cofresí traveled during this time, but he had associates on the east coast and may have taken advantage of eastern migration from Cabo Rojo.

Although he may have been captured and imprisoned in San Juan, he does not appear in contemporary records. However, Cofresí's associates Juan "El Indio" de los Reyes, Francisco Ramos and José "Pepe" Cartagena were released only months before his recorded reappearance.

"Last of the Caribbean Pirate"

By 1823, Cofresí was probably on the crew of the barbary pirate barquentine El Scipión, captained by José Ramón Torres and managed by his cousin, the first mayor of Mayagüez, José María Ramírez de Arellano.

All historians agree, since several of his friends and family members benefited from the sale of stolen goods. Cofresí may have joined to evade the authorities, perfecting skills he would use later in life.

El Scipión employed questionable tactics later associated with the pirate, such as flying the flag of Gran Colombia so other ships would lower their guard, as she did in capturing the British frigate Aurora and the American brigantine Otter. The capture of Otter led to a court order requiring restitution, affecting the crew.

At this time, Cofresí turned to piracy. Although the reasons behind his decision are unclear, several theories have been proposed by researchers.

In "Orígenes portorriqueños" Ramírez Brau speculates that Cofresí's time aboard El Scipión, or seeing a family member become a privateer, may have influenced his decision to become a pirate after the crew's pay was threatened by the lawsuit.

According to Acosta, a lack of work for privateers ultimately pushed Cofresí into piracy. The timing of this decision was crucial in establishing him as the dominant Caribbean pirate of the era.

Cofresí began his new career in early 1823, filling a role vacant in the Spanish Main since the death of Jean Lafitte, and was the last major target of West Indies anti-piracy_operations.

While piracy was heavily monitored and most pirates were rarely successful, Cofresí was confirmed to have looted at least eight vessels and has been credited with over 70 captures.

Unlike his predecessors, Cofresí is not known to have imposed a pirate code on his crew. His leadership was enhanced by an audacious personality, a trait acknowledged even by his pursuers.

According to 19th-century reports, he had a rule of engagement that when a vessel was captured, only those willing to join his crew were permitted to live.

Cofresí's influence extended to many civil informants and associates, forming a network which took 14 years after his death to fully dismantle.

The earliest document linked to Cofresí's modus operandi is a letter dated July 5, 1823, from Aguadilla, Puerto Rico which was published in the St. Thomas Gazette.

The letter reported that a brigantine, loaded with coffee and West Indian indigo from La Guairá, was boarded by pirates on June 12, 1823.

The hijackers ordered the ship brought to Isla de Mona, incorrectly anglicized as "Monkey Island", a small island in the eponymous passage between Puerto Rico and Hispaniola, where its captain and crew were ordered to unload the cargo.

After this was done, the pirates reportedly killed the sailors and sank the brigantine. Both of Cofresí's brothers were soon involved in his operation, helping him move loot and deal with captured ships.

Juan Francisco was able to gather information about maritime traffic in his work at the port, presumably forwarding it to his brother.

The pirates communicated with their accomplices through coastal signs, and their associates on land warned them of danger. The system was probably used to identify loaded vessels as well.

According to Puerto Rican historian Aurelio Tió, Cofresí shared his loot with the needy, especially family members and close friends and was considered the Puerto Rican equivalent of Robin Hood.

Acosta disagrees, saying that any acts of generosity were probably opportunistic. Cardona Bonet's research suggests that Cofresí organized improvised markets in Cabo Rojo, where the stolen goods would be informally sold.

According to this theory, merchant families would buy goods for resale to the public. The process was facilitated by local collaborators, such as French smuggler Juan Bautista Buyé.

On October 28, 1823, months after the El Scipión case was settled, Cofresí attacked a ship registered to the harbor of Patillas. He robbed the small fishing boat of 800 pesos in cash.

Cofresí attacked with other members of his gang and that of another pirate, Manuel Lamparo, who was connected to British pirate Samuel McMorren, also known as Juan Bron.

That week, he also led the capture of John, an American yacht. Out of Newburyport and captained by Daniel Knight. It was on its way to Mayagüez.

The ship was captured by a ten-ton boat armed with a swivel gun near Desecheo Island. Cofresí's group, consisting of seven pirates armed with sabers and muskets, stole $1,000 in cash, tobacco, tar and other provisions and the vessel's square rig and mainsail.

Cofresí ordered the crew to head for Santo Domingo, threatening to kill everyone aboard if they were seen at any Puerto Rican port. Despite the threat, Knight went to Mayagüez and reported the incident.

Old map of Hispaniola and Puerto Rico

Map of the area where Cofresí and his men usually operated. They were Puerto Rico, Mona, Vieques, Crab Island, Culebra, Saona, Hispaniola and Saint Thomas.

It was soon established that some of the pirates were from Cabo Rojo since they disembarked there. Undercover agents were sent to the town to track them, and new mayor Juan Font y Soler requested resources to deal with a larger group which was out of control.

The connections between the pirates and local sympathizers made arresting them difficult.

The central government, frustrated with Cabo Rojo's inefficiency, demanded the pirates' capture and western Puerto Rico military commander José Rivas was ordered to use pressure on local authorities.

Although Cofresí was tracked to the beach in Piñones, near his brothers' homes in Guayanilla. The operation only recovered the John's sails, meat, flour, cheese, lard, butter and candles.

The pirates escaped aboard a boat. A detachment caught Juan José Mateu and charged him with conspiracy. His confession connected Cofresí to the two hijackings. Cofresí's sudden success was an odd thing, nearly a century after the end of the Golden Age of Piracy.

By this time, joint governmental efforts had destroyed widespread buccaneering by Anglo-French seamen, primarily based on Jamaica and Tortuga, which had turned the Caribbean into a haven for pirates

NORMA IRIS PAGAN MORALES

attacking shipments from the region's Spanish colonies. This made his capture a priority.

By late 1823, the pursuit on land probably forced Cofresí to move his main base of operations to Mona. The following year, he was often there.

This base, initially a temporary refuge with Barrio Pedernales his stable outpost, became more heavily used. Easily accessible from Cabo Rojo, Mona had been associated with pirates for more than a century; it was visited by William Kidd, who landed in 1699 after fleeing with a load of gold, silver, and iron.

A second pirate base was found at Saona, an island south of Hispaniola.

In November, several sailors aboard El Scipión took advantage of her officers' shore leave and mutinied, seizing control of the ship.

The vessel, repurposed as a pirate ship, began operating in the Mona Passage and was later seen at Mayagüez before disappearing from the record.

Cofresí was connected to El Scipión by pirate Jaime Márquez, who admitted under police questioning on Saint Thomas that boatswain Manuel Reyes Paz was a Cofresí associate.

The confession hints that the ship was captured by Hispaniola authorities. Cofresí is recorded in eastern Hispaniola, then part of the unified Republic of Haiti, modern-day Dominican Republic, where his crew reportedly rested off Puerto Plata province.

On one excursion, the pirates were intercepted by Spanish patrol boats off the coast of Samaná Province. With no apparent escape route, Cofresí is said to have ordered the vessel's sinking and it sailed into Bahía de Samaná before coming to rest near the town of Punta Gorda.

This created a diversion, allowing him and his crew to escape in skiffs they rowed to shore and adjacent wetlands, where the larger Spanish ships could not follow.

The remains of the ship, reportedly full of stolen goods, have not been found.

In an article in the May 9, 1936, issue of Puerto Rico Ilustrado, Eugenio Astol described an 1823 incident between Cofresí and Puerto Rican physician and politician Pedro Gerónimo Goyco.

The 15-year-old Goyco traveled alone on a boat to a Santo Domingo school for his secondary education. In mid-voyage, Cofresí intercepted the ship, and the pirates boarded it.

Cofresí assembled the passengers, asking their names and those of their parents. When he learned that Goyco was among them, the pirate ordered a change of course. They landed on a beach near Mayagüez, where Goyco was freed.

Cofresí explained that he knew Goyo's father, an immigrant from Herceg Novi named Gerónimo Goicovich who had settled in Mayagüez.

Goyco returned home safely, later attempting the voyage again. The elder Goicovich had favored members of Cofresí's family, despite their association with a pirate.

Goyco grew up to become a militant abolitionist, like Ramón Emeterio Betances and Segundo Ruiz Belvis.

Cofresí's actions quickly gained the attention of the Anglo-American nations, who called him "Cofrecinas" a mistranslated, onomatopoeic variant of his last name.

Commercial agent and US Consul Judah Lord wrote to Secretary of State John Quincy Adams, describing the El Scipión situation and the capture of John. Adams relayed the information to Commodore David Porter, leader of the anti-piracy West Indies Squadron, who sent several ships to Puerto Rico.

On November 27 Cofresí sailed from his base on Mona with two boats armed with pivot gun cannons.

They assaulted another American ship, the brigantine William Henry. The Salem Gazette reported that the following month a boat sailed from Santo Domingo to Saona, capturing 18 pirates, including Manuel Reyes Paz, and a "considerable quantity" of leather, coffee, indigo, and cash.

The International Manhunt

Cofresí's victims were locals and foreigners, and the region was economically destabilized. When he boarded Spanish vessels, he usually targeted immigrants brought by the royal decree of 1815, ignoring his fellow criollos.

The situation was complicated by several factors, most of them geopolitical. The Spanish Empire had lost most of its possessions in the New World, and her last two territories. They were Puerto Rico and Cuba who faced economic problems and political unrest.

To undermine the commerce of former colonies, Spain stopped issuing letters of marque. This left sailors unemployed, and they gravitated towards Cofresí and piracy.

On the diplomatic front, the pirates assaulted foreign ships while flying the Flag of Spain, angering nations who had reached an agreement about the return of ships captured by corsairs and compensation for losses.

Aware that the problem had developed international overtones, Spanish-appointed governor of Puerto Rico Lt. Gen. Miguel Luciano de la Torre y Pando in 1822–1837. This made Cofresí's capture a priority.

By December 1823, other nations joined the effort to combat Cofresí, sending warships to the Mona Passage.

Gran Colombia sent two corvettes, Bocayá and Bolívar, under the command of former privateer and Jean Lafitte associate Renato Beluche.

The British assigned the brig-sloop HMS Scout to the region after the William Henry incident.

On January 23, 1824, de la Torre implemented anti-piracy measures in response to Spanish losses and political pressure from the United States, ordering that pirate be tried in a military tribunal with the defendants considered enemy combatants.

De la Torre ordered the pursuit of pirates, bandits, and those aiding them, issuing medals, certificates and bounties in gold and silver as rewards.

Manuel Lamparo was captured on Puerto Rico's east coast, and some of his crew joined Cofresí and other fugitives.

United States Secretary of the Navy Samuel L. Southard ordered David Porter to assign ships to the Mona Passage, and the commodore sent the boat USS Weasel and the brigantine USS Spark.

The ships were to investigate the zone, gathering information at Saint Barthelemy and St. Thomas with the goal of destroying the base at Mona.

Although Porter warned that the pirates were reportedly well-armed and -supplied, he said the crews would probably not find any loot at the base because of the proximity of eastern Puerto Rican ports.

On February 8, 1824, the Spark arrived at Mona, conducted reconnaissance, and landed. A suspicious boat was seen, but Captain John T. Newton decided not to chase her.

The crew found a small settlement with an empty hut and other buildings, a chest of medicine, sails, books, an anchor, and documents from William Henry.

Newton ordered the base and a large canoe found in the vicinity destroyed and reported his findings to the Secretary of the Navy.

According to another report, the ship sent was the USS Beagle. In this account, several pirates evaded the Beagle's crew.

Attacks on two brigantines were reported by Renato Beluche on February 12, 1824 and published in El Colombiano several days later.

The first was Boniton, captained by Alexander Murdock, which sailed with a load of cocoa from Trinidad and was intercepted En route to Gibraltar.

The second, Bonne Sophie, sailed from Havre de Grace under the command of a man named Chevanche with dry goods bound for Martinique.

In both cases, the sailors were beaten and imprisoned, and the ships were robbed.

The ships were part of a convoy escorted by the Bolívar off Puerto Real, Cabo Rojo. Cofresí captained a ship identified by Beluche as a pailebot, a small boat.

Although Bolívar could not capture her, her crew described the vessel as painted black, armed with a rotating cannon, and having a crew of twenty unidentified Puerto Rican men.

Cofresí was presumably leading the vessels to dock at Pedernales, where Mendoza and his brother could facilitate the distribution of loot with the aid of official inertia. From there, other associates usually used Boquerón Bay for transportation and ensured that the loot reached stores in Cabo Rojo and nearby towns.

In this region Cofresí's influence extended to government and the military, with the Ramírez de Arellano family involved in the smuggling and sale of his loot.

On land the loot, hidden in sacks and barrels, was brought to Mayagüez, Hormigueros or San Germán for distribution. When Beluche returned to Colombia, he published an article critical of the situation in the press. La Gaceta de Puerto Rico countered, accusing him of stealing Bonne Sophie and connecting him to the pirates.

On February 16, 1824, de la Torre mandated a more-aggressive pursuit and prosecution of pirates.

In March the governor ordered a search for the boat Caballo Blanco, reportedly used in the boarding of Boniton and Bonne Sophie and similar attacks.

In private communication with Mayagüez military commander José Rivas, he asked Rivas to find someone trustworthy who could launch a mission to capture "the so-called Cofresin" and to notify him personally of the pirate's arrest.

Authorizing the use of force, the governor described Cofresí as "one of the evil ones that I am pursuing" and acknowledged that the pirate was protected by Cabo Rojo authorities.

The mayor was unable or unwilling to cooperate, despite orders from de la Torre.

Rivas tracked Cofresí to his house twice but found it empty…

When the captain lost contact with the pirate and his wife, he was also unable to communicate with the mayor. A similar search was undertaken in San Germán, whose mayor reported to de la Torre on March 12, 1824.

Martinique governor François-Xavier Donzelot wrote to de la Torre on March 22, concerned about the capture of Bonne Sophie and the impact of piracy on maritime commerce.

This brought France into the search for Cofresí. In March 23 de la Torre authorized France to patrol the Puerto Rican coast and commissioned a frigate, Flora.

The mission was led by a military commander named Mallet, who was ordered to the west coast and pursue the pirates "until he was able to trap and destroy them".

Although Flora arrived three days after the operation's approval, the attempt was unsuccessful. Rivas then assigned Joaquín Arroyo, a retired Pedernales militiaman, to monitor activity near Cofresí's house.

There were 1824 wanted poster, offering a bounty in gold and silver for Cofresí's capture....

In April 1824, Rincon mayor Pedro García authorized the sale of a vessel owned by Juan Bautista de Salas to Pedro Ramírez. Ramírez, who may have been a member of the Ramírez de Arellano family, lived in Pedernales and was a neighbor of Cofresí's brothers and Cristobal Pabón Davila.

On April 30, shortly after acquiring the ship, Ramírez sold it to Cofresí, who used it as a pirate flagship. The irregularity of the transactions was quickly noticed, urging an investigation of García.

The scandal weakened his already-frail authority, and Matías Conchuela intervened as the governor's representative.

De la Torre asked the mayor of Añasco, Thomás de la Concha, to retrieve the records and verify their accuracy. The investigation, led by public prosecutor José Madrazo of the Regimento de Granada's Military Anti-Piracy Commission, concluded with Bautista's imprisonment and sanctions for García.

Several members of the Ramírez de Arellano family were prosecuted, including the former mayors of Añasco and Mayagüez, Manuel and José María, Tómas and Antonio.

Others with the same last name but unclear parentage, such as Juan Lorenzo Ramirez, were also linked to Cofresí.

Several unsuccessful searches were carried out in Cabo Rojo by an urban militia led by Captain Carlos de Espada, and additional searches were made in San Germán.

On May 23, 1824, the Mayagüez military commander prepared two vessels and sent them to Pedernales in response to reported sightings of Cofresí. Rivas and the military captain of Mayagüez, Cayetano Castillo y Picado, boarded a ship commanded by Sergeant Sebastián Bausá.

Sailor Pedro Alacán, best known as the grandfather of Ramón Emeterio Betances and a neighbor of Cofresí, was captain of the second schooner. The expedition failed, only finding a military deserter named Manuel Fernández de Córdova.

Also known as Manuel Navarro, Fernández was connected to Cofresí through Lucas Branstan, a merchant from Trieste who was involved in Bonne Sophie incident.

In the meantime, the pirates fled toward southern Puerto Rico. Poorly supplied after his hasty retreat, Cofresí docked at Jobos Bay on June 2, 1824. About a dozen pirates invaded the hacienda of Francisco Antonio Ortiz, stealing his cattle.

The group then broke into a second estate, owned by Jacinto Texidor, stole plantains, and resupplied their ship. It is now believed that Juan José Mateu gave the pirates refuge in one of his haciendas, near Jobos Bay.

The next day the news reached Guayama mayor Francisco Brenes, who quickly contacted the military and requested operations by land and sea.

He was told that there were not enough weapons in the municipality for a mission of that scale. Brenes then requested supplies from Patillas, which rushed him twenty guns. The pirates then fled the municipality and traveled west.

On June 9, 1824, Cofresí led an assault on the boat San José y Las Animas off the coast of Tallaboa in Peñuelas. The ship was en route between Saint Thomas and Guayanilla with over 6,000 pesos' worth of dry goods for Félix and Miguel Mattei, who were aboard.

The Mattei brothers are now believed to have been anti-establishment smugglers related to Henri La Fayette Villaume Ducoudray Holstein and the Ducoudray Holstein Expedition.

The boat, owned by Santos Lucca, sailed with captain Francisco Ocasio and a crew of four. Often used to transport cargo throughout the southern region and Saint Thomas, she made several trips to Cabo Rojo.

When Cofresí began the chase, Ocasio headed landward. The brothers abandoned ship and swam ashore, from where they watched the ship's looting.

Portugués was second-in-command during the boarding of San José y las Animas, and Joaquín "El Campechano" Hernández was a crew member. The pirates took most of the merchandise, leaving goods valued at 418 pesos, three reales and 26 maravedi.

Governor Miguel de la Torre was visiting nearby municipalities at the time, which occupied the authorities. The cargo from San José y Las Animas, containing clothing belonging to the brothers and a painting was later found at Cabo Rojo.

Days later, a small boat commanded by Luis Sánchez and Francisco Guilfuchi left Guayama in search of Cofresí. Unable to find him, they returned on June 19, 1824. The Patillas and Guayama enacted measures, monitored by the governor, which were intended to prevent further visits.

De la Torre continued his tour of the municipalities, ordering Rivas to focus on the Cabo Rojo area when he reached Mayagüez. The task was given to Lieutenant Antonio Madrona, leader of the Mayagüez fort.

Madrona assembled troops and left for Cabo Rojo, launching an operation on June 17, 1824, which ended with the arrest of pirate Eustaquio Ventura de Luciano at the home of Juan Francisco. The troops came close to capturing a second associate, Joaquín "El Maracaybero" Gómez.

Madrona then began a surprise attack at Pedernales. They found Cofresí and several of his associates, including Juan Bey, his brother Ignacio, and his brother-in-law Juan Francisco Creitoff.

The pirates had only one option and was to flee on foot. The Cofresí brothers escaped, but Creitoff and Bey were captured and tried in San Germán.

Troops later visited Creitoff's house, where they found Cofresí's wife and mother-in-law. They questioned the women. The women confirmed the brothers' identities.

The authorities continued searching the homes of those involved and those of their families, where they found quantities of stolen goods hidden and prepared for sale. Madrona also found burned loot on a nearby hill.

Juan Francisco Cofresí, Ventura de Luciano and Creitoff were sent to San Juan with other suspected associates. Of this group the pirate's brother, Luis de Río, and Juan Bautista Buyé were prosecuted as accomplices instead of pirates. Ignacio was later arrested and charged as an accomplice.

The Mattei brothers filed a claim against shopkeeper Francisco Betances that some of his merchandise was cargo from San José y Las Animas.

In response to a tip, José Mendoza and Rivas organized an expedition to Mona. On June 22, 1824, Pedro Alacán assembled a party of eight volunteers. Among them Joaquín Arroyo, possibly Mendoza's source.

He lent a small sailboat he co-owned, the Avispa, once used by Cofresí's brothers to José Pérez Mendoza and Antonio Gueyh. There were eight volunteers. The locally coordinated operation intended to ambush and apprehend Cofresí in his hideout.

The expedition left the coast of Cabo Rojo with Action Stations in place. Despite unfavorable sea conditions, the party arrived at their destination. However, as soon as they disembarked Avispa was lost.

Although most of the pirates were captured without incident, Cofresí's second in-command Juan Portugués was shot to death in the back and dismembered by crewmember Lorenzo Camareno. Among the captives was a man identified as José Rodríguez, but Cofresí was not with his crew.

Five days later, they returned to Cabo Rojo on a ship confiscated from the pirates with weapons. Three prisoners and Portugués' head and right hand, probably for identification when claiming the reward.

Rivas contacted de la Torre, informing him of further measures to track the pirates.[136] The governor publicized the expedition, writing an account which was published in the government newspaper La Gaceta del Gobierno de Puerto Rico on July 9, 1824.

Alacán was honored by the Spanish government, receiving the ship recovered from the pirates as compensation for the loss of the Avispa. Mendoza and the crew were also honored.

Cofresí reportedly escaped in one of his ships with "Campechano" Hernández, resuming his attacks soon after the ambush. Shortly after the Mona expedition, Ponce mayor José Ortíz de la Renta began his own search for Cofresí.

On June 30, 1824, the boat Unión left with 42 sailors commanded by captain Francisco Francheschi. After three days, the search was abandoned, and the ship returned to Ponce. The governor enacted more measures to capture the pirates, including the commission of gunboats.

De la Torre ordered the destruction of any hut or abandoned ship which might aid Cofresí in his escape attempts, an initiative carried out on the coasts of several municipalities.

Again, acting based on information obtained by interrogation, the authorities tracked the pirates during the first week of July.

Although José "Pepe" Cartagena, a local mulatto and Juan Geraldo Bey were found in Cabo Rojo and San Germán. Respectively, Cofresí avoided the troops.

On July 6, 1824, Cartagena resisted arrest and was killed in a shootout, with the developments again featured in La Gaceta del Gobierno de Puerto Rico.

During the next few weeks, a joint initiative by Rivas and the west coast mayors led to the arrest of Cofresí associates Gregorio del Rosario, Miguel Hernández, Felipe Carnero, José Rodríguez, Gómez, Roberto Francisco Reifles, Sebastián Gallardo, Francisco Ramos, José Vicente and a slave of Juan Nicolás Bey, Juan Geraldo's father, known as Pablo. However, the pirate again evaded the net.

In his confession, Pablo testified that Juan Geraldo Bey was an accomplice of Cofresí. Sebastián Gallardo was captured on July 13, 1824 and tried as a collaborator.

The defendants were transported to San Juan, where they were prosecuted by Madrazo in a military tribunal overseen by the governor. The trial was plagued by irregularities, including Gómez' allegation that the public attorney had accepted a bribe of 300 pesos from Juan Francisco.

During the searches, the pirates stole a "durable, copper-plated boat" from Cabo Rojo and escaped. The ship was originally stolen in San Juan by Gregorio Pereza and Francisco Pérez, both arrested during the search for Caballo Blanco and given to Cofresí.

When the news became public, mayor José María Hurtado asked residents for help…

On August 5, 1824, Antonio de Irizarry found the boat at Punta Arenas, a cape in the Joyuda barrio. The mayor quickly organized his troops, reaching the location on horseback.

Aboard the ship they found three rifles, three guns, a carbine, a cannon, ammunition, and supplies. After an unsuccessful search of nearby woods, the mayor sailed the craft to Pedernales and turned it over to Mendoza.

A group left behind continued the search but did not find anyone. If the pirates had fled inland, Hurtado alerted his colleagues in the region about the find.

The mayor resumed the search but abandoned it due to a rainstorm and poor directions. Peraza, Pérez, José Rivas del Mar, José María Correa, and José Antonio Martinez were later arrested, but Cofresí remained free.

On August 5, 1824, the pirate and a skeleton crew captured the sailboat María off the coast of Guayama as she completed a run between Guayanilla and Ponce. It was under the command of Juan Camino.

After boarding the ship, they decided not to rob her, since a larger craft was sailing towards them. The pirates fled west, intercepting a second boat, La Voladora, off Morillos.

Cofresí did not steal her either, instead requesting information from captain Rafael Mola. That month a ship commanded by the pirates prowled the port of Fajardo, taking advantage of the lack of gunboats capable of pursuing their shallow-draft vessels.

Shortly afterwards, the United States ordered captain Charles Boarman of the USS Weasel to monitor the western waters of Puerto Rico as part of an international force. The ship located a small vessel commanded by the pirates off Culebra, but it fled to Vieques and ran inland into dense vegetation. Boarman could only recover the ship.

The Danish ship Jordenxiold was intercepted off Isla Palominos on September 3, 1824, as she completed a voyage from Saint Thomas to Fajardo. The pirates stole goods and cash from the passengers.

This incident attracted the attention of the Danish government, which commissioned the Santa Cruz, a 16-gun brigantine commanded by Michael Klariman to monitor the areas off Vieques and Culebra.

On September 8 and 9, 1824, a hurricane named, Nuestra Señora de la Monserrate, struck southern Puerto Rico and passed directly over the Mona Passage. Cofresí and his crew were caught in the storm, which drove their ship towards Hispaniola.

According to historian Enrique Ramírez Brau, an expedition weeks later by Fajardo commander Ramón Aboy to search Vieques, Culebra and the Windward Islands for pirates was after Cofresí.

The operation used the boat Aurora, owned by Nicolás Márquez and Flor de Mayo, owned by José María Marujo. After weeks of searching, the team failed to locate anything of interest.

Continuing to drift, Cofresí and his crew were captured after his ship reached Santo Domingo. Sentenced to six years in prison, they were sent to a keep named Torre del Homenaje. Cofresí and his men escaped, were recaptured, and again imprisoned.

The group escaped again, breaking the locks on their cell doors, and climbing down the prison walls on a stormy night on a rope made from their clothing. With Cofresí were two other inmates, a man known as Portalatín and Manuel Reyes Paz, former boatswain of El Scipión.

After reaching the province of San Pedro de Macorís, the pirates bought a ship. They sailed from Hispaniola in late September to Naguabo, where Portalatín disembarked. From there they went to the island of Vieques, where they set up another hideout and regrouped.

The big Challenge to the West Indies Squadron

By October 1824, piracy in the region was dramatically reduced, with Cofresí the remaining target of concern. However, that month Peraza, Pérez, Hernández, Gallardo, José Rodríguez, and Ramos escaped from jail. Three former members of Lamparo's crew, a man of African descent named Bibián Hernández Morales, Antonio del Castillo and Juan Manuel de Fuentes Rodríguez also broke out.

They were joined by Juan Manuel "Venado" de Fuentes Rodríguez, Ignacio Cabrera, Miguel de la Cruz, Damasio Arroyo, Miguel "El Rasgado" de la Rosa and Juan Reyes.

Those traveling east met with Cofresí, who welcomed them on his crew. The pirate was in Naguabo looking for recruits after his return from Hispaniola. Hernández Morales, an experienced knife fighter, was second-in-command of the new crew.

At the height of their success, they had a flotilla of three ships and a boat. The group avoided capture by hiding in Ceiba, Fajardo, Naguabo, Jobos Bay and Vieques. When Cofresí sailed the east coast, he reportedly flew the flag of Gran Colombia.

On October 24, 1824, Hernández Morales led a group of six pirates in the robbery of Cabot, Bailey & Company in Saint Thomas, making off with U.S. $5,000.

On October 26, 1824, the USS Beagle, commanded by Charles T. Platt, navigated by John Low, and carrying shopkeeper George Bedford, with a list of stolen goods, which were reportedly near Naguabo left Saint Thomas.

Platt sailed to Vieques, following a tip about a pirate ship. Beagle opened fire, interrupting the capture of a sip from Saint Croix, but the pirates docked at Punta Arenas in Vieques and fled inland.

One, identified as Juan Felis, was captured after a shootout. When Platt disembarked in Fajardo to contact Juan Campos, a local associate of Bedford, the authorities accused him of piracy and detained him. The officer was later freed, but the pirates escaped.

Commodore Porter's reaction to what was later known as the Fajardo Affair led to a diplomatic crisis which threatened war between Spain and the United States. Campos was later found to be involved in the distribution of loot.

With more ships, Cofresí's activity near Culebra and Vieques peaked by November 1824. The international force reacted by sending more warships to patrol the zone.

France provided the Gazelle, a brigantine, and the frigate Constancia. After the Fajardo incident, the United States increased its flotilla in the region, with the USS Beagle joined by the boats USS Grampus and USS Shark in addition to the previously commissioned Santa Cruz and Scout.

Despite unprecedented monitoring, Cofresí grew bolder. John D. Sloat, captain of Grampus, received intelligence placing the pirates in a ship out of Cabo Rojo.

On the evening of January 25, 1825, Cofresí sailed a boat towards Grampus, which was patrolling the west coast. In position, the pirate commanded his crew, armed with sabers and muskets to open fire and ordered the ship to stop. When Sloat gave the order to counterattack, Cofresí sailed into the night.

Although a rowing boat and cutters from Grampus were sent after the pirates, they failed to find them after a two-hour search.

The pirates sailed east and docked at Quebrada de las Palmas, a river in Naguabo. From there, Cofresí, Hernández Morales, Juan Francisco "Ceniza" Pizarro and De los Reyes crossed the mangroves and vegetation to the Quebrada barrio in Fajardo.

Joined by a fugitive, Juan Pedro Espinoza and his group robbed the house of Juan Becerril. They hid in a house nearby in Río Abajo barrio.

Two days later Cofresí again led his flotilla out to sea and targeted San Vicente, a Spanish sloop making its way back from Saint Thomas. Cofresí attacked with two ships, ordering his crew to fire muskets and blunderbusses. Sustaining heavy damage, San Vicente finally escaped because he was near port.

On February 10, 1825, Cofresí looted the Neptune ship. The merchant ship, with a cargo of fabric and provisions, was attacked while its dry goods were unloaded at dockside in Jobos Bay.

Neptune was owned by Salvador Pastorisa, who was supervising the unloading. Cofresí began the charge in a ship, opening musket fire on the crew. Pastoriza fled in a rowboat.

Despite a bullet wound, Pastoriza identified four of the eight to ten pirates, including Cofresí...

An Italian living in Puerto Rico, Pedro Salovi, was reportedly second-in-command during the attack. The pirates pursued and shot those who fled. Cofresí sailed Neptune out of Jobos Port, a harbor in Jobos Bay, near Fajardo, and adopted the vessel as a pirate ship.

Guayama mayor Francisco Brenes doubled his patrol. Salovi was soon arrested and informed on his shipmates. Hernández Morales led another ship, intercepting Beagle off Vieques.

After a battle, the pirate ship was captured, and Hernández Morales was transported to St. Thomas for trial. After being sentenced to death, he escaped from prison and disappeared for years.

According to a St. Thomas resident, on February 12, 1825, the pirates retaliated by setting fire to a town on the island. That week, Neptune captured a Danish boat belonging to W. Furniss, a company based in Saint Thomas, off the Ponce coast with a load of imported merchandise.

After the assault, Cofresí and his crew abandoned the ship at sea. Later seen floating with broken masts, it was presumed lost.

A short time later, Cofresí and his crew boarded another ship owned by the company near Guayama, again stealing and abandoning her. Like its predecessor, it was seen near Caja de Muertos, Dead Man's Chest, before disappearing.

Evading Beagle, Cofresí returned to Jobos Bay. On February 15, 1825, the pirates arrived in Fajardo. Three days later, John Low picked up a six-gun sloop, Anne, commonly known by her Spanish name Ana or La Ana, which he had ordered from boat-builder Toribio Centeno and registered in St. Thomas.

Centeno sailed the ship to Fajardo, where he received permission to dock at Quebrada de Palmas in Naguabo. As its new owner Low accompanied him, remaining aboard while cargo was loaded.

That night Cofresí led a group of eight pirates, silently boarded the ship. They forced the crew to jump overboard. During the capture, Cofresí reportedly picked $20 from Low's pocket.

Despite having to "walk the plank", Low's crew survived. They reported the assault to the governor of Saint Thomas. Low probably attracted the pirates' attention by docking near one of their hideouts. His work on the Beagle rankled, and they were hungry for revenge after the capture of Hernández Morales.

Low met Centeno at his hacienda, where he told the Spaniards about the incident and later filed a formal complaint in Fajardo. Afterwards, he and his crew sailed to Saint Thomas.

Although another account suggests that Cofresí bought Anne from Centeno for twice Low's price, legal documents verify that the builder was paid by Low. Days later, Cofresí led his pirates to the Humacao shipyard. They stole a cannon from a gunboat and ordered by Miguel de la Torre to follow the pirates that it was under construction.

The crew armed themselves with weapons found on the ships they boarded. After the hijacking, Cofresí adopted Anne as his flagship.

Although she is popularly believed to have been renamed El Mosquito, all official documents use her formal name. Anne was quickly used to intercept a merchant off the coast of Vieques who was completing a voyage from Saint Croix to Puerto Rico.

Like others before it, the fate of the captured ship and its crew is unknown. The Spanish countered with an expedition from the port of

Patillas. Captain Sebastián Quevedo commanded a small boat, Esperanza, to find the pirates but was unsuccessful after several days at sea.

At the same time, de la Torre pressured the regional military commanders to act against the pirates and undercover agents monitored maritime traffic in most coastal towns. The pirates docked Anne in Jobos Bay before sunset, a pattern reported by the local militia to southern region commander Tomás de Renovales.

At this time the pirates sailed Anne towards Peñuelas, where the ship was recognized. Cofresí's last capture was on March 5, 1825, when he commanded the hijacking of a boat owned by Vicente Antoneti in Salinas.

By the spring of 1825, the flotilla led by Anne was the last substantial pirate threat in the Caribbean. The incursion which finally ended Cofresí's operation began to be reveal.

When Low arrived at his home base in Saint Thomas with news of Anne's hijacking, a Puerto Rican ship reported a recent sighting.

Sloat requested three international ships, with Spanish and Danish papers, from the Danish governor collaborating with Pastoriza and Pierety.

All four of Cofresí's victims left port shortly after the authorization on March 4. The task force was made up of Grampus, San José y Las Animas. There was an unidentified vessel belonging to Pierety and a third boat staffed by volunteers from a Colombian frigate.

After sighting Anne while they negotiated the involvement of the Spanish government in Puerto Rico, the task force decided to split up.

San José y Las Animas found Cofresí the next day and mounted a surprise attack. The sailors aboard hid while Cofresí, recognizing the ship as a local merchant vessel, gave the order to attack it.

When Anne was within range, the crew of San José y las Animas opened fire. Startled, the pirates countered with cannon and musket fire while attempting to outrun the ship. Unable to shake off San José y las Animas and having lost two members of his crew, Cofresí grounded Anne and fled inland.

While a third pirate fell during the landing, most scattered throughout rural Guayama and adjacent areas. Cofresí, injured, was accompanied by two crew members.

Half of his crew was captured shortly afterwards, but the captain remained at large until the following day. At midnight a local trooper, Juan Cándido Garay, and two other members of the Puerto Rican militia spotted Cofresí.

The trio ambushed the pirate, who was hit by a gun fire while he was fleeing. Despite his injury, Cofresí fought back with a knife until he was subdued by militia machetes.

After their capture, the pirates were held at a prison in Guayama before their transfer to San Juan.

Cofresí met with mayor Francisco Brenes, offering him 4,000 pieces of eight, which he claimed to possess, in exchange for his freedom.

Although a key component of modern myth, this is the only historical reference to Cofresí's hiding any treasure. Brenes declined the bribe.

Cofresí and his crew remained in Castillo San Felipe del Morro in San Juan for the rest of their lives.

On March 21, 1825, the pirate's reputed servant, known only as Carlos, was arrested in Guayama.

A Military Prosecution/ No Civil Trial

Cofresí received a council of war trial, with no possibility of a civil trial. The only right granted the pirates was to choose their lawyers. The arguments the attorneys could make were limited. Their role was just a formality. José Madrazo was again the prosecutor.

The case was rushed. This was very odd because other cases as serious as this one, took months or years. Cofresí was reportedly tried as an insurgent corsair and listed as such in a subsequent explanatory action in Spain. This was in accordance with measures enacted by Governor Miguel de la Torre the year before.

It is thought that the reason for the irregularities was that the Spanish government was under international inspection, with several neutral countries filing complaints about pirate and privateer attacks in Puerto Rican waters.

There was also additional pressure due to the start of David Porter's court-martial in the United States for invading the municipality of Fajardo.

The ministry rushed the Cofresí trial,_denying him and his crew defense_witnesses or testimony, required by trial protocol.

The trial was based on the pirates' confessions, with their legitimacy or circumstances not established.

The other pirates on trial were Manuel Aponte Monteverde of Añasco and Vicente del Valle Carbajal of Punta Espada or Santo Domingo.

There were also Vicente Ximénes of Cumaná, Antonio Delgado of Humacao, Victoriano Saldaña of Juncos, Agustín de Soto of San Germán, Carlos Díaz of Trinidad de Barlovento, Carlos Torres of Fajardo, Juan Manuel Fuentes of Havana, and José Rodríguez of Curaçao.

Torres stood out as an African and Cofresí's slave. Among the few sentenced for piracy who were not executed, his sentence was to be sold at public auction with his price earmarked for trial costs.

Cofresí confessed to capturing a French ship in Vieques, a Danish boat, a sailing ship from St. Thomas, a brigantine, and a ship from eastern Hispaniola.

There was another ship with a load of cattle in Boca del Infierno. A ship from which he stole 800 pieces of eight in Patillas, and an American vessel with a cargo worth 8,000 pieces of eight abandoned and burned in Punta de Peñones.

Under pressure, Cofresi was stubborn that he was unaware of the current whereabouts of the vessels or their crews and that he had never killed anyone. His testimony was corroborated by the other pirates.

Yet, according to a letter sent to Hezekiah Niles' Weekly Register Cofresí admitted off the record that he had killed nearly 400 people but no Puerto Ricans. The pirate also confessed that he burned the cargo of an American vessel to throw off the authorities.

The defendants' social status and association with criminals or outlaws' elements dictated the course of events. Captain José Madrazo served as judge and prosecutor of the one-day trial. Governor Miguel de la Torre may have influenced the process, negotiating with Madrazo beforehand.

On July 14, 1825, U.S. Congressman Samuel Smith accused Secretary of State Henry Clay of pressuring the Spanish governor to execute the pirates.

On the morning of March 29, 1825, a firing squad was assembled to carry out the sentence handed down to the pirates. The public execution, which had many spectators, was supervised by the Regimento de Infantería de Granada between eight and nine a.m. Catholic priests were present to hear confessions and offer comfort. As the pirates prayed, they were shot before the silent crowd.

Although San Felipe del Morro is the accepted execution site, Alejandro Tapia y Rivera, whose father was a member of the Regimento de Granada, places their execution near Convento Domenico in the Baluarte de Santo Domingo part of present-day Old San Juan.

According to historian Enrique Ramírez Brau, in a final act of defiance Cofresí refused to have his eyes covered after he was tied to a chair, and he was blindfolded by soldiers.

Richard Wheeler said that the pirate stated that after killing three or four hundred people, it would be strange if he was not accustomed to death.

Cofresí supposedly said he had "killed four hundred persons with his own hands, but never to his knowledge had he killed a native of Puerto Rico."

Cofresí's last words were reportedly, "I have killed hundreds with my own hands, and I know how to die. Fire!"

According to several of the pirates' death certificates, they were buried on the shore next to the Santa María Magdalena de Pazzis Cemetery.

Hernández Morales and several of his associates received the same treatment. Cofresí and his men were buried behind the cemetery, on what is now a luxurious green hill overlooking the cemetery wall. Contrary to local folklore, they were not buried in Old San Juan Cemetery, Cementerio Antiguo de San Juan. Their execution as criminals made them ineligible for burial in the Catholic cemetery.

A letter from Sloat to United States Secretary of the Navy Samuel L. Southard implied that at least some of the pirates were intended to be "beheaded and quartered, and their parts sent to all the small ports around the island to be exhibited". Spanish authorities continued to arrest Cofresí associates until 1839.

At this time, defendants were required to pay trial expenses, and Cofresí's family was charged 643 pieces of eight, two reales and 12 maravedi.

Contemporary documents suggest that Juana Creitoff, with little or no support from Cofresí's brothers and sisters, was left with the debt. His brothers distanced themselves from the trial and their brother's legacy, and Juan Francisco left Cabo Rojo for Humacao.

Juan Ignacio also evidently disassociated himself from Creitoff and her daughter and one of Juan Ignacio's granddaughters ignored Bernardina and her descendants.

Due to Cofresí's squandering of his treasure, his only asset the Spanish government could seize was Carlos. Appraised at 200 pesos, he was sold to Juan Saint Just for 133 pesos.

After the auction costs were paid, only 108 pesos and 2 reales were left. The remainder was paid by Félix and Miguel Mattei after they made a deal with the authorities giving them the cargo of the San José y las Animas in return for future accountability. Juana Creitoff died a year later.

Bernardina later married a Venezuelan immigrant, Estanislao Asencio Velázquez, continuing Cofresí's blood lineage in Cabo Rojo to this day. She had seven children. José Lucas, María Esterlina, Antonio Salvador, Antonio Luciano, Pablo, María Encarnación and Juan Bernardino.

One of Cofresí's most notable descendants was Ana González, better known by her married name Ana G. Méndez.

Cofresí's great-granddaughter, Méndez was directly descended from the Cabo Rojo bloodline through her mother Ana González Cofresí.

Known for her interest in education, she was the first member of her branch of the Cofresí family to earn a high-school diploma and university degree.

A teacher, Méndez founded the_Puerto Rico High School of Commerce during the 1940s, when most women did not complete their education.

By the turn of the 21st century her initiative had evolved into the Ana G. Méndez University System, the largest group of private universities in Puerto Rico.

Other branches of the Cofresí family include Juan Francisco's descendants in Ponce, and Juan Ignacio's lineage persists in the western region.

Internationally, the Kupferschein family remains in Trieste. Another family member was Severo Colberg Ramírez, speaker of the House of Representatives of Puerto Rico during the 1980s. Colberg made efforts to popularize Cofresí, particularly the heroic legends which followed his death.

He was related to the pirate through his sister Juana, who married Germán Colberg.

After Cofresí's death, items associated with him have been preserved or placed on display. His birth certificate is at San Miguel Arcángel Church with those of other notable figures, including Ramón Emeterio Betances and Salvador Brau.

Earrings said to have been worn by Cofresí were owned by Ynocencia Ramírez de Arellano, a maternal cousin. Her great-great-grandson, collector Teodoro Vidal Santoni, gave them to the National Museum of American History in 1997 and the institution displayed them in a section devoted to Spanish colonial history.

Locally, documents are preserved in the Institute of Puerto Rican Culture's General Archive of Puerto Rico, the Ateneo Puertorriqueño, the University of Puerto Rico's General Library and Historic Investigation Department and the Catholic Church's Parochial Archives.

Outside Puerto Rico, records can be found at the National Archives Building and the General Archive of the Indies.

Let me inform you that the official documents relating to Cofresí's trial and execution have been lost...

CHAPTER 41

Grito de Lares

Many Spanish colonies had gained their independence by the mid-1850s.

In Puerto Rico, there were two groups: the loyalists, who were loyal to Spain, and the independentistas, who advocated independence.

In 1866, <u>Dr. Ramón Emeterio Betances</u>, <u>Segundo Ruiz Belvis</u>, and other independence advocates met in New York City where they founded the Revolutionary Committee of Puerto Rico.

An outcome of this project was a plan to send an armed expedition from the Dominican Republic to invade the island.

Several revolutionary groups were formed in the western towns and cities of Puerto Rico.

Two of the most important groups were at Mayagüez, led <u>by Mathias Brugman</u> and code-named <u>"Capa Prieto"</u> at Lares, code-named "Centro Bravo" and headed by Manuel Rojas.

"Centro Bravo" was the main center of operations and was in the Rojas plantation of El Triunfo. Manuel Rojas was named "Commander of the Liberation Army" by Betances. Mariana Bracetti, Manuel's sister-in-law, was named "Leader of the Lares Revolutionary Council."

Upon the request of Betances, Bracetti knitted the first flag of Puerto Rico also known as the revolutionary Flag of Lares, Bandera de Lares.

Ramón Emeterio Betances

The Spanish authorities discovered plot that Ramon Emeterio Betances had. They were able to confiscate Betances's armed ship before it arrived in Puerto Rico.

The mayor of the town of Camuy, Manuel González, leader of that town's revolutionary group, was arrested and charged with treason. He learned that the Spanish Army was aware of the independence plot and escaped to warn Manuel Rojas.

Alerted, the revolutionists decided to start the revolution as soon as possible, and set the date for September 28, 1868.

Mathias Brugman and his men joined with Manuel Rojas's men and with about 800 men and women, marched on and took the town of Lares. This was to be known as "Grito de Lares", The Cry of Lares.

The revolutionists entered the town's church and placed Mariana Bracetti's revolutionary flag on the High Altar as a sign that the revolution had begun.

They declared Puerto Rico to be the "Republic of Puerto Rico" and named Francisco Ramírez its President. Manuel and his poorly armed followers proceeded to march on to the town of San Sebastián, armed only with clubs and machetes.

The Spanish Army had been forewarned and awaited with superior firepower. The revolutionists were met with deadly fire. The revolt failed.

Many revolutionists were killed, and at least 475, including Manuel Rojas and Mariana Bracetti, were imprisoned in the jail of Arecibo, and sentenced to death. Others fled and went into hiding.

Mathias Brugman was hiding in a local farm where he was betrayed by a farmer named Francisco Quiñones; he was captured and executed on the spot.

In 1869, fearing another revolt, the Spanish Crown disbanded the Puerto Rican Militia, which had been composed almost entirely of native-born Puerto Ricans, also, the Compañia de Artilleros Morenos de Cangrejos, a separate company of black Puerto Ricans.

They then organized the Volunteer Institute, composed entirely of Spaniards and their sons.

CHAPTER 42

Intentona de Yauco

During the Intentona de Yauco, the current Puerto Rican Flag was flown on the island for the first time.

Leaders of El Grito de Lares who were in exile in New York City joined the Puerto Rican Revolutionary Committee, founded on December 8, 1895, to continue the quest for independence.

In 1897, with the aid of <u>Antonio Mattie Lluberas and Fidel Velez</u>, the local leaders of the independence movement of the town of Yauco, they organized another uprising, which became known as the Intentona de Yauco.

On March 26, 1897, there was a second and last major attempt to overthrow the Spanish government. The local conservative political factions, which believed that such an attempt would be a threat to their struggle for autonomy, opposed such an action.

Rumors of the planned event spread to the local Spanish authorities, who acted swiftly and put an end to what would be the last major uprising in the island to Spanish colonial rule.

<u>Cuba</u>

<u>General Juan Ríus Rivera, Commander-in-Chief of the Cuban Liberation Army</u>In 1869, the incoming governor of Puerto Rico<u>, Jose Laureano Sanz</u>, to ease tensions in the island, dictated a general amnesty

and released all who were involved with the Grito de Lares revolt from prison.

Both Mariana Bracetti and Manuel Rojas were released. Bracetti lived her last years in the town of Añasco, while Rojas was deported to Venezuela. Many of the former prisoners joined the Cuban Liberation Army and fought against Spain.

Among the many Puerto Ricans who volunteered to fight for Cuba's independence were Juan Ríus Rivera, Francisco Gonzalo Marín, also known as "Pachin Marín" and José Semidei Rodríguez.

Juan Ríus Rivera as a young man met and befriended Betances. He eventually joined the pro-independence movement in the island. He became a member of the Mayagüez revolutionary group "Capá Prieto" under the command of Brugman.

Ríus, did not participate directly in the revolt because at the time he was studying law in Spain, however, he was an avid reader about information pertaining to the Antilles and learned about the failed revolt.

He interrupted his studies and traveled to the United States where he went to the Cuba Revolutionary "Junta" and offered his services. He joined the Cuban Liberation Army and was given the rank of general and fought alongside Gen. Máximo Gómez in Cuba's Ten Years' War.

He later fought alongside Gen. Antonio Maceo Grajales and upon Maceo's death was named Commander-in-Chief of the Cuban Liberation Army. After Cuba gained its independence, Gen. Juan Ríus Rivera became an active political figure in the new nation.

Francisco Gonzalo Marín was a poet and journalist in Puerto Rico who joined the Cuban Liberation Army upon learning of the death of his brother Wecenlao in the battlefields of Cuba. Marin, who was given the rank of lieutenant, befriended, and fought alongside José Martí.

In November 1897, Lt. Marin died from the wounds he received in a battle against the Spanish Army.

José Semidei Rodríguez from Yauco, Puerto Rico, fought in various battles in the Cuban War of Independence,1895–1898.

After Cuba gained its independence, he joined the Cuban National Army with the rank of brigadier general. Semidei Rodríguez continued to serve in Cuba as a diplomat upon his retirement from the military.

CHAPTER 43

Spanish American War

In 1890, Captain Alfred Thayer Mahan, a member of the Navy War Board and leading U.S. strategic thinker, wrote a book titled The Influence of Sea Power upon History.

He argued for the creation of a large and powerful navy modeled after the British Royal Navy.

Part of his strategy called for the acquisition of colonies in the Caribbean Sea which would serve as coaling and naval stations, and which would serve as strategic points of defense upon the construction of a canal in the Isthmus.

William H. Seward, the former Secretary of State under the administrations of various presidents, among them Abraham Lincoln and Ulysses Grant, had stressed that a canal be built either in Honduras, Nicaragua or Panama and that the United States annex the Dominican Republic and purchase Puerto Rico and Cuba.

The idea of annexing the Dominican Republic failed to receive the approval of the U.S. Senate and Spain did not accept the 160 million dollars the U.S. offered for Puerto Rico and Cuba.

Since 1894, the Naval War College had been formulating plans for war with possible adversaries. One of these plans included military operations in Puerto Rican waters.

Not only was Puerto Rico considered valuable as a naval station, Puerto Rico and Cuba were also major producers of sugar, a valuable commercial commodity the United States lacked.

The United States declared war on Spain in 1898 following the loss of the battleship USS Maine in Havana harbor, Cuba.

One of the United States' principal objectives in the Spanish American War was to take control of Spanish possessions Puerto Rico and Cuba in the Atlantic, and the Philippines and Guam in the Pacific.

CHAPTER 44

3rd Provisional Battalion of Puerto Rico

The Spanish sent the 1st, 2nd, and 3rd Puerto Rican Provisional Battalions to defend Cuba against the American invaders.

The 1st Puerto Rican Provisional Battalion, composed of the Talavera Cavalry and Krupp artillery, was sent to Santiago de Cuba where they fought American forces in the Battle of San Juan Hill.

The Puerto Rican Battalion suffered a total of 70% casualties including dead, wounded, MIAs and prisoners. The invasion of Puerto Rico by the American military forces was known as the Puerto Rican Campaign.

On May 10, 1898, Spanish forces under the command of Captain Ángel Rivero Méndez in the fortress of San Cristóbal in San Juan, exchanged fire with the USS Yale, and on May 12 a fleet of 12 American ships bombarded San Juan.

On June 25, the USS, Yosemite arrived in San Juan and blockaded the port. Captains Ramón Acha Caamaño and José Antonio Iriarte, both natives of Puerto Rico, were among those who defended the city from Fort San Felipe del Morro. They had three batteries under their command, which were armed with at least three 15 cm Ordóñez cannons.

The battle lasted three hours and resulted in the death of Justo Esquivies, the first Puerto Rican soldier to die in the Puerto Rican Campaign.

On July 25, 1898, General Nelson A. Miles landed at the southern town of Guánica and began advancing towards Ponce and then San Juan.

Part of the Hacienda Desideria, owned by Antonio Mariani, where the Battle of Yauco took place in 1898.

One of the most notable battles during the Puerto Rico Campaign occurred between combined Spanish forces and Puerto Rican volunteers, led by <u>Captain Salvador Meca and Lieutenant Colonel</u> <u>Francisco Puig</u>, and American forces led by Brigadier General George A. Garretson on July 26, 1898.

The Spanish forces engaged the 6th Massachusetts in the Battle of Yauco. Puig and his forces suffered 2 officers and 3 soldiers wounded and 2 soldiers dead. The Spanish forces were ordered to retreat.

The Puerto Rican Campaign was short compared to the other campaigns. The Puerto Ricans who resided in the southern and western towns and villages resented Spanish rule and tended to view the Americans as their liberators, thereby making the invasion much easier.

The 1st, 2nd and 3rd Puerto Rican Provisional Battalions were in Cuba defending that island, which may have also contributed. However, the Americans met resistance from the Spanish forces and Puerto Rican Volunteers and were engaged in the following battles:

Battle of Fajardo
Battle of Guayama
Battle of the Guamani River Bridge
Battle of Coamo
Battle of Silva Heights
Battle of Asomante

On August 13, 1898, the Spanish American War ended, and the Spanish surrendered without other major incidents. Some Puerto Rican leaders such as José de Diego and Eugenio María de Hostos expected the United States to grant the island its independence.

Believing that Puerto Rico would gain its independence, a group of men staged an uprising in Ciales which became known as "<u>El Lentamente de Ciales</u>" or the "<u>Ciales Uprising of 1898</u>" and proclaimed Puerto Rico to be a republic.

The Spanish authorities who were unaware that the cease fire had been signed brutally suppressed the uprising.

The total casualties of the Puerto Rican Campaign were 450 dead or wounded Spanish and Puerto Ricans, 4 dead and 39 wounded Americans.

Upon the signing of the Treaty of Paris on December 10, 1898, Puerto Rico became a territory of the United States. The Spanish troops had already left by October 18, 1898.

The United States named General Nelson A. Miles military governor of Puerto Rico.

On July 1, 1899, "The Porto Rico Regiment of Infantry, United States Army" was created, and approved by the U.S. Congress on May 27, 1908.

The regiment was a segregated, all-volunteer unit made up of 1,969 Puerto Ricans.

CHAPTER 45

Puerto Rican commander in the Philippines

In 1897, before the onset of fighting in Puerto Rico, Juan Alonso Zayas, born in San Juan, was a second lieutenant in the Spanish Army. He received orders to head for the Philippines to take command of the 2nd Expeditionary Battalion stationed in Baler.

He arrived in Manila, the capital, in May 1897. There, he took a vessel and headed for Baler, on the island of Luzon. The distance between Manila and Baler is 62 miles (100 km); if traveled through the jungles and badly built roads, the actual distance was 144 miles (230 km).

At that time, a system of communication between Manila and Baler was almost non-existent. The only way Baler received news from Manila was by way of vessels.

The Spanish colonial government was under constant attack from local Filipino groups who wanted independence. Zayas's mission was to protect Baler against any possible attack.

Among his plans for the defense of Baler was to convert the local church of San Luis de Tolosa into a fort.

The independence advocates, under the leadership of Colonel Calixto Vilacorte, were called "insurgents", Tagalo, by the Spanish.

On June 28, 1898, they demanded the surrender of the Spanish army.

The Spanish governor of the region, Enrique de las Morena y Fossi, refused. The Filipinos immediately attacked Baler in a battle that was to last for seven months.

Despite being outnumbered and suffering hunger and disease, the battalion did not surrender.

In the meantime, Zayas and the rest of the battalion were totally unaware of the Spanish American War.

In August 1898, hostilities between the United States and Spain came to an end. The Philippines became a U.S. possession in accordance with the Treaty of Paris.

In May 1899, the battalion at Baler learned of the Spanish American War and its aftermath.

On June 2, 1899, the battalion's commander, <u>Lieutenant Martín Cerezo</u>, surrendered to the Tagalos. The surrender was dependent upon several conditions, including the Spaniards not being treated as prisoners of war and being allowed to travel to a ship that would take them back to Spain. The 32 survivors of Zayas Battalion were sent to Manila, where they boarded a ship for Spain.

In Spain, they were given a hero's welcome and became known as los Ultimos de Baler "the Last of Baler".

CHAPTER 46

Porto Rico Provisional Regiment of Infantry

On March 2, 1898, Congress authorized the creation of the first body of native troops in Puerto Rico.

On June 30, 1901, the "Porto Rico Provisional Regiment of Infantry" came into being. An Act of Congress, approved on May 27, 1908, reorganized the regiment as part of the "regular" Army.

Since the native Puerto Rican officers were Puerto Rican citizens and not citizens of the United States, they were required to undergo a new physical examination to determine their fitness for commissions in the Regular Army and to take an oath of U.S. citizenship with their new officers' oath.

Puerto Rico National Guard
Major General Luis R. Esteves (Army)

In 1906, a group of Puerto Ricans met with the appointed Governor Winthrop, and suggested the organization of a Puerto Rico National Guard.

The petition failed because the U.S. Constitution prohibits the formation of any armed force within the United States and its territories without the authorization of Congress.

On June 19, 1915, <u>Major General Luis R. Esteves</u> of the U.S. Army became the first Puerto Rican and the first Hispanic to graduate from the United States Military Academy at West Point, New York.

While he attended West Point, he tutored classmate Dwight D. Eisenhower in Spanish; a second language was required to graduate.

He was a second lieutenant in the 8th Infantry Brigade under the command of John J. Pershing when he was sent to El Paso, Texas in the Pancho Villa Expedition.

From El Paso, he was sent to the town of Polvo, where he was appointed mayor and judge by its citizens. Esteves helped organize the 23rd Battalion, which would be composed of Puerto Ricans and be stationed in Panama during World War I. He also played a key role in the formation of the <u>Puerto Rico National Guard.</u>

CHAPTER 47

During World War I Events

In 1904, Camp Las Casas was established in Santurce under the command of <u>Lt. Colonel Orval P. Townshend</u>. The Porto Rico Regiment was assigned to the camp. The regiment consisted of two battalions of the former Porto Rico Provisional Regiment of Infantry.

<u>Lieutenant Teófilo Marxuach</u> was the officer of the day at El Morro Castle on March 21, 1915.

The Odenwald, built in 1903, not to be confused with the German World War II war ship which carried the same name, was an armed German supply ship which tried to force its way out of the San Juan Bay and deliver supplies to the German submarines waiting in the Atlantic Ocean.

<u>Lt. Marxuach</u> gave the order to open fire on the ship from the walls of the fort. Sergeant Encarnacion Correa manned a machine gun and fired warning shots with little effect.

Marxuach fired a shot from a cannon located at the Santa Rosa battery of "El Morro" fort, in what is the first shot of World War I fired by the regular armed forces of the United States against any ship flying the colors of the Central Powers, forcing the Odenwald to stop and to return to port where its supplies were confiscated. The Odenwald was confiscated by the United States and renamed SS Newport. It was assigned to the U.S. Shipping Board, where it served until 1924 when it was retired.

As more countries became involved in World War I, the U.S. Congress approved the Jones–Shafroth Act, which imposed United States citizenship upon Puerto Ricans.

Those who were eligible, except for women, were expected to serve in the military. About 20,000 Puerto Ricans were drafted during World War I.

On May 3, 1917, the regiment recruited 1,969 men. The 295th and 296 Infantry Regiments were created in Puerto Rico.

In November 1917, the first military draft, enlistment, lottery in Puerto Rico was held in the island's capital, San Juan.

Eustaquio Correa was the first Puerto Rican to be drafted into the Armed Forces of the United States.

On May 17, 1917, the Porto Rico Regiment of Infantry was deployed to guard the Panama Canal. One of the Puerto Ricans who distinguished himself during World War I was Lieutenant Frederick Lois Riefkohl of the US Navy, who on August 2, 1917.

He became the first known Puerto Rican to be awarded the Navy Cross. The Navy Cross was awarded to Lt. Riefkohl for his actions in an engagement with an enemy submarine.

Lt. Riefkohl, who was also the first Puerto Rican to graduate from the United States Naval Academy, served as a rear admiral in World War II.

Frederick L. Riefkohl's brother, Rudolph William Riefkohl also served. Riefkohl was commissioned a second lieutenant and assigned to the 3rd Heavy Artillery Regiment in France, where he participated in the Meuse-Argonne Offensive.

According to the United States War Department, after the war he served as Captain of Coastal Artillery at the Letterman Army Medical Center in Presidio of San Francisco, in California in 1918.

He played an instrumental role in helping the people of Poland overcome the 1919 typhus epidemic.

By 1918, the Army realized there was a shortage of physicians specializing in anesthesia, a low salary specialty, who were required in military operating rooms.

To address the need, the Army began hiring women physicians as civilian contract employees. The first Puerto Rican woman doctor to serve in the Army under contract was Dr. Dolores Piñero from San Juan.

She was assigned to the San Juan base hospital where she worked as an anesthesiologist during the mornings and in the laboratory during the afternoons.

In New York, some Puerto Ricans joined the 369th Infantry Regiment, which was mostly composed of African Americans. They were not allowed to fight alongside their white counterparts but did serve as part of a French division.

They fought on the Western Front in France, and their reputation earned them the nickname of "the Harlem Hell Fighters" by the Germans.

Among them was Rafael Hernández Marín, considered by many as Puerto Rico's greatest composer.

The 369th was awarded French Croix de guerre for battlefield gallantry by the French government.

On January 6, 1914, First Lieutenant Bernard L. Smith established the Marine Section of the Navy Flying School in the island municipal Culebra.

As the number of Marine Aviators grew so did the desire to separate from Naval Aviation.

The Marine Corps Aviation Company in Puerto Rico consisted of 10 officers and 40 enlisted men.

The first USMC plane: a Curtiss C-3 in Culebra, Puerto Rico.

The Porto Rico Regiment returned to Puerto Rico in March 1919 and was renamed the 65th Infantry Regiment under the Reorganization Act of June 4, 1920.

It is estimated that 18,000 Puerto Ricans from the Porto Rico Regiment served in the war and that 335 were wounded by chemical gas experimentation the United States conducted as part of its active chemical weapons program in Panama.

Neither the military nor the War Department of the United States kept statistics regarding the total number of Puerto Ricans who served in the regular units of the Armed Forces, United States mainland forces.

It is known that four Puerto Ricans died in combat, but it is impossible to determine the exact number of Puerto Ricans who served and died in World War I.

The need for a Puerto Rican National Guard unit became apparent to Major General Luis R. Esteves, who had served as an instructor of

Puerto Rican Officers for the Porto Rico Regiment of Infantry at Camp Las Casas in Puerto Rico.

His request was approved by the government and Puerto Rican Legislature.

In 1919, the first regiment of the Puerto Rican National Guard was formed, and General Luis R. Esteves became the first official Commandant of the Puerto Rican National Guard.

CHAPTER 48

Interwar years "THE BANANA WAR"

<u>The Second Nicaraguan Campaign</u> 1926–1933

After World War I, Puerto Ricans fought on foreign shores as members of the United States Marine Corps.

Civil war broke out in Nicaragua during the first months of 1926. Upon the request of the Nicaraguan government, 3,000 U.S. Marines were sent ashore to establish a neutral zone for the protection of American citizens. The American intervention was also known as the <u>Banana Wars.</u>

In 1926, <u>Captain Pedro del Valle</u> served with the Gendarmerie of Haiti for three years.

During that time, he also became active in the war against <u>Augusto Sandino in Nicaragua.</u>

In 1927, <u>Lieutenant Jaime Sabater</u>, from San Juan, Puerto Rico graduated from United States Naval Academy.

<u>Private Rafel Toro</u>, from Humacao, Puerto Rico, was part of the U.S. Marine Corps occupation force in Nicaragua, serving with the Guardia Nacional de Nicaragua.

On July 25, 1927, <u>Private Toro</u> was assigned to advance guard duty in Nueva Segovia. As he rode into town, he was attacked; returning fire, he was able to hold back the enemy until reinforcements arrived. He was mortally wounded in this action and was posthumously awarded the Navy Cross.

Rif War 1920

After the Spanish American War, members of the Spanish forces and civilians who were loyal to the Spanish Crown were allowed to return to Spain.

Those who returned took with them their Puerto Rican spouses and children. Among those who were born in Puerto Rico and who would go on to serve in the Rif War as members of the Spanish military were General Manuel Goded Llopis and Captain Felix Arenas Gaspar.

The Rif War was a rebellion against Spanish colonial rule in Spanish Morocco, a Spanish protectorate, in 1919.

During the Rif War Gaspar, who was born in San Juan, distinguished himself in combat. He was posthumously awarded the Cruz Laureada de San Fernando "Laureate Cross of Saint Ferdinand", Spain's version of the United States' Medal of Honor, for his actions in the defense of his company.

Spanish Civil War 1936–1939

Puerto Ricans fought on both sides during the Spanish Civil War. The Spanish Civil War was a major conflict in Spain that started after an attempted coup d'état by parts of the army, led by the Fascist General Francisco Franco, against the government of the Second Spanish Republic.

Puerto Ricans fought on both factions involved; the "Nationalists" as members of the Spanish Army and the "Loyalists", Republicans, as members of the Abraham Lincoln International Brigade.

Among the Puerto Ricans who fought alongside General Franco and the Nationalists was General Manuel Goded Llopis, 1882–1936.

Llopis, who was born in San Juan, was named Chief of Staff of the Spanish Army of Africa after his victories in the Rif War, took the Balearic Islands and by order of Franco, suppressed the rebellion of Asturias.

Llopis was sent to lead the fight against the Anarchists in Catalonia, but his troops were outnumbered. He was captured and was sentenced to die by firing squad.

Among the many Puerto Ricans who fought for the Second Spanish Republic as members of the Abraham Lincoln Brigade, was Lieutenant Carmelo Delgado Delgado. He was a leader of the Puerto Rican Nationalist Party from Guayama.

At the beginning of the Spanish Civil War, Delgado was in Spain studying for a law degree.

Delgado was an anti-fascist who believed the Spanish Nationalists were traitors. He fought in the Battle of Madrid but was captured and sentenced to die by firing squad on April 29, 1937.

World War II
Pearl Harbor of the Atlantic

In 1940, when Germany attacked Great Britain, President Franklin Delano Roosevelt ordered the construction of a protected anchorage in the Atlantic, at Ceiba, Puerto Rico, as Pearl Harbor in Hawaii.

The site was meant to provide anchorage, docking, repair facilities, fuel, and supplies for 60% of the Atlantic Fleet.

The naval base, which was named U.S. Naval Station Roosevelt Roads, became the largest naval installation in the world in landmass.

In May 2003, after six decades of existence, the base was officially shut down by the U.S. Navy.

In 1939, a survey was conducted of possible air base sites. It was determined that Punta Borinquen was the best site for a major air base.

Later that year, Major Karl S. Axtater assumed command of what was to become Borinquen Army Airfield, later renamed Ramey Air Force Base.

The first squadron based at Borinquen Field was the 27th Bombardment Squadron, consisting of nine Douglas B-18A Bolo medium bombers.

In 1940, the air echelon of the 25th Bombardment Group, 14 B-18A aircraft and two Northrop A-17 aircraft, arrived at the base from Langley Field.

Throughout the war, many squadrons rotated through the airbase, which was supported by numerous antiaircraft, coastal artillery and support units.

Borinquen Field was also used as a part of the ferrying route for aircraft being moved from Florida to the Middle East and PBM Mariners taking off from Naval Air Station San Juan in 1943.

CHAPTER 49

The Puerto Rico National Guard Army Founder

In October 1940, the 295th and 296th Infantry Regiments of the Puerto Rican National Guard, founded by <u>Major General Luis R. Esteves</u>, were called into Federal Active Service, and assigned to the Puerto Rican Department in accordance with the existing War Plan Orange.

There were no Puerto Rican military-related fatalities in the Japanese attack of Pearl Harbor, although one Puerto Rican civilian was killed.

Daniel LaVerne was an amateur boxer who was working at Pearl Harbor's Red Hill underground fuel tank construction project when the Japanese attacked.

He died because of the injuries which he received during the attack. His name is listed among the 2,338 Americans killed or mortally wounded on December 7, 1941, in the Remembrance Exhibit on the back lawn of the USS Arizona Memorial Visitor Center at Pearl Harbor.

It is estimated by the Department of Defense that 65,034 Puerto Ricans served in the U.S. military during World War II.

Soldiers from the island, serving in the 65th Infantry Regiment, participated in combat in the European Theater, in Germany and Central Europe.

Those who resided in the mainland of the United States were assigned to regular units of the military and served either in the European or Pacific theaters of the war.

Some families had multiple members join the Armed Forces. Seven brothers of the Medina family known as "The Fighting Medinas", fought in the war. They came from Río Grande, Puerto R

In some cases, Puerto Ricans, were subject to the racial discrimination which at that time was widespread in the United States.

"The Fighting Medinas"

World War II was also the first conflict in which women, other than nurses, were allowed to serve in the U.S. Armed Forces. However, when the United States entered World War II, Puerto Rican nurses volunteered for service but were not accepted into the Army or Navy Nurse Corps.

As a result, many of the volunteers migrated to the mainland U.S. to work in the factories which produced military equipment.

In 1944, the Army Nurse Corps decided to actively recruit Puerto Rican nurses so that Army hospitals would not have to deal with the language barriers when tending to wound Hispanic soldiers.

Among them was Second Lieutenant Carmen Lozano Dumler, who became one of the first Puerto Rican female military officers.

In 1944, the Army sought to recruit up to 200 Puerto Rican women for the Women's Army Corps (WAC). Over 1,000 applications were received.

The Puerto Rican WAC unit, designated Company 6, 2nd Battalion, 21st Regiment of the Women's Army Auxiliary Corps, was a segregated Hispanic unit.

It was assigned to the New York Port of Embarkation after basic training at Fort Oglethorpe, Georgia.

The WACs were assigned to work in military offices which planned the shipment of troops around the world.

Among them was PFC Carmen García Rosado, who in 2006, authored and published a book titled "LAS WACS, Participacion de la Mujer Boricua en la Segunda Guerra Mundial", The WACs – The participation of the Puerto Rican women in the Second World War, the first book to document the experiences of the first 200 Puerto Rican women who participated in said conflict.

NORMA IRIS PAGAN MORALES

According to <u>García Rosado</u>, one of the hardships which Puerto Rican women in the military were subjected to was social and racial discrimination against the Latino community, which at the time was widespread in the United States.

Puerto Rican Army nurses, 296th Station Hospital, Camp Tortuguero, Vega Baja, PR.

The 149th Women's Army Auxiliary Corps, WAAC, Post Headquarters Company was the first WAAC Company to go overseas, setting sail from New York Harbor for Europe in January 1943.

The unit arrived in Northern Africa on January 27, 1943 and rendered overseas duties in Algiers within General Dwight D. Eisenhower's theater headquarters.

<u>Tech4 Carmen Contreras-Bozak</u>, a member of this unit, was the first Hispanic to serve in the Women's Army Corps as an interpreter and in numerous administra.

The 65th Infantry, after an extensive training program in 1942, was sent to Panama to protect the Pacific and the Atlantic sides of the isthmus in 1943.

On November 25, 1943, <u>Colonel Antulio Segarra</u>, proceeded Col. John R. Menclenhall as Commander of the 65th Infantry, thus becoming the first Puerto Rican Regular Army officer to command a Regular Army regiment.

On January 12, 1944, the 296th Infantry Regiment departed from Puerto Rico to the Panama Canal Zone.

In April 1945, the unit returned to Puerto Rico and soon after was sent to Honolulu, Hawaii.

The 296th arrived on June 25, 1945 and was attached to the Central Pacific Base Command at Kahuku Air Base.

<u>Lieutenant Colonel Gilberto José Marxuach</u>, "The Father of the San Juan Civil Defense", was the commander of both the 1114th Artillery Co. and the 1558th Engineers Co.

In January 1944, the 65th Infantry Regiment was moved from Panama to Fort Eustis in Newport News, Virginia in preparation for overseas deployment to North Africa.

An advance party was sent to Casablanca on 16 March, with the remainder of the regiment arriving by 5 April 1944.

For some Puerto Ricans, this would be the first time that they were away from their homeland.

Being away from their homeland for the first time would serve as an inspiration for compositions of two Bolero's; "En mi viejo San Juan" by Noel Estrada and "Despedida", My Good-bye, a farewell song written by Pedro Flores and interpreted by Daniel Santos.

By April 29, 1944, the regiment had landed in Italy and moved on to Corsica.

On 1 October 1944, the 65th Infantry landed in France and was committed to action on the Maritime Alps at Peira Cava.

On December 13, 1944, the 65th Infantry, under the command of Lieutenant Colonel Juan César Cordero Davila, relieved the 2nd Battalion, 442nd Infantry Regiment, a regiment which was made up of Japanese Americans under the command of Col. Virgil R. Miller, a native of Puerto Rico.

The 3rd Battalion fought against and defeated Germany's 34th Infantry Division's 107th Infantry Regiment. There were 17 battle casualties. These included Pvt. Sergio Sanchez-Sanchez and Sergeant Angel Martinez, from the town of Sabana Grande, who were the first two Puerto Ricans from the 65th Infantry to be killed in combat.

On March 18, 1945, the regiment was sent to the District of Mannheim and assigned to military occupation duties. [citation needed] In all, the 65th Infantry participated in the campaigns of Naples-Fogis, Rome-Arno, central Europe and of the Rhineland.

It was during this conflict that CWO2 Joseph B. Aviles, Sr., a member of the United States Coast Guard and the first Hispanic American to be promoted to Chief Petty Officer, "received a war-time promotion to Chief Warrant Officer, November 27, 1944, thus becoming the first Hispanic American to reach that level as well."

Aviles, who served in the United States Navy as Chief Gunner's Mate in World War I, spent most of the war at St. Augustine, Florida training recruits.

Commanders

Lt. Gen. Pedro del Valle, (USMC)
This was first time that Puerto Ricans played important roles as commanders in the Armed Forces of the United States. Besides Lieutenant Colonel Juan César Cordero Dávila who served with the 65th Infantry and Colonel Virgil R. Miller, a West Point graduate, born in San Germán, Puerto Rico, who was the regimental commander of the 442d Regimental Combat Team, a unit which was composed of "Nisei", second generation Americans of Japanese descent, that rescued Lost Texas Battalion of the 36th Infantry Division, in the forests of the Vosges Mountains in northeastern France.

Colonel Virgilio N. Cordero, Jr.,1893–1980, was a battalion commander of the 31st Infantry Regiment on December 8, 1941, when Japanese attacked Philippines.

Cordero was named regimental commander of the 52nd Infantry Regiment of the new Filipino Army, thus becoming the first Puerto Rican to command a Filipino Army regiment.

The Bataan Defense Force surrendered on April 9, 1942, and Cordero and his men underwent brutal torture and humiliation during the Bataan Death March and nearly four years of captivity.

He was one of nearly 1,600 members of the 31st Infantry who were taken as prisoners. Half of these men died while prisoners of the Japanese forces.

After Cordero gained his freedom, when the Allied troops defeated the Japanese, he continued serving in the military until 1953.

Seven Puerto Ricans, all graduates of the United States Naval Academy, served in command positions in the Navy and the Marine Corps.

Lieutenant General Pedro Augusto del Valle was the first Hispanic Marine Corps general. He played a key role in the Guadalcanal Campaign and the Battle of Guam and became the Commanding General of the First Marine Division.

Del Valle played an instrumental role in the defeat of the Japanese forces in Okinawa and oversaw the reorganization of Okinawa.

Admiral Horacio Rivero, Jr., USN, who later became the first Puerto Rican to become a four-star admiral; Captain Marion Frederic Ramírez de Arellano, USN, the first Hispanic submarine commanding officer.

As submarine commander of the USS Balao, SS-285, he is credited with sinking two Japanese ships.

Celestino Benítez Rear Admiral Rafael, USN, a highly decorated submarine commander who was the recipient of two Silver Star Medal.

Rear Admiral José M. Cabanillas, USN, who was the executive officer of the USS Texas which participated in the invasions of North Africa and Normandy, D-Day.

Rear Admiral Edmund Ernest García, USN, commander of the destroyer USS Sloat who saw action in the invasions of Africa, Sicily, and France

Rear Admiral Frederick Lois Riefkohl, USN, the first Puerto Rican to graduate from the Naval Academy and recipient of the Navy Cross

Colonel Jaime Sabater, Sr., USMC, who commanded the 1st Battalion, 9th Marines during the Bougainville amphibious operations Sabater also participated in the Battle of Guam, July 21 – August 1, 1944, as executive officer of the 9th Marines. He was wounded in action on July 21, 1944, and awarded the Purple Heart.

The Remarkable Combatants

Among the many Puerto Ricans who distinguished themselves in combat were Sergeant First Class Agustín Ramos Calero and the first three Puerto Ricans to be awarded the Distinguished Service Cross: PFC. Luis F. Castro, Private Anibal Irrizarry, and PFC Joseph R. Martinez. Sergeant First Class Agustín Ramos Calero was awarded a total of 22 decorations and medals his actions in Europe, making him the most decorated Puerto Rican soldier of World War II.

CHAPTER 50

The Aviators

Puerto Ricans also served in the United States Army Air Forces.

In 1944, Puerto Rican aviators were sent to the Tuskegee Army Airfield in Tuskegee, Alabama to train the famed 99th Fighter Squadron of the Tuskegee Airmen.

A few Puerto Ricans who served in the Royal Canadian Air Force, the British Royal Air Force.

Human experimentation

Puerto Rican soldiers were subject to human experimentation by the United States Armed Forces.

On Panama's San Jose Island, Puerto Rican soldiers were exposed to mustard gas to see if they reacted differently than their "white" counterparts.

According to Susan L. Smith of the University of Alberta, the researchers were searching for evidence of race-based differences in the responses of the human body to mustard gas exposure.

Demobilization
LTJG Maria Rodriguez Denton

The American participation in the Second World War came to an end in Europe on May 8, 1945.

At this time, the western Allies celebrated "V-E Day", Victory in Europe Day, upon Germany's surrender, and in the Asian theater on August 14, 1945 "V-J Day" .

This happened with Victory over Japan Day, when the Japanese surrendered by signing the Japanese Instrument of Surrender.

Lieutenant Junior Grade Maria Rodriguez Denton, U.S. Navy, born in Guanica, Puerto Rico, was the first woman from Puerto Rico who became an officer in the United States Navy as member of the WAVES.

It was LTJG Denton who forwarded the news, through channels, to President Harry S. Truman that the war had ended.

On October 27, 1945, the 65th Infantry sailed home from France. Arriving at Puerto Rico on November 9, 1945.

They were received by the local population as national heroes and given a victorious reception at the Military Terminal of Camp Buchanan.

According to the book "Historia Militar De Puerto Rico", Military history of Puerto Rico, by historian Col. Héctor Andrés Negroni, the men of the 65th Infantry were awarded the following military decorations: 2 Silver Stars, 22 Bronze Stars, and 90 Purple Hearts.

The 295th Regiment returned on February 20, 1946, from the Panama Canal Zone, and the 296th Regiment on March 6. Both regiments were awarded the American Theater streamer and the Pacific Theater streamer. They were inactivated that same year.

According to the 4th Report of the Director of Selective Service of 1948, a total of 51,438 Puerto Ricans served in the Armed Forces during World War II, however the Department of Defense in its report titled "Number of Puerto Ricans serving in the U.S. Armed Forces during National Emergencies" stated that the total of Puerto Ricans who served was 65,034 and from that total 2,560 were listed as wounded.

Unfortunately, the exact total amount of Puerto Ricans who served in World War II in other units, besides those of Puerto Rico, cannot be determined because the military categorized Hispanics under the same heading as whites. The only racial groups to have separate statistics kept were African Americans and Asian Americans.

CHAPTER 51

Revolt against the United States

During the mid-1940s, various pro-independence groups, such as the Puerto Rican Independence Party, which believed in gaining the island's independence through the electoral process.

The Puerto Rican Nationalist Party believed in the concept of armed revolution existed in Puerto Rico.

On October 30, 1950, the nationalists, under the leadership of Dr. Pedro Albizu Campos staged uprisings in the towns of Ponce, Mayagüez, Naranjito, Arecibo, Utuado, San Juan, San Juan Nationalist revolt and Jayuya.

The National Guard, commanded by the Puerto Rico Adjutant General Major General Luis R. Esteves and under the orders of Gov. Luis Muñoz Marín, occupy Jayuya.

The most notable of these occurred in Jayuya in what became known as El Grito de Jayuya, Jayuya Uprising.

Nationalist leader Blanca Canales led the armed nationalists into the town and attacked the police station. A small battle with the police occurred; one officer was killed, and three others were wounded before the rest dropped their weapons and surrendered.

The nationalists cut the telephone lines and burned the post office. Canales led the group into the town square where the illegal light blue version of the Puerto Rican Flag was raised. It was against the law to carry a Puerto Rican Flag from 1898 to 1952.

In the town square, Canales gave a speech and declared Puerto Rico a free Republic. The town was held by the nationalists for three days.

The United States declared martial law in Puerto Rico and sent the Puerto Rico National Guard to attack Jayuya. The town was attacked by U.S. bomber planes and ground artillery.

Even though part of the town was destroyed, news of this military action was prevented from spreading outside of Puerto Rico.

It was called an incident between Puerto Ricans. The top leaders of the nationalist party, including Albizu Campos and Blanca Canales, were arrested and sent to jail to serve long prison terms.

Griselio Torresola, Albizu Campos's bodyguard, was in the United States at the time of the Jayuya Uprising. Torresola and fellow nationalist Oscar Collazo, were to assassinate President Harry S. Truman.

On November 1, 1950, they attacked the Blair House where Torresola and a policeman, Leslie Coffelt, lost their lives.

Oscar Collazo was arrested and sentenced to death. His sentence was later commuted to life imprisonment by President Truman, and he eventually received a presidential pardon.

CHAPTER 52

Cold War 1947–1991

After World War II a geopolitical, ideological, and economic struggle emerged between the United States and the Soviet Union and their respective allies.

Popularly named the Cold War, open hostilities never occurred between the main parties involved. Instead, it involved a nuclear and conventional weapons arms race, networks of military alliances, economic warfare and trade embargoes, propaganda, espionage, and smaller conflicts.

The Cold War was a period of geopolitical tension between the United States and the Soviet Union and their respective allies, the Western Bloc and the Eastern Bloc, which began following World War II.

Historians do not fully agree on its starting and ending points, but the period is generally considered to span the 1947 Truman Doctrine which was on 12 March 1947 until the 1991 dissolution of the Soviet Union, 26 December 1991.

The term cold war is used because there was no large-scale fighting directly between the two superpowers, but they each supported major regional conflicts known as proxy wars. The conflict was based around the ideological and geopolitical struggle for global influence by these two superpowers, following their temporary alliance and victory against Nazi Germany in 1945.

Aside from the nuclear arsenal development and conventional military deployment, the struggle for dominance was expressed via indirect means such as psychological warfare, propaganda campaigns, espionage, far-reaching embargoes, rivalry at sports events and technological competitions such as the Space Race.

The Western Bloc was led by the United States as well as the other First World nations of the Western Bloc that were generally liberal democratic but tied to a network of authoritarian states, most of which were their former colonies.

The Eastern Bloc was led by the Soviet Union and its Communist Party, which had an influence across the Second World and was also tied to a network of authoritarian states.

The US government supported anti-communist and right-wing governments and uprisings across the world, while the Soviet government funded left-wing parties and revolutions around the world.

As nearly all the colonial states achieved independence in the period 1945–1960, they became Third World battlefields in the Cold War.

The first phase of the Cold War began shortly after the end of the Second World War in 1945. The United States and its allies created the NATO military alliance in 1949 in the apprehension of a Soviet attack and termed their global policy against Soviet influence containment.

The Soviet Union formed the Warsaw Pact in 1955 in response to NATO. Major crises of this phase included the 1948–1949 Berlin Blockade, the 1927–1949 Chinese Civil War, the 1950–1953 Korean War, the 1956 Hungarian Revolution, the 1956 Suez Crisis, the Berlin Crisis of 1961 and the 1962 Cuban Missile Crisis.

The US and the USSR competed for influence in Latin America, the Middle East, and the decolonizing states of Africa, Asia, and Oceania.

Following the Cuban Missile Crisis, a new phase began that saw the Sino-Soviet split between China and the Soviet Union complicate relations within the Communist sphere, while France, a Western Bloc state, began to demand greater autonomy of action.

The USSR invaded Czechoslovakia to suppress the 1968 Prague Spring, while the US experienced internal turmoil from the civil rights movement and opposition to the Vietnam War.

In the 1960s–1970s, an international peace movement took root among citizens around the world. Movements against nuclear weapons testing and for nuclear disarmament took place, with large anti-war protests.

By the 1970s, both sides had started making allowances for peace and security, ushering in a period of détente that saw the Strategic Arms Limitation Talks and the US opening relations with the People's Republic of China as a strategic counterweight to the USSR.

Several self-proclaimed Marxist governments were formed in the second half of the 1970s in the Third World, including Angola, Mozambique, Ethiopia, Cambodia, Afghanistan, and Nicaragua.

Détente collapsed at the end of the decade with the beginning of the Soviet–Afghan War in 1979. The early 1980s was another period of elevated tension. The United States increased diplomatic, military, and economic pressures on the Soviet Union, at a time when it was already suffering from economic stagnation.

In the mid-1980s, the new Soviet leader Mikhail Gorbachev introduced the liberalizing reforms of glasnost "openness", c. 1985 and perestroika, "reorganization", 1987 and ended Soviet involvement in Afghanistan in 1989.

Pressures for national sovereignty grew stronger in Eastern Europe, and Gorbachev refused to militarily support their governments any longer.

In 1989, the fall of the Iron Curtain after the Pan-European Picnic and a peaceful wave of revolutions, except for Romania and Afghanistan, overthrew almost all communist governments of the Eastern Bloc.

The Communist Party of the Soviet Union itself lost control in the Soviet Union and was banned following an abortive coup attempt in August 1991.

This in turn led to the formal dissolution of the USSR in December 1991, the declaration of independence of its constituent republics and the collapse of communist governments across much of Africa and Asia. The United States was left as the world's sole superpower.

The Cold War and its events have left a significant legacy. It is often referred to in popular culture, especially with themes of espionage and the threat of nuclear warfare.

The Cuban Missile Crisis of 1962 was the most important direct confrontation. The Korean and Vietnam War were among the major civil wars polarized along Cold War lines.

CHAPTER 53

The Puerto Rico Air National Guard

The Air National Guard (ANG), also known as the Air Guard, is a federal military reserve force of the United States Air Force, as well as the air militia of each U.S. state, the District of Columbia, the Commonwealth of Puerto Rico, and the territories of Guam and the U.S. Virgin Islands. It, along with each state's, districts, commonwealths, or territory's Army National Guard component, makes up the National Guard of each state and the districts, commonwealths and territories as applicable.

When Air National Guard units are used under the jurisdiction of the state governor, they are fulfilling their militia role. However, if federalized by order of the President of the United States, Air National Guard units become an active part of the United States Air Force.

They are jointly administered by the states and the National Guard Bureau, a joint bureau of the Army and Air Force that oversees the United States National Guard.

Air National Guard operating forces are structured where each of the 50 U.S. states, the Commonwealth of Puerto Rico, the territories of Guam and the U.S. Virgin Islands, and the District of Columbia of the United States, houses at least one wing. Each wing is either assigned aircraft, or aircraft are shared with a unit of the active-duty Air Force or the Air Force Reserve under an "Associate" arrangement.

The ANG of the territories of Guam and the Virgin Islands have no aircraft assigned and perform ground support functions. Air National Guard activities may be located on active-duty air force bases, air reserve bases, naval air stations/joint reserve bases, or air national guard bases and stations which are either independent military facilities or collocated as tenants on civilian-controlled joint civil-military airports.

ANG units typically operate under Title 32 USC. However, when operating under Title 10 USC all ANG units are operationally gained by an active-duty Air Force major command, MAJCOM, or the United States Space Force.

ANG units of the Combat Air Forces, CAF, based in the Continental United States, CONUS, plus a single air control squadron of the Puerto Rico ANG, are gained by the Air Combat Command, ACC.

CONUS-based ANG units in the Mobility Air Forces, MAF, plus the Puerto Rico ANG's airlift wing and the Virgin Islands ANG's civil engineering squadron are gained by the Air Mobility Command, AMC.

Most ANG units fall under either ACC or AMC, however, there remain a few exceptions, such as the Alaska ANG, Hawaii ANG and Guam ANG, whose CAF and MAF units are operationally gained by Pacific Air Forces.

PACAF, while a smaller number of ANG units in CONUS are operationally gained by Air Education and Training Command AETC, Air Force Global Strike Command, AFGSC, Air Force Special Operations Command, AFSOC, and United States Air Forces in Europe - Air Forces Africa, USAFE-AFAFRICA.

Colonel Mihiel Gilormini was named commander of the 198th Fighter Squadron in Puerto Rico.

Gilormini and Colonel Alberto A. Nido, together with Lieutenant Colonel Jose Antonio Muñiz, played an instrumental role in the creation of the Puerto Rico Air National Guard on November 23, 1947.

The Puerto Rico Air National Guard is a part of the Air Reserve Component, ARC, of the United States Air Force.

Both Gilormini and Nido were eventually promoted to brigadier general and served as commanders of PRANG.

In 1963, the Air National Guard Base, at the San Juan International airport in Puerto Rico, was renamed "Muñiz Air National Guard Base" in honor of Lt. Col. Jose Antonio Muñiz who died on July 4, 1960, when his F-86 crashed during takeoff during the 4th of July festivities in Puerto Rico.

CHAPTER 54

USS Cochino incident

Cochino was named for the Cochino, a triggerfish found in the Atlantic. Her keel was laid down by Electric Boat Company of Groton, Connecticut. She was launched on 20 April 1945 sponsored by Mrs. M.E. Serat, and commissioned on 25 August 1945 with Commander W.A. Stevenson in command.

Cochino joined the U.S Atlantic Fleet, cruising East Coast and Caribbean Sea waters from her home port of Key West, Florida. In the late 1940s she received a GUPPY II conversion which streamlined her hull and increased her engine power.

On 18 July 1949, Cochino put to sea for a cruise to Britain, and arctic operations.

In August 1949, the USS Cochino and USS Tusk sailed along the Kola Peninsula to determine whether the USSR had detonated an atomic bomb.

Her group ran through a violent polar gale off Norway, and the jolting's received by Cochino played their part on 25 August in causing an electrical fire and battery explosion, followed by the generation of both hydrogen and chlorine gases.

Defying the most unfavorable possible weather conditions, Commander.

Later Rear Admiral, Rafael Celestino Benítez, 1917–1999, commanding officer of Cochino, and his men fought for 14 hours to save the submarine displaying great seamanship and courage. But a second battery explosion on August 26 made "Abandon Ship" the only possible order, and Cochino sank.

Tusk's crew rescued all Cochino's men except for Robert Wellington Philo, a civilian engineer. Six sailors from Tusk were lost during the rescue.

Cochino is one of four United States Navy submarines to be lost since the end of World War II. The others are USS Stickleback, USS Thresher, and USS Scorpion.

The USS Cochino, SS-345, was a Gato-class submarine under the command of Commander Rafael Celestino Benítez.

On August 12, 1949, the Cochino, along with the USS Tusk, SS-426, departed from Portsmouth, United Kingdom. Both diesel submarines were supposed to be on a cold-water training mission, however, according to Blind Man's Bluff.

The Untold Story of American Submarine Espionage, the submarines were part of an American intelligence operation. They had snorkels that allowed them to spend long periods underwater, largely invisible to an enemy, and they carried electronic gear designed to detect far-off radio signals.

The mission of the Cochino and the Tusk was to eavesdrop on communications that revealed the testing of submarine-launched Soviet missiles that might soon carry nuclear warheads. It was the first American undersea spy mission of the Cold War.

The mission was cut short when one of the Cochino's 4,000-pound batteries caught fire. Benitez directed the firefighting, trying both to save the ship and his crew from the toxic gases.

The crew members of the Tusk rescued all except one Cochino crew member and convinced Benitez, who was the last man on the Cochino, to board the Tusk.

The Cochino sank off the coast of Norway two minutes after Benitez's departure. Benitez retired from the Navy in 1957 as a rear admiral.

Sixty-one thousand Puerto Ricans served in the Korean War, including 18,000 Puerto Ricans who enlisted in the continental United States.

On August 26, 1950, the 65th Infantry Regiment departed from Puerto Rico and arrived in Pusan, Korea on September 23, 1950.

It was during the long sea voyage that the 65th Infantry was nicknamed the "Borinqueneers". The name is a combination of the words "Borinquen" the Taíno name for Puerto Rico and "Buccaneers".

Among the hardships suffered by the Puerto Ricans after they arrived in Korea was the lack of warm clothing during the cold, harsh winters. The enemy made many attempts to encircle the regiment, but each time they failed because of the many casualties inflicted by the 65th.

In December 1950, U.S. Marines found themselves at the Chosin Reservoir area. The 65th was part of a task force which enabled the Marines to withdraw from Hangu-Ri.

Among the battles and operations in which the 65th participated was the operation "Killer" of January 1951, becoming the first regiment to cross the Han River.

In April 1951, the regiment participated in the Uijonber Corridor drives and in June 1951, the 65th was the third regiment to cross the Han Ton River.

Master Sergeant Juan E. Negrón received the Medal of Honor posthumously on March 18, 2014, for his courageous actions while serving as a member of Company L, 65th Infantry Regiment, 3d Infantry Division during combat operations against an armed enemy in Kalma-Eri, Korea on April 28, 1951.

The 65th helped push the advance from Ch'orwon towards P'yonggang in June and then assisted in breaking the Iron Triangle of Hill 717 in July 1951.

In late November 1951, the 65th successfully fought off an attack by two battalion-sized enemy units. Colonel Juan César Cordero Dávila was named commander of 65th Infantry on February 1, 1952, thus becoming one of the highest-ranking ethnic officers in the Army.

Commencing on July 3, 1952, the regiment defended the main line of resistance (MLR) for 47 days and saw action at Cognac, King, and Queen with successful attacks on Chinese positions.

In September 1952, the 65th Infantry was holding on to a hill known as Outpost Kelly. Chinese Communist forces that had joined the

North Koreans overran the hill in what became known as the Battle of Outpost Kelly.

The 65th Infantry Regiment launched several efforts to retake the position but was overwhelmed by Chinese artillery and driven off on 24 September.

In October the regiment also saw action in the Cherwon Sector and on Iron Horse, around Hill 391, which became known as Jackson Heights.

In June 1953, the 2nd Battalion, 65th Infantry Regiment conducted a series of successful raids on Hill 412 in support of a position called Outpost Harry, and later the regiment conducted several successful raids in addition to defending defensive positions near the base of the Iron Triangle until the armistice was signed in July.

CHAPTER 55

The 65th Infantry

Distinctions Awarded

The 65th Infantry was credited with battle participation in nine campaigns.

Among the distinctions awarded to the members of the 65th were a Medal of Honor, 10 Distinguished Service Crosses, 256 Silver Stars and 595 Bronze Stars.

According to El Nuevo Día newspaper, May 30, 2004, a total of 756 Puerto Ricans lost their lives in Korea and a total of 3,630 men were wounded, from all four branches of the U.S. Armed Forces. More than half of these were from the 65th Infantry, not including non-Puerto Ricans.

The 65th Infantry returned to Puerto Rico and was disabled in 1956. However, <u>Major General Juan César Cordero Dávila</u>, Puerto Rico's Adjutant General 1958–65, persuaded the Department of the Army to transfer the 65th Infantry from the regular Army to the Puerto Rican National Guard.

This was the only unit ever transferred from active component Army to the Army Guard.

The Mass Court-Martials

After the fighting around Outpost Kelly, <u>Col. Cordero Dávila</u> was relieved of his command by Col. Chester B. DeGavre, a West Point graduate and a "continental" officer from the mainland United States and the officer staff of the 65th was replaced with non-Hispanic officers.

DeGavre ordered that the unit stop calling itself the Borinqueneers, cut their special rations of rice and beans, ordered the men to shave off their mustaches and had one of them wear signs that read "I am a coward".

Throughout October 1952, the 65th's morale declined and casualties around Jackson Heights mounted; by early November a patrol from Company L refused to follow their platoon leader across a river in the Chorwon Valley.

In December 1952, 162 Puerto Ricans of the 65th Infantry were arrested, 95 were court-martialed, and 91 were found guilty and sentenced to prison terms ranging from 1 to 18 years of hard labor.

It was the largest mass court martial of the Korean War. The Secretary of the Army Robert T. Stevens moved quickly to remit the sentences and granted clemency and pardons to all those involved. Though the men who were court-martialed were pardoned in 1954, a campaign was later started to obtain a formal exoneration.

An Army report released in 2001 blamed the breakdown of the 65th on the following factors: a shortage of officers and noncommissioned officers, a rotation policy that removed combat-experienced leaders and soldiers, tactics that led to high casualties, an ammunition shortage, communication problems between largely white, English-speaking officers and Spanish-speaking Puerto Rican enlisted men, and declining morale.

The report also found bias in the prosecution of the Puerto Ricans, citing instances of continental soldiers who were not charged after refusing to fight in similar circumstances, before and after Jackson Heights.

CHAPTER 56

The Cuban Missile Crisis

The Cuban Missile Crisis, also known as the October Crisis of 1962, the Caribbean Crisis or the Missile Scare, was a 35-day, 16 October – 20 November 1962.

It was a confrontation between the United States and the Soviet Union, which escalated into an international crisis when American deployments of missiles in Italy and Turkey were matched by Soviet deployments of similar ballistic missiles in Cuba.

Despite the short time frame, the Cuban Missile Crisis remains a defining moment in US national security and nuclear war preparation. The confrontation is often considered the closest the Cold War came to escalating into a full-scale nuclear war.

In response to the presence of American Jupiter ballistic missiles in Italy and Turkey, and the failed Bay of Pigs Invasion of 1961, Soviet First Secretary Nikita Khrushchev agreed to Cuba's request to place nuclear missiles on the island to deter a future invasion.

An agreement was reached during a secret meeting between Khrushchev and Cuban Prime Minister Fidel Castro in July 1962, and construction of several missiles launch facilities started later that summer.

Meanwhile, campaigning for the 1962 United States elections was underway, and the White House denied charges for months that it was ignoring dangerous Soviet missiles 90 mi, 140 km, from Florida.

The missile preparations were confirmed when an Air Force U-2 spy plane produced clear photographic evidence of medium-range R-12,

NATO code name SS-4 and intermediate-range R-14, NATO code name SS-5, ballistic missile facilities.

When this was reported to President John F. Kennedy, he then convened a meeting of the nine members of the National Security Council and five other key advisers, in a group that became known as the Executive Committee of the National Security Council, EXCOMM.

During this meeting, President Kennedy was originally advised to carry out an air strike on Cuban soil to compromise Soviet missile supplies, followed by an invasion of the Cuban mainland.

After careful consideration, President Kennedy chose a less aggressive course of action, to avoid a declaration of war. After consultation with EXCOMM, Kennedy ordered a naval "quarantine" on October 22 to prevent further missiles from reaching Cuba.

By using the term "quarantine", rather than "blockade" an act of war by legal definition, the United States was able to avoid the implications of a state of war.

The US announced it would not permit offensive weapons to be delivered to Cuba and demanded that the weapons already in Cuba be dismantled and returned to the Soviet Union.

After several days of tense negotiations, an agreement was reached between Kennedy and Khrushchev: publicly, the Soviets would dismantle their offensive weapons in Cuba and return them to the Soviet Union, subject to United Nations verification, in exchange for a US public declaration and agreement to not invade Cuba again.

Secretly, the United States agreed with the Soviets that it would dismantle all the Jupiter MRBMs which had been deployed to Turkey against the Soviet Union. There has been debate on whether Italy was included in the agreement as well.

While the Soviets dismantled their missiles, some Soviet bombers remained in Cuba, and the United States kept the naval quarantine in place until November 20, 1962.

When all offensive missiles and the Ilyushin Il-28 light bombers had been withdrawn from Cuba, the blockade was formally ended on November 20, 1962.

The negotiations between the United States and the Soviet Union pointed out the necessity of a quick, clear, and direct communication line between the two superpowers.

As a result, the Moscow–Washington hotline was established. A series of agreements later reduced US–Soviet tensions for several years, until both parties eventually resumed expanding their nuclear arsenals.

Admiral Horacio Rivero, Jr.

The Cuban Missile Crisis was a tense confrontation between the Soviet Union and the United States over the Soviet deployment of nuclear missiles in Cuba.

On October 22, 1962, Admiral Horacio Rivero, Jr. was the commander of the American fleet sent by President John F. Kennedy to set up a quarantine, blockade, of the Soviet ships.

On October 28, 1962, Soviet Premier Nikita Khrushchev ordered the removal of the Soviet missiles in Cuba, and Kennedy ordered an end of the quarantine of Cuba on November 20, 1962.

This brought the end to the crisis. Rivero later served as U.S. Ambassador to Spain,1972–1975.

CHAPTER 57

Puerto Ricans serving during the Vietnam War

During the Vietnam War, an estimated 48,000 Puerto Ricans served in the four branches of the armed forces.

According to a report by the Department of Defense, titled "Number of Puerto Ricans serving in the U.S. Armed Forces during National Emergencies" the total number of Puerto Ricans who died was 455 with 3,775 wounded.

A total of 17 men were listed as Missing in Action (MIA), and of these, PFC Humberto Acosta-Rosario is the only one whose body was never found.

Five Puerto Ricans were awarded the Medal of Honor for actions during the Vietnam War: Staff Sergeant Felix M. Conde-Falcon, Spc4 Héctor Santiago Colón, Captain Eurípides Rubio, PFC Carlos Lozada, and Captain Humbert Roque Versace.

Lance Corporal José L. Rivera, Corporal Miguel Rivera-Sotomayor, and Sergeant Angel Mendez, members of the United States Marine Corps, were awarded the Navy Cross for their heroic actions.

Mendez was posthumously awarded the Navy Cross for his actions on March 16, 1967, for saving the life of his platoon commander, Lieutenant Ronald D. Castille. He is one of the seven justices of the Supreme Court of Pennsylvania.

U.S. Senator Charles Schumer has recommended that Mendez' award be upgraded to the Medal of Honor.

Another highly decorated soldier in the Vietnam War was Sergeant First Class Jorge Otero Barreto from the town of Vega Baja, Puerto Rico. He was awarded 38 decorations, among them 2 Silver Star Medals, 5 Bronze Star Medals with "V" for Valor, 4 Army Commendation Medals, 5 Purple Heart Medals and 5 Air Medals.

On September 22, 2015, the Public Broadcasting Service (PBS) documentary. "On Two Fronts: Latinos & Vietnam" by producer Mylène Moreno of Souvenir Pictures, Inc., aired nationwide on PBS and is part of PBS Stories of Service.

The documentary focuses on the totality of the Latino experience in Vietnam, not just Puerto Ricans.

Other Puerto Ricans who served in Vietnam and had distinguished military careers include Major General Salvador E. Felices, Rear Admiral Diego E. Hernández, Colonel Héctor Andrés Negroni and Brigadier General Ruben A. Cubero who in 1991 became the first person of Hispanic heritage to be named Dean of Faculty of the United States Air Force Academy.

Two Puerto Ricans who served in Vietnam held positions in the Administration of President George W. Bush. They are Dr. Richard Carmona, a former Green Beret who was awarded two Purple Hearts and was appointed Surgeon General in March 2002, and Major General William A. Navas Jr., who was awarded the Bronze Star Medal and was named Assistant Secretary of the Navy on June 6, 2001.

CHAPTER 58

Operation El Dorado Canyon

The 1986 United States bombing of Libya, code-named Operation El Dorado Canyon, consisted of air strikes by the United States against Libya on Tuesday 15 April 1986.

The attack was carried out by the U.S. Air Force, U.S. Navy, and U.S. Marine Corps via air strikes, in retaliation for the West Berlin discotheque bombing ten days earlier.

There were 40 reported Libyan casualties, and one U.S. plane was shot down. One of the claimed Libyan deaths was of a baby girl, reported to be Muammar Gaddafi's daughter, Hana Gaddafi.

However, there are doubts as to whether she was really killed, or whether she even existed.

Libya represented a high priority for President Ronald Reagan shortly after his 1981 inauguration. Libyan leader Muammar Gaddafi was firmly anti-Israel and had supported violent organizations in the Palestinian territories and Syria.

There were reports that Libya was attempting to become a nuclear power and Gaddafi's occupation of Chad, which was rich in uranium, was of major concern to the United States. Gaddafi's ambitions to set up a federation of Arab and Muslim states in North Africa were alarming to U.S. interests.

Furthermore, then-Secretary of State Alexander Haig wanted to take proactive measures against Gaddafi because he had been using former

Central Intelligence Agency (CIA) operatives to help set up terrorist camps, most notably Edwin P. Wilson and Frank E. Terpil.

After the December 1985 Rome and Vienna airport attacks, which killed 19 and wounded approximately 140, Gaddafi indicated that he would continue to support the Red Army Faction, the Red Brigades, and the Irish Republican Army if the European governments supported anti-Gaddafi Libyans.

After years of occasional skirmishes with Libya over Libyan territorial claims to the Gulf of Sidra, the United States contemplated a military attack to strike targets within the Libyan mainland. In March 1986, the United States, asserting the 12-nautical-mile, 22 km; 14 mi; limit to territorial waters according to international law, sent a carrier task force to the region.

Libya responded with aggressive counter-maneuvers on 24 March that led to a naval engagement in the Gulf of Sidra.

On 5 April 1986, Libyan agents bombed "La Belle" nightclub in West Berlin, killing three people, including a U.S. serviceman, and injuring 229 people.

West Germany and the United States obtained cable transcripts from Libyan agents in East Germany who were involved in the attack.

More detailed information was retrieved years later when Stasi archives were investigated by the reunited Germany. Libyan agents who had carried out the operation from the Libyan embassy in East Germany were identified and prosecuted by Germany in the 1990s.

The attack mission against Libya had been preceded in October 1985 by an exercise in which the 20th TFW stationed at RAF Upper Heyford airbase in the UK, which was equipped with F-111Es, received a top-secret order to launch a simulated attack mission on 18 October, with ten F-111Es armed with eight 500-lb practice bombs, against a simulated airfield located in Newfoundland, Canada south of CFB Goose Bay.

The mission was designated Operation Ghost Rider. The mission was a full rehearsal for a long-range strike against Libya. The mission was completed successfully, except for one aircraft that had all but one of its eight bombs hang up on one of its wing racks. The lessons learned were passed on to the 48th TFW which was equipped with the newer "F" models of the F-111.

Elements of the then-secret 4450th Tactical Group (USAF) were put on standby to fly the strike mission against Libya. Over 30 F-117s had already been delivered to Tactical Air Command (USAF) and were operating from Tonopah Test Range Airport in Nevada. Commanders in the North Africa/Mediterranean theaters knew nothing about the capabilities of the F-117, or that the aircraft even existed.

Within an hour of the planned launch of the F-117s, the Secretary of Defense scrubbed the stealth mission, fearing a compromise of the secret aircraft and its development program.

The air strike was carried out with conventional U.S. Navy and U.S. Air Force aircraft. The F-117 would remain completely unknown to the world for several more months, before being unveiled in 1988 and featured prominently in media coverage of Operation Desert Storm.

For the Libyan raid, the United States was denied overflight rights by France, Spain, and Italy as well as the use of European continental bases, forcing the Air Force portion of the operation to be flown around France and Spain, over Portugal and through the Straits of Gibraltar, adding 1,300 miles, 2,100 km, each way and requiring multiple aerials refueling. The French refusal alone added 2,800 km.

French President François Mitterrand refused overflight clearance because the United States was interested in limited action in Libya while France was more interested in major action that would remove Gaddafi from power.

Another factor in the French decision was the United States' last-minute failure to participate in a retaliatory air raid on Iranian positions after the 1983 Beirut barracks bombings.

On April 14, 1986, in response to acts of terrorism sponsored by Libyan leader Muammar al-Gaddafi. In particular, the Berlin disco bombing of April 6, 186 and against the backdrop of heightened tension and clashes between the Libyan and U.S. Navies over Libya's disputed territorial water claims in the Gulf of Sidra.

The United States launched a surprise attack on key facilities in Tripoli and other parts of Libya. The attack was code-named Operation El Dorado Canyon.

With the acceptance of the British government, 24 U.S. Air Force F-111F fighter-bombers took off from U.S. air bases in England.

Attacking in the pre-dawn hours of April 15, 1986, their main purposes were 22 airfields, terrorist training camps, and other military installations.

Captain Fernando L. Ribas-Dominicci was one of the pilots who participated in the Libyan air raid. His F-111 was shot down over the Gulf of Sidra off the Libyan coast. Ribas-Dominicci and his weapons systems officer, Captain Paul F. Lorence, were the only U.S. casualties. Al-Qaddafi, who was also personally targeted, escaped harm, but his daughter was killed.

CHAPTER 59

The Gulf War and Operation Restore Hope

The Gulf War was an armed campaign waged by a United States-led coalition of 35 countries against Iraq in response to the Iraqi invasion and annexation of Kuwait.

On 2 August 1990, the Iraqi military invaded the neighboring State of Kuwait, and had fully occupied the country within two days.

Different speculations have been made regarding the true intents behind the invasion, including Iraq's inability to pay Kuwait the more than US$14 billion that it had borrowed to finance its military efforts during the Iran–Iraq War, and Kuwait's surge in petroleum production levels which kept revenues down for Iraq.

Throughout much of the 1980s, Kuwait's oil production was above its mandatory OPEC quota, which kept international oil prices down.

Iraq interpreted Kuwait's refusal to decrease its oil production as an act of aggression towards the Iraqi economy.

The invasion of Kuwait was met with international condemnation, and economic sanctions against Iraq were immediately imposed by the United Nations Security Council in response. British prime minister Margaret Thatcher and American president George H. W. Bush deployed troops and equipment into Saudi Arabia and urged other countries to send their own forces to the scene. In response to the call, an array of nations joined the U.S.-led coalition, forming the largest military alliance since World War II.

The bulk of the coalition's military forces were from the United States, with Saudi Arabia, the United Kingdom, and Egypt as the largest lead-up contributors, in that order. Kuwait and Saudi Arabia paid around US$32 billion of the US$60 billion cost.

The initial conflict to expel Iraqi forces from Kuwait began with an aerial and naval bombardment on 17 January 1991, which continued for five weeks.

During this period, Iraq began to launch missiles into Israel with the aim of provoking a response by the Israeli military, which the Iraqi leadership expected to prompt the coalition's Muslim states to withdraw and therefore jeopardize the alliance against Iraq.

As the Iraqi missile campaign against Israel failed to generate the desired response, Iraq also launched Scud missiles at coalition targets stationed in Saudi Arabia. This was followed by a ground assault by the coalition into Iraqi-occupied Kuwait on 24 February.

The offensive was a decisive victory for coalition forces, who liberated Kuwait and promptly began to advance past the Iraq–Kuwait border into Iraqi territory. 100 hours after the beginning of the ground campaign, the coalition ceased its advance and declared a ceasefire. Aerial and ground combat was confined to Iraq, Kuwait, and areas straddling the Iraq–Saudi Arabia border.

The war marked the introduction of live news broadcasts from the front lines of the battle, principally by the American network CNN.

It has also earned the nickname Video Game War after the daily broadcast of images from cameras onboard American bombers during Operation Desert Storm.

The Gulf War has gained notoriety for including three of the largest tank battles in American military history.

Captain Manuel Rivera Jr., (USMC)

In 1990, 1,700 Puerto Rican National Guardsmen were among the 20,000 Hispanics deployed to the Persian Gulf in Operations Desert Shield and Desert Storm as part of the Gulf War.

NORMA IRIS PAGAN MORALES

Four Puerto Ricans lost their lives, including <u>Captain Manuel Rivera, Jr.</u> of the Marine Corps, a Puerto Rican from the South Bronx, who on January 22, 1991, became the first Marine, and therefore the first Hispanic, to be killed in Operation Desert Shield.

Rivera was killed during a support mission over the Persian Gulf. On January 30, 1991, the U.S. House of Representatives paid tribute to Rivera.

During this era Haydee Javier Kimmich, from Cabo Rojo, Puerto Rico, was the highest-ranking Hispanic female in the Navy when she was promoted to the rank of captain, O-6.

Kimmich was assigned as the Chief of Orthopedics at the Navy Medical Center in Bethesda and reorganized their Reservist Department during Operation Desert Storm. In 1998, she was selected as the woman of the year in Puerto Rico.

Operation Restore Hope

Was an American military operation with the support of the United Nations that was formed to deliver humanitarian aid and restore order to the African nation of Somalia, then suffering from severe famine, anarchy, and domination by several warlords following the collapse of Siad Barre's Marxist government and the outbreak of the Somali Civil War.

On January 30, 1993, <u>Private First-Class Domingo Arroyo, Jr.</u>, a Marine from Puerto Rico, became the first of the 44 American soldiers killed during the operation. His patrol was ambushed near Mogadishu, the capital of Somalia, by forces controlled by Somali warlords.

238

CHAPTER 60

21st century campaigns

September 11 attacks

On September 11, 2001, 19 militants associated with the Islamic extremist group al Qaeda hijacked four airplanes and carried out suicide attacks against targets in the United States.

Two of the planes were flown into the twin towers of the World Trade Center in New York City, a third plane hit the Pentagon in Arlington, Virginia, just outside Washington, D.C., and the fourth plane crashed in a field in Shanksville, Pennsylvania.

Almost 3,000 people were killed during the 9/11 terrorist attacks, which triggered major U.S. initiatives to combat terrorism and defined the presidency of George W. Bush.

World Trade Center

On September 11, 2001, at 8:45 a.m. on a clear Tuesday morning, an American Airlines Boeing 767 loaded with 20,000 gallons of jet fuel crashed into the north tower of the World Trade Center in New York City.

The impact left a gaping, burning hole near the 80th floor of the 110-story skyscraper, instantly killing hundreds of people and trapping hundreds more in higher floors.

As the evacuation of the tower and its twin got underway, television cameras broadcasted live images of what initially appeared to be a freak accident.

Then, 18 minutes after the first plane hit, a second Boeing 767 United Airlines Flight 175 appeared out of the sky, turned sharply toward the World Trade Center, and sliced into the south tower near the 60th floor.

The collision caused a massive explosion that showered burning debris over surrounding buildings and onto the streets below. It immediately became clear that America was under attack.

The hijackers were Islamic terrorists from Saudi Arabia and several other Arab nations. Reportedly financed by the al Qaeda terrorist organization of Saudi fugitive Osama bin Laden, they were allegedly acting in retaliation for America's support of Israel, its involvement in the Persian Gulf War and its continued military presence in the Middle East.

Some of the terrorists had lived in the United States for more than a year and had taken flying lessons at American commercial flight schools. Others had slipped into the country in the months before September 11 and acted as the "muscle" in the operation.

The 19 terrorists easily smuggled box-cutters and knives through security at three East Coast airports and boarded four early-morning flights bound for California, chosen because the planes were loaded with fuel for the long transcontinental journey.

Soon after takeoff, the terrorists commandeered the four planes and took the controls, transforming ordinary passenger jets into guided missiles.

As millions watched the events unfolding in New York, American Airlines Flight 77 circled over downtown Washington, D.C., before crashing into the west side of the Pentagon military headquarters at 9:45 a.m.

Jet fuel from the Boeing 757 caused a devastating inferno that led to the structural collapse of a portion of the giant concrete building, which is the headquarters of the U.S. Department of Defense.

All told, 125 military personnel and civilians were killed in the Pentagon, along with all 64 people aboard the airliner.

Less than 15 minutes after the terrorists struck the nerve center of the U.S. military, the horror in New York took a catastrophic turn when the south tower of the World Trade Center collapsed in a mass dust and smoke.

The structural steel of the skyscraper, built to withstand winds more than 200 miles per hour and a large conventional fire, could not withstand the tremendous heat generated by the burning jet fuel.

At 10:30 a.m., the north building of the twin towers collapsed. Only six people in the World Trade Center towers at the time of their collapse survived. Almost 10,000 others were treated for injuries, many severe.

Meanwhile, a fourth California-bound plane, United Flight 93, was hijacked about 40 minutes after leaving Newark Liberty International Airport in New Jersey.

Because the plane had been delayed in taking off, passengers on board learned of events in New York and Washington via cell phone and Airphone calls to the ground.

Knowing that the aircraft was not returning to an airport as the hijackers claimed, a group of passengers and flight attendants planned an insurrection.

One of the passengers, Thomas Burnett, Jr., told his wife over the phone that "I know we're all going to die. There's three of us who are going to do something about it. I love you, honey."

Another passenger, Todd Beamer, was heard saying "Are you guys ready? Let's roll" over an open line.

Sandy Bradshaw, a flight attendant, called her husband and explained that she had slipped into a galley and was filling pitchers with boiling water. Her last words to him were "Everyone's running to first class. I've got to go. Bye."

The passengers fought the four hijackers and are suspected to have attacked the cockpit with a fire extinguisher.

The plane then flipped over and sped toward the ground at upwards of 500 miles per hour, crashing in a rural field near Shanksville in western Pennsylvania at 10:10 a.m.

All 44 people aboard were killed. Its intended target is not known, but theories include the White House, the U.S. Capitol, the Camp David presidential retreat in Maryland or one of several nuclear power plants along the eastern seaboard.

A total of 2,996 people were killed in the 9/11 attacks, including the 19 terrorist hijackers aboard the four airplanes. Citizens of 78 countries died in New York, Washington, D.C., and Pennsylvania.

At the World Trade Center, 2,763 died after the two planes slammed into the twin towers.

That figure includes:

343 firefighters and paramedics
23 New York City police officers
37 Port Authority police officers

Those Por Authority police officers were struggling to complete an evacuation of the buildings and save the office workers trapped on higher floors.

At the Pentagon, 189 people were killed, including 64 on American Airlines Flight 77, the airliner that struck the building.

On Flight 93, 44 people died when the plane crash-landed in Pennsylvania.

America Responds to the Attacks

At 7 p.m., President George W. Bush, who was in Florida at the time of the attacks and had spent the day being shuttled around the country because of security concerns, returned to the White House.

At 9 p.m., he delivered a televised address from the Oval Office, declaring, "Terrorist attacks can shake the foundations of our biggest buildings, but they cannot touch the foundation of America. These acts shatter steel, but they cannot dent the steel of American resolve."

In a reference to the eventual U.S. military response he declared, "We will make no distinction between the terrorists who committed these acts and those who harbor them."

Operation Enduring Freedom, the American-led international effort to oust the Taliban regime in Afghanistan and destroy Osama bin Laden's terrorist network based there, began on October 7, 2001.

Within two months, U.S. forces had effectively removed the Taliban from operational power, but the war continued, as U.S. and coalition forces attempted to defeat a Taliban insurgency campaign based in neighboring Pakistan.

Osama bin Laden, the mastermind behind the September 11th attacks, remained at large until May 2, 2011, when he was finally tracked down and killed by U.S. forces at a hideout in Abbottabad, Pakistan.

In June 2011, then-President Barack Obama announced the beginning of large-scale troop withdrawals from Afghanistan; it took until August 2021 for all U.S. forces to withdraw.

Department of Homeland Security Is Created

In the wake of security fears raised by 9/11 and the mailing of letters containing anthrax that killed two and infected 17, The Homeland Security Act of 2002 created the Department of Homeland Security.

It was signed into law by President George W. Bush on November 25, 2002. Today, the Department of Homeland Security is a cabinet responsible for preventing terror attacks, border security, immigrations and customs and disaster relief and prevention.

The act was followed two days later by the formation of the National Commission on Terrorist Attacks Upon the United States. The bipartisan "9/11 Commission," as it came to be known, was charged with investigating the events that led up to September 11th.

The 9/11 Commission Report was released on July 22, 2004. It named Khalid Sheikh Mohammed, the accused mastermind behind 9/11, "the principal architect of the 9/11 attacks."

Mohammed led propaganda operations for al Qaeda from 1999-2001. He was captured on March 1, 2003, by the Central Intelligence Agency and Pakistan's Inter-Services Intelligence and interrogated before being imprisoned in Guantanamo Bay detention camp with four other accused terrorists charged with 9/11-related war crimes.

The use of torture, including waterboarding, during Khalid Sheikh Mohammed's interrogation has received international attention. In August 2019, a U.S. military court judge in Guantánamo Bay, Cuba set a trial date for Mohammed and the other four men charged with plotting the 9/11 terrorist attacks to begin in 2021; it was later postponed because of the COVID-19 pandemic.

Economic Impact of 9/11

The 9/11 attacks had an immediate negative effect on the U.S. economy. Many Wall Street institutions, including the New York Stock Exchange, were evacuated during the attacks.

On the first day of trading after the attacks, the market fell 7.1 percent, or 684 points. New York City's economy alone lost 143,000 jobs a month and $2.8 billion wages in the first three months.

The heaviest losses were in finance and air transportation, which accounted for 60 percent of lost jobs. The estimated cost of the World Trade Center damage is $60 billion. The cost to clean the wreckage at Ground Zero was $750 million.

Five Ways 9/11 Changed America
9/11 Victim Compensation Fund

Thousands of first responders and people working and living in lower Manhattan near Ground Zero were exposed to toxic fumes and particles emanating from the towers as they burned and fell.

By 2018, 10,000 people were diagnosed with 9/11-related cancer.

From 2001 to 2004, over $7 billion dollars in compensation was given to families of the 9/11 victims and the 2,680 people injured in the attacks.

Funding was renewed on January 2, 2011, when President Barack Obama signed The James Zadroga 9/11 Health and Compensation Act into law.

Named for James Zadroga, a New York City Police officer who died of respiratory disease he contracted after rescuing people from the rubble at Ground Zero, the law continued health monitoring and compensation for 9/11 first responders and survivors.

In 2015, funding for the treatment of 9/11-related illness was renewed for five more years at a total of $7.4 billion. The Victim Compensation Fund was set to stop accepting claims in December 2020.

On July 29, 2019, then-President Trump signed a law authorizing support for the September 11 Victim Compensation Fund through 2092.

Previously, administrators had cut benefits by up to 70 percent as the $7.4 billion fund depleted. Vocal lobbyists for the fund included Jon Stewart, 9/11 first responder John Feal and retired New York Police Department detective and 9/11 responder Luis Alvarez, who died of cancer 18 days after testifying before Congress.

9/11 Anniversary and Memorial

On December 18, 2001, Congress approved naming September 11 "Patriot Day" to commemorate the anniversary of the 9/11 attacks. In 2009, Congress named September 11 a National Day of Service and Remembrance.

The first memorials to September 11 came in the immediate wake of the attacks, with candlelight vigils and flower tributes at U.S. embassies around the world.

In Great Britain, Queen Elizabeth sang the American national anthem during the changing of the guard at Buckingham Palace.

Rio de Janeiro put up billboards showing the city's Christ the Redeemer statue embracing the New York City skyline.

For the first anniversary of the attacks in New York City in 2002, two bright columns of light were shot up into the sky from where the Twin Towers once stood.

The "Tribute in Light" then became an annual installation run by the Municipal Art Society of New York. On clear nights, the beams are visible from over 60 miles away.

A World Trade Center Site Memorial Competition was held to select an appropriate permanent memorial to the victims of 9/11. The winning design by Michael Arad, "Reflecting Absence," now sits outside the museum in an eight-acre park.

It consists of two reflecting pools with waterfalls rushing down where the Twin Towers once rose into the sky.

The names of all 2,983 victims are engraved on the 152 bronze panels surrounding the pools, arranged by where individuals were on the day of the attacks, so coworkers and people on the same flight are memorialized together.

The site was opened to the public on September 11, 2011, to commemorate the 10-year anniversary of 9/11.

The National September 11 Memorial & Museum followed, opening on the original World Trade Center site in May 2014. The Freedom Tower, also on the original World Trade Center site, opened in November 2014.

On September 11, 2001, United Airlines Flight 93 was hijacked by four members of al-Qaeda as part of the September 11 attacks.

The hijackers' specific target was the United States Capitol. Among the pilots available that day of the 113th Wing of the DC Air National Guard were Lieutenant Colonel Marc H. Sasseville and Lieutenant Heather Penney.

They were given the mission of finding the United Airlines Flight 93 and destroying it. Since their fighters were not armed with missiles and carrying dummy ammunition from a recent training mission, they might have been required to ram the passenger aircraft.

It was not until hours later that they would learn United 93 had already gone down in a field outside Shanksville, Pennsylvania, killing all 44 people aboard including the four hijackers.

In 2001, Noel Zamot was assigned to the Directorate of Operations, United States Space Command, Paterson Air Force Base in Colorado as Deputy Chief of Operations Integration.

According to the United States Air Force, Zamot's mission as Deputy Chief of Operations in the aftermath of the September 11 attacks was to integrate emerging national capabilities into a joint counter terrorism operation.

He developed concepts for long-term Information Operations and Space Control activities for the U.S. enabling a multi-spectral combat response.

He was also involved in the development of the Special Access Program (SAP) systems and in the development of new counter-space capabilities which resulted in a more effective counter-terrorism operation across three combat zones.

When he retired from the Air Force, he was commandant of the Test Pilot School at Edwards Air Force Base.

On 11 September 2001, unimaginable horror came to our country as terrorists turned airliners filled with innocent people into lethal weapons.

As one terrible blow after another hit in New York City, at the Pentagon and in Pennsylvania, ordinary Americans, citizens, and citizen-soldiers -- responded heroically to these extraordinary events.

The Army Reserve are particularly proud of their own who displayed the highest qualities of courage and selflessness on 11 September, whether that meant rushing into the World Trade Center, regardless of personal safety concerns, helping injured comrades out of the turning Pentagon or organizing rescue and recovery activities.

We especially remember those we lost on 11 September. There were the five citizen soldiers of the 77th Regional Support Command (RSC) who were members of the Fire Department of New York.

They, along with hundreds of their comrades, died saving the lives of thousands of others at the World Trade Center. There was the 77th RSC Judge Advocate...

General officer, also at work in his civilian job, who died in Tower Two of the World Trade Center. There was the retired colonel, a security chief for an investment company in Tower o got all but six of his firm's 2,700 employees out safely and then lost his life when he went back to find those still missing.

There was also the Active Guard Reserve (AGR) colonel and the retired AGR colonel who were at their appointed place of duty in the Pentagon at the time that place of duty became the point of impact.

These are the names of those we should never forget our first casualties in the war on terrorism:

Warrant Officer 1 Ronald P. Bucca, fire marshal, Fire Department of New York (FDNY), killed during rescue efforts at the World Trade Center.

Staff Sergeant Frederick J. Ill, captain, FDNY, killed during rescue efforts at the World Trade Center.

Retired Colonel Ronald F. Golinski, Department of Army Civilian, killed while on duty at the Pentagon.

Colonel William H. Pohlmann, lawyer, working on the 91st floor of Tower Two, killed at the World Trade Center.

Sergeant Shawn Powell, fireman, FDNY, killed during rescue efforts at the World Trade Center.

Retired Colonel Rick Rescorla, director of security for Morgan Stanley in Tower Two killed while helping others escape at the World Trade Center.

Colonel David M. Scales, AGR officer, killed while on duty at the Pentagon.

Captain Mark P. Whiteford, fireman, FDNY, killed during rescue efforts at the World Trade Center.

These were not our only heroes on 11 September, nor did the Army Reserve's response end after the initial attacks. It was only beginning. Army Reservists on site in the Pentagon and New York City took immediate action to help the injured, to try to reach other survivors, and to assist other rescue workers.

Even as rescue workers fought the flames, the Army Reserve response grew, across America, with crisis action teams standing up and in full operation in every major Army Reserve command headquarters within hours. Military Police units quickly took up station at key facilities.

In New York City, the 77th RSC reacted swiftly to the disaster, quickly appropriating, and delivering hundreds of support items in short order to assist in the disaster recovery effort.

Equally quick to respond and critical to the rescue and recovery operation were the Army Reserve Emergency Preparedness Liaison Officers in the New York City area.

They arrived on the scene immediately to facilitate support requests from civilian agencies as quickly and effectively as possible.

Thousands of trained and ready Army Reserve men and women came forward, first as volunteers and then in response to the partial mobilization ordered by the president on 14 September, just three days after the attacks.

Among the first soldiers to move out and begin operations was the 311th Quartermaster Company, Mortuary Affairs, from Aguadilla, Puerto Rico.

Seventy-two hours after the call went out for volunteers from the 311th, they had deployed to the Pentagon and were searching through wreckage for the remains of victims.

By the time the unit was mobilized a week later, it had already been "at war" for a week.

Two of our Military History Detachments have worked hard to capture the events of 11 September and the weeks that followed from the perspective of the Army Reserve.

The 311th Military History Detachment from Fort Totten, N.Y., commanded by Major Robert Bensburg, and the 90th Military History Detachment from San Antonio, Texas, commanded by Captain Suzanne Summers was called up soon after 11 September.

The 311th was assigned to cover the New York City story and the 90th covered the Washington, D.C., area.

The soldiers of these two small detachments gathered information and material, documented what had taken place and conducted numerous oral history interviews with participants.

In doing their mission, they had to go into the damaged section of the Pentagon and look out over what is now known as Ground Zero in New York City.

They interviewed survivors of the Pentagon attack and others who had performed the horrific task of recovering those who had not survived. They talked with heroes and those who supported the heroes.

Reserve's role in the global war on terrorism, the beginning of what was and continues to be a decisive and extraordinarily rapid response to a national crisis.

This is the beginning of a story that will not end until the United States achieves the inevitable victory over the terrorists.

The Army Reserve was on the front lines of this war when it began on 11 September 2001.

CHAPTER 61

Iraq and Afghanistan

At just short of 20 years, the now ending U.S. combat mission in Afghanistan was America's longest war. The average Americans tended to forget about it.

It has received significantly less oversight from Congress than the Vietnam War. Its death toll is in the many tens of thousands.

Because the U.S. borrowed most of the money to pay for it, generations of Americans will be burdened by the cost of paying it off.

Here's a look at the U.S. led war in Afghanistan, by the numbers, as the Taliban in a lightning offensive take over much of the country before the United States' Aug. 31 deadline for ending its combat role and as the U.S. speeds up American and Afghan evacuations.

A lot of the data below is from Linda Bilmes of Harvard University's Kennedy School and from the Brown University Costs of War project.

The United States between 2003 and 2011 fought the Afghanistan and Iraq wars at the same time, and many American troops served tours in both wars, some figures as noted cover both post 9/11 U.S. wars.

THE LONGEST WAR

The percentage of U.S. population born since the 2001 attacks plotted by al-Qaida leaders who were sheltering in Afghanistan: Roughly one out of every four.

THE HUMAN COST

American service members killed in Afghanistan through April: 2,448. U.S. contractors: 3,846.

Afghan national military and police: 66,000.
Other allied service members, including from other NATO member states: 1,144.
Afghan civilians: 47,245.
Taliban and other opposition fighters: 51,191.
Aid workers: 444.
Journalists: 72.

AFGHANISTAN AFTER NEARLY 20 YEARS OF U.S. OCCUPATION

The percentage drop-in infant mortality rate since U.S., Afghan and other allied forces overthrew the Taliban government, which had sought to restrict women and girls to the home: About 50.
Percentage of Afghan teenage girls able to read today: 37.

OVERSIGHT BY CONGRESS:

Date Congress authorized U.S. forces to go after culprits in Sept. 11, 2001, attacks: Sept. 18, 2001.
Number of times U.S. lawmakers have voted to declare war in Afghanistan:
Number of times lawmakers on Senate Appropriations defense subcommittee addressed costs of Vietnam War, during that conflict: 42
Number of times lawmakers in same subcommittee have mentioned costs of Afghanistan and Iraq wars, through mid-summer 2021: 5.
Number of times lawmakers on Senate Finance Committee have mentioned costs of Afghanistan and Iraq wars since Sept. 11, 2001, through mid-summer 2021: 1.

PAYING FOR A WAR ON CREDIT, NOT IN CASH:

Amount President Harry Truman temporarily raised top tax rates to pay for Korean War: 92%.

Amount President Lyndon Johnson temporarily raised top tax rates to pay for Vietnam War: 77%.

Amount President George W. Bush cut tax rates for the wealthiest, rather than raise them, at outset of Afghanistan and Iraq wars: At least 8%.

Estimated amount of direct Afghanistan and Iraq war costs that the United States has debt financed as of 2020: $2 trillion.

Estimated interest costs by 2050: Up to $6.5 trillion.

THE WARS END. THE COSTS DON'T

Amount Bilmes estimates the United States has committed to pay in health care, disability, burial, and other costs for roughly 4 million Afghanistan and Iraq veterans: more than $2 trillion.

Period those costs will peak after 2048.

Specialist Lizbeth Robles

In the 21st century, Puerto Ricans have participated in the military campaigns of Afghanistan and Iraq, in what the United States and its allies refer to as the War on Terror.

Among those killed in Iraq are the first three Puerto Rican women to die in a foreign combat zone.

They are Specialist Frances M. Vega, Specialist Lizbeth Robles and Specialist Aleina Ramirez Gonzalez.

On November 2, 2003, Specialist Frances M. Vega became the first female Puerto Rican soldier born in the United States to die in a war zone.

A ground-to-air missile fired by protestors in Fallujah hit the Chinook transport helicopter Vega was in; she was one of 16 soldiers who lost their lives in the crash that followed.

On March 1, 2005, Specialist Lizbeth Robles became the first female Puerto Rican soldier born on the island to die in Iraq when her Humvee was involved in an accident.

On July 10, 2007, <u>Captain María Inés Ortiz</u>, who was assigned to a hospital in an area known as the "Green Zone" in Baghdad, Iraq, became the first Puerto Rican nurse to die in combat and the first Army nurse to die in the Iraq War after the area came under a heavy mortar attack.

<u>Specialist Hilda I. Ortiz Clayton</u>, who was of Puerto Rican descent, was a U.S. Army combat photographer killed in 2013 when a mortar exploded during an Afghan training exercise; she was able to photograph the explosion that killed her and four Afghan soldiers.

The 55th Signal Company named their annual competitive award for combat camera work "The Spc. Hilda I. Clayton Best Combat Camera (COMCAM) Competition" in her honor.

CHAPTER 62

Monument of Remembrance

"El Monumento de la Recordación"

Over 1,225 Puerto Ricans have died while serving the United States. The names of those who died in combat are inscribed in "El Monumento de la Recordación", Monument of Remembrance, which was unveiled on May 19, 1996. It is situated in front of the Capitol Building in San Juan, Puerto Rico.

On Veterans Day, November 11, 2013, a group representing the Puerto Rican community in Connecticut placed a floral arrangement on the tomb of Augusto Rodrigues, who fought in the American Civil War, recognizing him as Puerto Rico's first known U.S. Armed Forces veteran.

Puerto Rico's Military History

The recorded military history of Puerto Rico encompasses the period from the 16th century, when Spanish conquistadores battled native Taínos in the rebellion of 1511, to the present employment of Puerto Ricans in the United States Armed Forces in the military campaigns in Afghanistan and Iraq.

Puerto Rico was part of the Spanish Empire for four centuries, during which the people of Puerto Rico defended themselves against invasions from the British, French, and Dutch. Puerto Ricans fought alongside General Bernardo de Gálvez during the American Revolutionary War in the battles of Baton Rouge, Mobile, Pensacola and St. Louis. During the mid-19th century, Puerto Ricans residing in the United States fought in the American Civil War.

In the 1800s, the quest for Latin American independence from Spain spread to Puerto Rico, in the short-lived revolution known as the Grito de Lares and culminating with the Intentado de Yauco.

Puerto Rico was invaded by the United States during the Spanish American War. After the war ended, Spain officially ceded the island to the United States under the terms established in the Treaty of Paris of 1898.

Puerto Rico became a United States territory and the "Porto Rico Regiment", Puerto Rico's name was changed to Porto Rico, was established on the island.

Upon the outbreak of World War I, the U.S. Congress approved the Jones–Shafroth Act, which extended United States citizenship the Puerto Rican House of Delegates rejected US citizenship with limitations upon Puerto Ricans and made them eligible for the military draft.

Since then, as citizens of the United States, Puerto Ricans have participated in every major United States military engagement.

During World War II, Puerto Ricans participated in the Pacific and Atlantic theaters, not only as combatants but also as commanders. It was during this conflict that Puerto Rican nurses were allowed to participate as members of the WAACs.

Four Puerto Ricans were awarded the Medal of Honor, the highest military honor in the United States, for their actions during the Korean War. The members of Puerto Rico's 65th Infantry Regiment distinguished themselves in combat in the Korean War and were honored with the Congressional Gold Medal.

During the Vietnam War five Puerto Ricans were awarded the Medal of Honor. Presently, Puerto Ricans continue to serve in the military of the United States.

The main enemies of Spain at the time were the English and the Dutch. They, however, were not the only enemies that Spain faced in the forced them to retreat. The only settlement that remained was San Juan.

In 1585, war broke out between England and Spain. The Anglo-Spanish War was not limited to Europe extending to Spanish and English territories in America.

In November 1595, Sir Francis Drake, the vice-admiral in command of the Royal Navy fleet attempted an attack in the Spanish Armada. Sir John Hawkins also attempted an unsuccessful invasion of San Juan. Both Hawkins and Drake died of poor health during the struggle.

On June 15, 1598, the English fleet, led by George Clifford, landed in Santurce. They held the island for several months. He was forced to abandon the island upon an outbreak of bump-twisted sickness among his troops.

In 1599, 400 additional soldiers and 46 cannons were sent to the island along with a new governor, Alonso de Mercado, to rebuild the city.

CHAPTER 63

American Civil War

Lieutenant Augusto Rodríguez

During the 1800s, commerce existed between the ports of the eastern coast of the United States and Puerto Rico

Ships sailed to and from the U.S. and Puerto Rico. Many of them settled in places such as New York, Connecticut, and Massachusetts.

Upon the outbreak of the American Civil War, many Puerto Ricans joined the ranks of the United States military armed forces, however since Puerto Ricans were Spanish subjects they were inscribed as Spaniards.

The 1860 census of New Haven, Connecticut, shows there were 10 Puerto Ricans living there. Among of them was Augusto Rodriguez who joined the 15th Connecticut Regiment (a.k.a. Lyon Regiment) in 1862.

During the Civil War, Rodriguez, who reached the rank of lieutenant, served in the defenses of Washington, D.C. He also led his men in the Battles of Fredericksburg and Wyse Fork. The regiment was gathered out on June 27, 1865, and he was discharged in New Haven on July 12, 1865.

Slave revolts

Up until 1873, when slavery was abolished in Puerto Rico, the wealth accumulated by many landowners in Puerto Rico derived mainly from the exploitation of slaves. Slavery, in the meantime, is generating its opposition disobedience, uprisings and flights.

In Puerto Rico there were many minor slave revolts in which the slaves clashed with the military establishment.

In July 1821, Marcos Xiorro, a bozal slave, planned and organized a conspiracy against the slave masters and the colonial government of Puerto Rico.

According to his plot, which was to be carried out on July 27, during the festival celebrations for Santiago, St. James, several slaves were to escape from various plantations in Bayamón.

This included the haciendas of Angus McBean, C. Kortnight, Miguel Andino and Fernando Fernández.

They were then to proceed to the sugarcane fields of Miguel Figueres and retrieve cutlasses and swords which were hidden in those fields.

Xiorro, together with a slave from the McBean plantation named Mario and another slave named Narciso, would lead the Bayamon's slaves and Toa Baja to capture the city of Bayamón. They would then burn the city and kill those who were not black.

After this, they would all unite with slaves from the adjoining towns of Río Piedras, Guaynabo, and Palo Seco. With this critical mass of slaves, all armed and supported from a series of quick victories, they would then invade the capital city of San Juan. This is where they would declare Xiorro as their king....

Unfortunately for the slave conspirators, the plot was revealed by a fellow slave to the authorities.

The mayor of Bayamón mobilized 500 soldiers. The ringleaders and followers of the conspiracy were captured immediately. A total of 61 slaves were imprisoned in Bayamón and San Juan.

The ringleaders were executed and the fate of Xiorro remains a mystery. There were other minor revolts up until the abolition of slavery in the island became official.

Revolt against Spain

General Antonio Valero de Bernabe, the "Liberator from Puerto Rico"

In 1822, there was an attempt, known as the Ducoudray Holstein Expedition, conceived, carefully planned, and organized by General Henri La Fayette Villaume Ducoudray Holstein to invade Puerto Rico and declare it a republic.

This invasion was different from all its ancestors since none before had intended to make Puerto Rico an independent nation and use the Taino name "Boricua" as the official name of the republic. It was also intended more as a business project than a patriotic effort.

It was the first time an invasion intended to make the city of Mayagüez the capital of the island. However, plans of the invasion were soon disclosed to the Spanish authorities and the plot never materialized.

CHAPTER 64

United Provinces of New Granada

In the early 19th century, the Spanish colonies, in what is known as the Latin American wars of independence, began to revolt against Spanish rule.

Antonio Valero de Bernabé was a Puerto Rican military leader known in Latin America as the "Liberator from Puerto Rico".

Valero was a recent graduate of the Spanish Military Academy when Napoleon Bonaparte convinced King Charles IV of Spain to permit him to pass through Spanish soil with the sole purpose of attacking Portugal.

When Napoleon refused to leave, the Spanish government declared war. Valero joined the Spanish Army and helped defeat Napoleon's army at the Siege of Saragossa. Valero became a hero; he was promoted to the rank of colonel and was awarded many decorations.

When Ferdinand VII assumed the throne of Spain in 1813, Valero became critical of the new king's policies towards the Spanish colonies in Latin America. He developed a strong hatred of the monarchy, resigned his commission in the army, and headed for Mexico.

There he joined the insurgent army headed by Agustin de Iturbide, in which Valero was named chief of staff.

He fought for and helped achieve Mexico's independence from Spain. After the Mexican victory, Iturbide proclaimed himself Emperor of Mexico.

Since Valero had developed anti-monarchist feelings following his experiences in Spain, he revolted against Iturbide. His revolt failed and he attempted to escape from Mexico by way of sea.

Valero was captured by a Spanish pirate, who turned him over to the Spanish authorities in Cuba. Valero was imprisoned but managed to escape with the help of a group of men that identified with Simón Bolívar's ideals.

Upon learning of Bolívar's dream of creating a unified Latin America, including Puerto Rico and Cuba, Valero decided to join him. Valero stopped in St. Thomas, where he established contacts with the Puerto Rican independence movement.

He then traveled to Venezuela, where he was met by General Francisco de Paula Santander.

He next joined Bolívar and fought alongside "The Liberator" against Spain, gaining his confidence and admiration. Valero was named Military Chief of the Department of Panama, Governor of Puerto Cabello, Chief of Staff of Colombia, Minister of War and Maritime of Venezuela, and in 1849 was promoted to the rank of brigadier general.

María de las Mercedes Barbudo

The meetings of the Puerto Rican Independence movement which met in St. Thomas were discovered by the Spanish authorities.

The members of the movement were either imprisoned or exiled.

In a letter dated October 1, 1824, which Venezuelan rebel leader José María Rojas sent to María de las Mercedes Barbudo, Rojas stated that the Venezuelan rebels had lost their principal contact with the Puerto Rican Independence movement in the Danish Island of Saint Thomas.

The secret communication which existed between the Venezuelan rebels and the leaders of the Puerto Rican independence movements was in danger of being discovered.

Mercedes Barbudo
First Puerto Rican Female Freedom Fighter

Mercedes Barbudo was known as the "first Puerto Rican female freedom fighter". She was a businesswoman who became a follower of the independence ideal for Puerto Rico upon learning that Bolivar dreamed of eventually engendering an American Revolution-style federation.

It would be known as the United Provinces of New Granada, between all the newly independent republics, with a government ideally set-up solely to recognize and uphold individual rights.

She was involved with the Puerto Rican Independence Movement which had ties with the Venezuelan rebels led by Simón Bolívar and who were against Spanish colonial rule in Puerto Rico.

Unknown to Mercedes Barbudo, the Spanish authorities in Puerto Rico under Governor Miguel de la Torre, were suspicious of the communication between her and the rebel groups of Venezuela.

The secret agents of the Spanish Government retained some of Mercedes mail and delivered it to Governor de la Torre. He ordered an investigation and had her mail confiscated.

The Government believed that the correspondence served as propaganda of the Bolivian ideals and that it would also serve to motivate Puerto Ricans to seek their independence.

Governor Miguel de la Torre ordered her arrest on the charge that she planned to overthrow the Spanish Government in Puerto Rico.

Since Puerto Rico did not have a women's prison, she was held without bail at the Castillo San Cristóbal...

Among the evidence which the Spanish authorities presented against her was Rojas letter. She was exiled to Cuba where she was able to escape. She made her way to Venezuela where she spent her final days.

CHAPTER 65

Puerto Rico Fort San Cristóbal Cannon

The Spanish government had received many complaints from the nations whose ships were attacked by Puerto Rican pirate Captain Roberto Cofresí.

Cofresí and his men had attacked eight ships, amongst them an American ship. The Spanish government, which routinely encouraged piracy against other nations, was pressured and felt obligated to pursue and capture the famous pirate.

In 1824, Captain John Slout of the U.S. Naval Forces and his schooner USS Grampus engaged Cofresí in a fierce battle. The pirate Cofresí was captured, along with eleven of his crew members, and turned over to the Spanish Government.

He was imprisoned in El Castillo del Morro in San Juan. Cofresi was judged by a Spanish Council of War, found guilty, and executed by firing squad on March 29, 1825.

On April 13, 1855, a mutiny broke out among the artillerymen at Fort San Cristóbal. They were protesting an extended two years of military service imposed by the island's Spanish governor, Garcia Cambia.

The mutineers pointed their cannons towards San Juan, creating a state of panic among the population.

Upon their surrender, the governor had the eight men arrested and sentenced to death by firing squad.

CHAPTER 66

Grito de Lares

Many Spanish colonies had gained their independence by the mid-1850s.

In Puerto Rico, there were two groups: the loyalists, who were loyal to Spain, and the "independentistas", who advocated independence.

In 1866, Dr. Ramón Emeterio Betances, Segundo Ruiz Belvis, and other independence advocates met in New York City where they founded the Revolutionary Committee of Puerto Rico.

An outcome of this project was a plan to send an armed expedition from the Dominican Republic to invade the island. Several revolutionary groups were formed in the western towns and cities of Puerto Rico.

Two of the most important groups were at Mayagüez, led by Mathias Brugman and code-named "Capa Prieto" and at Lares, code-named "Centro Bravo" and headed by Manuel Rojas.

"Centro Bravo" was the main center of operations and was in the Rojas plantation of El Triunfo. Manuel Rojas was named "Commander of the Liberation Army" by Betances. Mariana Bracetti, Manuel's sister-in-law, was named "Leader of the Lares Revolutionary Council."

Upon the request of Betances, Bracetti knitted the first flag of Puerto Rico also known as the revolutionary Flag of Lares, Bandera de Lares.

Ramón Emeterio Betances

The Spanish authorities discovered the plot and were able to confiscate Betances's armed ship before it arrived in Puerto Rico. The mayor of the town of Camuy, Manuel González, leader of that town's revolutionary group, was arrested and charged with treason.

He learned that the Spanish Army was aware of the independence plot and escaped to warn Manuel Rojas. Alerted, the revolutionists decided to start the revolution as soon as possible, and set the date for September 28, 1868.

Mathias Brugman and his men joined with Manuel Rojas's men and with about 800 men and women, marched on and took the town of Lares. This was to be known as "Grito de Lares", The Cry of Lares.

The revolutionists entered the town's church and placed Mariana Bracetti's revolutionary flag on the High Altar as a sign that the revolution had begun. They declared Puerto Rico to be the "Republic of Puerto Rico" and named Francisco Ramírez its President.

Manuel and his poorly armed followers proceeded to march on to the town of San Sebastián, armed only with clubs and machetes...

The Spanish Army had been forewarned and awaited with superior firepower. The revolutionists were met with deadly fire. The revolt failed, many revolutionists were killed, and at least 475, including Manuel Rojas and Mariana Bracetti, were imprisoned in the jail of Arecibo, and sentenced to death.

Others fled and went into hiding. Mathias Brugman was hiding in a local farm where he was betrayed by a farmer named Francisco Quiñones; he was captured and executed on the spot.

In 1869, fearing another revolt, the Spanish Crown disbanded the Puerto Rican Militia, which had been composed almost entirely of native-born Puerto Ricans, and the Compañia de Artilleros Morenos de Cangrejos, a separate company of black Puerto Ricans.

They then organized the Volunteer Institute, composed entirely of Spaniards and their sons...

Many Spanish colonies had gained their independence by the mid-1850s. In Puerto Rico, there were two groups: the loyalists, who were loyal to Spain, and the independentistas, who advocated independence.

In 1866, Dr. Ramón Emeterio Betances, Segundo Ruiz Belvis, and other independence advocates met in New York City where they founded the Revolutionary Committee of Puerto Rico. An outcome of this venture was a plan to send an armed expedition from the Dominican Republic to invade the island.

Several revolutionary cells were formed in the western towns and cities of Puerto Rico. Two of the most important cells were at Mayagüez, led by Mathias Brugman and code named "Capa Prieto" and at Lares, code-named "Centro Bravo" and headed by Manuel Rojas.

"Centro Bravo" was the main center of operations and was in the Rojas plantation of El Triunfo. Manuel Rojas was named "Commander of the Liberation Army" by Betances.

Mariana Bracetti, Manuel's sister-in-law was named "Leader of the Lares Revolutionary Council." Upon the request of Betances, Bracetti knitted the first flag of Puerto Rico also known as the revolutionary Flag of Lares, Bandera de Lares.

Ramón Emeterio Betances Original Lares Revolutionary Flag

The Spanish authorities discovered the plot and were able to confiscate Betances's armed ship before it arrived in Puerto Rico. The mayor of the town of Camuy, Manuel González, leader of that town's revolutionary cell, was arrested and charged with treason.

He learned that the Spanish Army was aware of the independence plot and escaped to warn Manuel Rojas. Alerted, the revolutionists decided to start the revolution as soon as possible, and set the date for September 28, 1868.

Mathias Brugman and his men joined with Manuel Rojas's men and with about 800 men and women, marched on and took the town of Lares. This was to be known as "Grito de Lares", The Cry of Lares.

The revolutionists entered the town's church and placed Mariana Bracetti's revolutionary flag on the High Altar as a sign that the revolution had begun.

They declared Puerto Rico to be the "Republic of Puerto Rico" and named Francisco Ramírez its President. Manuel and his poorly armed followers proceeded to march on to the town of San Sebastián, armed only with clubs and machetes.

The Spanish Army had been forewarned and awaited with superior firepower. The revolutionists were met with deadly fire. The revolt failed, many revolutionists were killed, and at least 475, including Manuel Rojas and Mariana Bracetti were imprisoned in the jail of Arecibo and sentenced to death.

Others fled and went into hiding. Mathias Brugman was hiding in a local farm where he was betrayed by a farmer named Francisco Quiñones; he was captured and executed on the spot.

In 1869, fearing another revolt, the Spanish Crown disbanded the Puerto Rican Militia, which had been composed almost entirely of native-born Puerto Ricans, and the Compañia de Artilleros Morenos de Cangrejos, a separate company of black Puerto Ricans.

They then organized the Volunteer Institute, composed entirely of Spaniards and their sons.

CHAPTER 67

The Current Flag Flown

During the Intentona de Yauco, the current Puerto Rican Flag was flown on the island for the first time

Leaders of El Grito de Lares who were in exile in New York City joined the Puerto Rican Revolutionary Committee, founded on December 8, 1895, to continue the quest for independence.

In 1897, with the aid of Antonio Mattei Lluberas and Fidel Velez, the local leaders of the independence movement of the town of Yauco, they organized another uprising, which became known as the Intentona de Yauco.

On March 26, 1897, there was a second and last major attempt to overthrow the Spanish government. The local conservative political factions, which believed that such an attempt would be a threat to their struggle for autonomy, opposed such an action.

Rumors of the planned event spread to the local Spanish authorities, who acted swiftly and put an end to what would be the last major uprising in the island to Spanish colonial rule.

Cuba

General Juan Ríus Rivera, Commander-in-Chief of the Cuban Liberation Army

In 1869, the incoming governor of Puerto Rico, Jose Laureano Sanz, to ease tensions in the island, dictated a general amnesty and released all who were involved with the Grito de Lares revolt from prison. Both Mariana Bracetti and Manuel Rojas were released. Bracetti lived her last years in the town of Añasco, while Rojas was deported to Venezuela.

Many of the former prisoners joined the Cuban Liberation Army and fought against Spain. Among the many Puerto Ricans who volunteered to fight for Cuba's independence were Juan Rius Rivera, Francisco Gonzalo Marín, also known as "Pachin Marín" and José Semidei Rodríguez.

Juan Rius Rivera as a young man met and befriended Betances. He eventually joined the pro-independence movement in the island. He became a member of the Mayagüez revolutionary cell "Capá Prieto" under the command of Brugman.

Rius, did not participate directly in the revolt because at the time he was studying law in Spain, however he was an avid reader about information pertaining to the Antilles and learned about the failed revolt.

He interrupted his studies and traveled to the United States where he went to the Cuba Revolutionary "Junta" and offered his services. He joined the Cuban Liberation Army and was given the rank of general and fought alongside Gen. Máximo Gómez in Cuba's Ten Years' War.

He later fought alongside Gen. Antonio Maceo Grajales and upon Maceo's death was named Commander-in-Chief of the Cuban Liberation Army.

After Cuba gained its independence, Gen. Juan Rius Rivera became an active political figure in the new nation.

Francisco Gonzalo Marín was a poet and journalist in Puerto Rico who joined the Cuban Liberation Army upon learning of the death of his brother Wecenlao in the battlefields of Cuba.

Marin, who was given the rank of lieutenant, befriended, and fought alongside José Martí.

In November 1897, Lt. Marin died from the wounds he received in a skirmish against the Spanish Army.

José Semidei Rodríguez from Yauco, Puerto Rico, fought in various battles in the Cuban War of Independence 1895–98.

After Cuba gained its independence, he joined the Cuban National Army with the rank of brigadier general. Semidei Rodríguez continued to serve in Cuba as a diplomat upon his retirement from the military.

CHAPTER 68

Spanish American War

In 1890, Captain Alfred Thayler Mahan, a member of the Navy War Board and leading U.S. strategic thinker, wrote a book titled The Influence of Sea Power upon History in which he argued for the creation of a large and powerful navy modeled after the British Royal Navy.

Part of his strategy called for the acquisition of colonies in the Caribbean Sea which would serve as coaling and naval stations, and which would serve as strategical points of defense upon the construction of a canal in the Isthmus.

This was not new, since William H. Stewart, the former Secretary of State under the administrations of various presidents, among them Abraham Lincoln and Ulysses Grant, had stressed that a canal be built either in Honduras, Nicaragua, or Panama and that the United States annex the Dominican Republic and purchase Puerto Rico and Cuba.

The idea of annexing the Dominican Republic failed to receive the approval of the U.S. Senate and Spain did not accept the 160 million dollars which the U.S. offered for Puerto Rico and Cuba.

Captain Mahan made the following statement to the War Department:

"Having therefore no foreign establishments either colonial or military, the ships of war of the United States, in war will be like land birds, unable to fly far from their own shores. To provide resting places for them where they can coal and repair. would be one of the first duties of a government proposing to itself the development of the power of the nation at sea"

Since 1894, the Naval War College had been formulating plans for war with Spain.

By 1896, the Office of Naval Intelligence had prepared a plan which including military operations in Puerto Rican waters. Not only was Puerto Rico considered a valuable as a naval station, Puerto Rico and Cuba were also abundant in valuable commercial commodity which the United States lacked, that commodity was sugar.

The United States declared war on Spain in 1898 following the sinking of the battleship USS Maine in Havana harbor, Cuba.

One of the United States' principal objectives in the Spanish American War was to take control of Spanish possessions Puerto Rico and Cuba in the Atlantic, and the Philippines and Guam in the Pacific.

The Spanish Crown sent the 1st, 2nd, and 3rd Puerto Rican Provisional Battalions to defend Cuba against the American invaders. The 1st Puerto Rican Provisional Battalion, composed of the Talavera Cavalry and Krupp artillery, was sent to Santiago de Cuba where they battled the American forces in the Battle of San Juan Hill. After the battle, the Puerto Rican Battalion suffered a total of 70% casualties which included their dead, wounded, MIA's and prisoners.

The invasion of Puerto Rico by the American military forces was known as the Puerto Rican Campaign.

On May 10, 1898, Spanish forces, under the command of Captain Ángel Rivero Méndez in the fortress of San Cristóbal in San Juan, exchanged fire with the USS Yale, and on May 12 a fleet of 12 American ships bombarded San Juan.

On June 25, 1898, the USS Yosemite arrived in San Juan and blockaded the port. Captains Ramón Acha Caamaño and José Antonio Iriarte, both natives of Puerto Rico, were among those who defended the city form Fort San Felipe del Morro.

They had 3 Batteries under their command, which were armed with at least three 15 cm Ordóñez cannons. The battle lasted 3 hours and resulted in the death of Justo Esquivies, the first Puerto Rican soldier to die in the Puerto Rican Campaign.

On July 25, 1898, General Nelson A. Miles entered the southern town of Guánica with 3,300 troops and faced a minor skirmish in their landing.

Part of the Hacienda Desideria, owned by Antonio Mariani, where the Battle of Yauco took place in 1898

One of the most notable battles during the Puerto Rico Campaign occurred between the Spanish forces and Puerto Rican volunteers, led by Captain Salvador Meca and Lieutenant Colonel Francisco Puig against the American forces led by Brigadier General George A. Garretson on July 26, 1898.

The Spanish forces engaged the 6th Massachusetts in a firefight in what became known as the Battle of Yauco. Puig and his forces suffered 2 officers and 3 soldiers wounded and 2 soldiers dead. The Spanish forces were ordered to retreat.

The Puerto Rican Campaign was short compared to the other campaigns because the Puerto Ricans who resided in the southern and western towns and villages resented Spanish rule and tended to view the Americans as their liberators, thereby making the invasion much easier and because, as stated before, the 1st, 2nd, and 3rd Puerto Rican Provisional Battalions where in Cuba defending that island.

The Americans met resistance from the Spanish forces and Puerto Rican Volunteers and were engaged in the following battles:

Battle of Fajardo, Battle of Guayama, Battle of the Guamani River Bridge, Battle of Coamo, Battle of Silva Heights and Battle of Asomante.

On August 13, 1898, the Spanish American War ended, and the Spanish surrendered without other major incidents. Some Puerto Rican leaders such as José de Diego and Eugenio María de Hostos expected the United States to grant the island its independence.

Believing that Puerto Rico would gain its independence, a group of men staged an uprising in Ciales which became known as "El Repartimiento de Ciales" or the "Ciales Uprising of 1898" and proclaimed Puerto Rico to be a republic.

The Spanish authorities who were unaware that the cease fire had been signed brutally suppressed the uprising. The total casualties of the

Puerto Rican Campaign were 450 dead or wounded Spanish and Puerto Ricans, and 4 dead and 39 wounded Americans.

Upon the signing of the Treaty of Paris on December 10, Puerto Rico became a territory of the United States. The Spanish troops had already left by October 18, and the United States named General Nelson A. Miles military governor of the island.

On July 1, 1899, "The Porto Rico Regiment of Infantry, United States Army" was created, and approved by the U.S. Congress on May 27, 1908. The regiment was a segregated, all-volunteer unit made up of 1,969 Puerto Ricans.

CHAPTER 69

Puerto Rican commander in the Philippines

In 1897, before the onset of fighting in Puerto Rico, Juan Alonso Zayas, born in San Juan, was a second lieutenant in the Spanish Army when he received orders to head for the Philippines to take command of the 2nd Expeditionary Battalion stationed in Baler. He arrived in Manila, the capital, in May 1897.

There he took a vessel and headed for Baler, on the island of Luzon. The distance between Manila and Baler is 62 miles,100 km; if traveled through the jungles and badly built roads, the actual distance was 144 miles, 230 km.

At that time a system of communication between Manila and Baler was almost non-existent.

The only way Baler received news from Manila was by way of vessels. The Spanish colonial government was under constant attack from local Filipino groups who wanted independence. Zayas's mission was to fortify Baler against any possible attack.

Among his plans for the defense of Baler was to convert the local church of San Luis de Tolosa into a fort.

The independence advocates, under the leadership of Colonel Calixto Vila Corte, were called "insurgents", Tagalogs, by the Spanish crown. On June 28, 1898, they demanded the surrender of the Spanish army.

The Spanish governor of the region, Enrique de las Morena y Fossa, refused; the Filipinos immediately attacked Baler in a battle that was to last for seven months.

Despite being outnumbered and suffering hunger and disease, the battalion did not capitulate. In the meantime, Zayas and the rest of the battalion were totally unaware of the Spanish American War that was going on.

In August 1898, the hostilities between the United States and Spain came to an end. The Philippines became a U.S. possession under the accordance of the Treaty of Paris.

In May 1899, the Battalion at Baler found out about the Spanish American War and its aftermath. They had been unaware that they had been fighting for a possession which was no longer theirs to fight for.

On June 2, 1899, the Battalion's commander, Lieutenant Martín Cerezo surrendered to the Tagalos only after some conditions were met.

Among the conditions were the following:

1. That the Spaniards are not treated as prisoners of war and
2. that they would not be harmed in their quest of reaching a Spanish ship which would take them back to Spain.

The 32 survivors of Zayas Battalion were sent to Manila, where they boarded a ship for Spain. In Spain, they were given a hero's welcome and became known as los Ultimos de Baler—"the Last of Baler".

CHAPTER 70

Porto Rico Provisional Regiment of Infantry

On March 2, 1898, Congress authorized the creation of the first body of native troops in Puerto Rico.

On June 30, 1901, the "Porto Rico Provisional Regiment of Infantry" came into being.

An Act of Congress, approved on May 27, 1908, reorganized the regiment as part of the "regular" Army.

Since the native Puerto Rican officers where Puerto Rican citizens and not citizens of the United States, they were required to undergo a new physical examination to determine their fitness for commissions in the Regular Army and to take an oath of U.S. citizenship with their new officers' oath.

In 1906, a group of Puerto Ricans met with the appointed Governor Winthrop, and suggested the organization of a Puerto Rican National Guard.

The petition failed because the U.S. Constitution prohibits the formation of any armed force within the United States and its territories without the authorization of Congress.

On June 19, 1915, Major General Luis R. Esteves of the U.S. Army became the first Puerto Rican and the first Hispanic to graduate from the United States Military Academy at West Point, New York.

While he attended West Point, he tutored classmate Dwight D. Eisenhower in Spanish; a second language was required in order to graduate.

He was a second lieutenant in the 8th Infantry Brigade of the army under the command of John J. Pershing when he was sent to El Paso, Texas in the Pancho Villa Expedition.

From El Paso, he was sent to the town of Polvo, where he was appointed mayor and judge by its citizens.

Esteves helped organize the 23rd Battalion, which would be composed of Puerto Ricans and be stationed in Panama during World War I.

He would also play a key role in the formation of the Puerto Rico National Guard.

CHAPTER 71

The Vargas Family

For the Vargas family, serving in the U.S. military while celebrating their Puerto Rican heritage has been a matter of pride and tradition.

Retired Army Lt. Col. Edwin Vargas, who served from 1972 to 1992, grew up as an "Army brat." His father had served in the Korean and Vietnam wars with the 65th Infantry Regiment.

"Every dog he had, he called 'Okie' for Okinawa," he said. "He was part of the occupation forces in Japan, had a break in service, came back during Korea and then in Vietnam.

They traveled as a family to Panama and Germany. They took leave saw most of Europe. It was wonderful for the whole family. It was an experience they loved.

Vargas wanted to follow in his footsteps as a child...

He admired his father and the other Puerto Rican pioneers who showed the U.S. that Puerto Ricans can fight as good as anybody, and because of that, it made things a little bit easier for him and for anybody who follows in his footsteps.

His father was wounded in Korea but still served in Vietnam. He retired as a sergeant first class after 22 years of service.

LANGUAGE BARRIER

During his own Army career, one of the challenges Vargas saw other Puerto Rican officers struggle with was the language. Many of the Puerto Rican officers he encountered spoke English with a heavy accent.

"When I went into the service, there were about 16 of us that went in together from the University of Puerto Rico in San Juan and the University of Puerto Rico Mayaguez campuses," he recalled. "Only six of us were able to serve long enough to retire.

Most of the guys who didn't stay were dinged because of communication. They had very thick accents, and sometimes it's hard to understand, so when they get rated, they get dinged on that and, unfortunately ... they get passed over and end up having to get out of the service."

RACISM

Vargas said he encountered some racism early on in his career, but his father had prepared him for it.

"It wasn't from my superiors, but I did run into some from my peers," he said. "My father had told me, 'Don't ever ask a soldier to do something you can't do and listen to your noncommissioned officers.' I knew I had to go above and beyond. I couldn't just settle for average. I knew I had to outdo my peers so that I could be considered to move forward."

His culture and family helped him cope with the tension.

"Puerto Ricans are a very close-knit family. Family is the center of everything," he said. "If anything goes wrong, you know the family is there to support you. When I went into the service as a lieutenant, I was 24 years old. I was already married and had a child."

PANAMA

Vargas' father wanted him to serve as an officer and told him not to go into the infantry or airborne specialties. Vargas did, anyway, believing that it would better prepare him for combat and leading troops.

"I was lucky that I commanded three companies in the Army," he explained. "I commanded a combat support company in the Demilitarized Zone, in Korea. I commanded a light infantry company in Panama, and I loved it. I' 'd go back there in a heartbeat. I finally commanded a headquarters company at Fort Buchanan, in Puerto Rico. Each command prepared me better for the next command."

In Panama, he said, he was an instructor at the School of the Americas, where he taught the commando course, a six-week ranger course conducted in the jungle.

KOREA

During his time serving in Korea in 1976, a North Korean contingent attacked a lieutenant and captain who were sent to trim a poplar tree. They were axed to death in Panmunjom.

"We were on alert for a number of weeks," Vargas remembered, "and one of our units ended up going in, tearing up some illegal roadblocks that the North Koreans had put in and cutting down the poplar tree, and that was the end of that."

While on another mission, he said, a South Korean company commander grabbed one of his South Korean armies augmentees because of a misunderstanding.

"He gave me, the soldier, back and we started socializing," Vargas said. "And he asked me where I was from. I said, 'I'm from Puerto Rico.' … That's when I started to learn about the 65th Infantry. He told me they were tremendous soldiers," Vargas said.

His father had served with the 65th Infantry Regiment, but Vargas knew little about the unit's history. Vargas said the South Koreans still speak highly of the 65th.

"They would fight with anything they had in their hands," Vargas said. "They did a wonderful job in slowing down the Chinese onslaught when they came in. They were tasked to hold them back. It made me feel so proud."

Vargas' careers also took him to South and Central America, where he trained with 1st Special Operations Command out of Fort Bragg, North Carolina.

"I went to several Central and South American countries," he said. "This is a Latino culture here, and it's so much different than the countries we went to. The one I could say it's most like was Costa Rica."

CONTINUING THE TRADITION

Vargas' son, former Army Spc. Edwin Vargas III served 11 years in the Puerto Rico Army National Guard as a military policeman and deployed to Kosovo. Vargas' son-in-law, medically retired Army Staff Sgt. Alfredo E. Ramirez, served four years as a communications signal support systems specialist and deployed to Iraq in 2010.

Both are proud to carry on the family tradition.

"I'm very proud of my grandfather. He has a Purple Heart. He never talks about the things he went through. I'm very proud of my dad, too," said Edwin Vargas. "Growing up as a Puerto Rican in the military, all the little Puerto Rican kids got together, all the family members, even though we were enlisted or officers, we all got together and had fun. I still have friends all over. We're always like a big family."

He added, "Besides, Puerto Ricans, we're very united, very family oriented, and we get along with everybody."

Ramirez said when he started hearing stories about the military from his wife's brother, he wanted to join.

"Since being a kid, I've always wanted to be in the military, but when she shared her experience with her father and her brother and I started hearing their stories, it gave me that push to take the tests and join the Army," he said.

Ramirez joined airborne school because of his father-in-law.

"I was the first one in the aircraft door," he said, "and I was like, 'Oh, my God' when they opened that door, and I looked down and I saw that the cars looked like little boxes."

"After that first jump, I loved it. It was awesome," he added, his face lighting up.

Ramirez's 5-year-old son, Alfredo, sometimes puts on his uniform hat and stands at attention. While watching a military movie, he will yell, "Hooah!" "He knows how to say 'Hooah,' and that makes me proud," Ramirez said.

PROUD TO SERVE

All members of the Vargas family said they are proud to have served on behalf of Puerto Rico and America.

"Our soldiers are as good as any soldiers in the world as long as they're properly trained and properly led," Vargas said. "They'll go to hell and back for their leadership. We're very proud of being part of the United States armed forces."

"I've grown up a lot, and I've made big changes in my life thanks to the military," Ramirez said. "If I could go back, I would do it.

Civilians, if you see a soldier in the street, shake their hands and make them feel better. Give them some motivation."

Edwin Vargas III agreed. "It doesn't matter if you come from Puerto Rico or from Utah," he said. "We're all soldiers. We're all American, and we're very proud of what we've done to serve our country and to be part of this big family of Americans."

CHAPTER 72

Our Heroes in Distant Territories...

Puerto Ricans have participated in many of the military conflicts in which the United States has been involved.

For example, they participated in the American Revolution, when volunteers from Puerto Rico, Cuba, and Mexico fought the British in 1779 under the command of General Bernardo de Galvez. This event took place from 1746 thru 1786.

Since the 18th century, Puerto Rican soldiers have continued to participate up to the present-day conflicts in Iraq and Afghanistan.

Let me remind you that Puerto Rico became a U.S. territory after the 1898. This was when the Treaty of Paris ended the Spanish American War...

After the Spanish American War, the United States appointed a military governor and soon the United States Army established itself in San Juan.

On March 2, 1899, the Army received funds and authorization from the United State to formally organize troops in Puerto Rico.

On March 24, 1899, the General Commander of the Puerto Rico Department, Mayor General Guy V. Henry ordered the creation of the Porto Rico Battalion of Volunteer Infantry.

This battalion was formed by four companies named A through D and was assigned to San Juan, Mayagüez and Ponce. The unit was activated on May 20, 1899, and it was led by Major Lorenzo Davinson.

Shortly afterwards, each company received additional men for a total of 112. Major Ebon Swift replaced Davison as the commander.

The validation of this move was notified in General Order 65, issued by the new General Commander Gen. George Davis.

On February 12, 1900, the Mounted Battalion was organized, and both were later designated Puerto Rico Regiment, U.S. Volunteers.

The following year, the units were renamed Puerto Rico Provisional Regiment of Infantry. The Band and First Battalion were sent to Washington on March 4, 1901, to participate in the inauguration of President McKinley.

On July 1, 1901, the United States Senate passed a bill which would require a strict mental and physical examination for those who wanted to join the regiment. It also approved the recruitment of native Puerto Rican civilians to be appointed the grade of second lieutenants for a term of four years if they passed the required tests.

On April 23, 1904, Congress authorized the recruitment of the local population as Second Lieutenants, leading to the recognition of Jaime Nadal, Henry Rexach, Pedro Parra, Eduardo Iriarte, Teofilo Marxuach, Eugenio de Hostos, Luis Emmanuelli and Pascual López.

In 1905, one of its battalions was sent to march along the First a Brigade of the First Division of the Regular Army during Roosevelt's inauguration. This was an act of Congress which was approved on May 27, 1908.

The regiment was then reorganized as part of the "regular" Army and the "Puerto Rico Provisional Regiment of Infantry" was renamed "Puerto Rico Regiment of Infantry".

Since the native Puerto Rican officers were Puerto Rican citizens and not citizens of the United States, they were required to undergo a new physical examination to determine their fitness so that they may be commission in the Regular Army.

They would then take an oath of United State citizenship with their new officers' oath.

By January 30, 1917, the Puerto Rico Regiment of Infantry was training in Camp Las Casas which was in Santurce. This location was part of San Juan in what is now known as "Residencial Las Casas".

Puerto Rico Regiment training in Camp Las Casas

In 1904, Camp Las Casas was established in Santurce under the command of Lt. Colonel Orval P. Townshend.

The Porto Rico Regiment was assigned to the camp. The regiment consisted of two battalions of the former Porto Rico Provisional Regiment of Infantry.

U.S. first shot of World War I fired in Puerto Rico

Lieutenant Teófilo Marxuach was the officer of the day at El Morro Castle on March 21, 1915.

The Odenwald, built in 1903, not to be confused with the German World War II war ship which carried the same name, was an armed German supply ship which tried to force its way out of the San Juan Bay and deliver supplies to the German submarines waiting in the Atlantic Ocean.

Lt. Marxuach gave the order to open fire on the ship from the walls of the fort. Sergeant Encarnacion Correa then manned a machine gun and fired warning shots with little effect.

Marxuach fired a shot from a cannon located at the Santa Rosa battery of "El Morro" fort, in what is the first shot of World War I fired by the regular armed forces of the United States against any ship flying the colors of the Central Powers, forcing the Odenwald to stop and to return to port where its supplies were confiscated.

The shots ordered by Lt. Marxuach were the first fired by the United States in World War I. The Odenwald was confiscated by the United States and renamed SS Newport.

It was assigned to the U.S. Shipping Board, where it served until 1924 when it was retired.

Many countries became involved in what became known as World War I, the U.S. Congress approved the Jones–Shafroth Act, which imposed United States citizenship upon Puerto Ricans.

Those who were eligible, except for women, were expected to serve in the military. About 20,000 Puerto Ricans were drafted during World War I.

On May 3, 1917, the Regiment recruited 1,969 men. The 295th and 296 Infantry Regiments were created in Puerto Rico.

In November 1917, the first military draft, conscription, lottery in Puerto Rico was held in the island's capital, San Juan. The first draft number was picked by Diana Yaeger, the daughter of the U.S. appointed governor of Puerto Rico Arthur Yager.

The number she picked was 1435 and it belonged to San Juan native Eustaquio Correa. Thus, Correa became the first Puerto Rican to be "drafted" into the Armed Forces of the United States.

On May 17, 1917, the Porto Rico Regiment of Infantry was sent to guard the Panama Canal in defense of the Panama Canal Zone One of the Puerto Ricans who distinguished himself during World War I was Lieutenant Frederick Lois Riefkohl of the US Navy, who on August 2, 1917, became the first known Puerto Rican to be awarded the Navy Cross.

The Navy Cross, which is the second highest medal after the Medal of Honor, that can be awarded by the U.S. Navy, was awarded to Lt. Riefkohl for his actions in an engagement with an enemy submarine. Lt. Riefkohl, who was also the first Puerto Rican to graduate from the United States Naval Academy, served as a rear admiral in World War II

Frederick L. Riefkohl's brother, Rudolph William Riefkohl also served. Riefkohl was commissioned a second lieutenant and assigned to the 63rd Heavy Artillery Regiment in France where he actively participated in the Meuse-Argonne Offensive.

According to the United States War Department, after the war he served as Captain of Coastal Artillery at the Letterman Army Medical Center in Presidio of San Francisco, in California in 1918. He played an instrumental role in helping the people of Poland overcome the 1919 typhus epidemic.

By 1918, the Army realized that there was a shortage of physicians specializing in anesthesia, a low salary specialty required in the military operating rooms. Therefore, the Army reluctantly began hiring women physicians as civilian contract employees.

The first Puerto Rican woman doctor to serve in the Army under contract was Dr. Dolores Piñero from San Juan. She was assigned to the San Juan base hospital where she worked as an anesthesiologist during the mornings and in the laboratory during the afternoons.

In New York, many Puerto Ricans joined the 369th Infantry Regiment which was mostly composed of Afro-Americans. They were not allowed to fight alongside their white counterparts; however, they were permitted to fight as members of a French unit in French uniforms. They fought along the Western Front in France, and their reputation earned them the nickname of "the Harlem Hell Fighters" by the Germans.

Among them was Rafael Hernández Marín, considered by many as Puerto Rico's greatest composer and his brother Jesus. The 369th was awarded French Croix de guerre for battlefield gallantry by the French President.

The first USMC plane: a Curtiss C-3 in Culebra, Puerto Rico.

Aviation in the United States Marine Corps was new. It came into existence on May 22, 1912, and the first major expansion of the Marine Corps' air component, of which Puerto Rico played a major rule, came with America's entrance into World War I.

On January 6, 1914, First Lieutenant Bernard L. Smith established the Marine Section of the Navy Flying School in the island municipal Culebra.

As the number of Marine Aviators grew so did the avid desire to separate from Naval Aviation.

By doing so, the Marine Aviation was designated as separate from the United States Naval Aviation. The creation of a "Marine Corps Aviation Company in Puerto Rico consisted of 10 officers and 40 enlisted men.

The Porto Rico Regiment returned to Puerto Rico in March 1919 and was renamed the 65th Infantry Regiment under the Reorganization Act of June 4, 1920.

It is estimated that <u>18,000 Puerto Ricans from the Porto Rico Regiment</u> served in the war and that <u>335 were wounded by the chemical gas experimentation which the United States</u> conducted as part of its active chemical weapons program in Panama.

Neither the military nor the War Department of the United States kept statistics regarding the total number of Puerto Ricans who served in the regular units of the Armed Forces, United States mainland forces, therefore, even though it is known that <u>four Puerto Ricans died in combat</u>, it is impossible to determine the exact number of Puerto Ricans who served and died in World War I.

The need for a Puerto Rican National Guard unit became apparent to Major General Luis R. Esteves, who had served as instructor of Puerto Rican Officers for the Porto Rico Regiment of Infantry at Camp Las Casas in Puerto Rico.

His request was met with the approval of the government and Puerto Rican Legislature.

In 1919, the first regiment of the Puerto Rican National Guard was formed, and General Luis R. Esteves became the first official Commandant of the Puerto Rican National Guard.

During this time, different units of the regiment were stationed at other forts throughout the island under the command of William P. Burnham.

Puerto Ricans were unaccustomed to the racial segregation policies of the United States which were also implemented in Puerto Rico and often refused to designate themselves as "white" or "black". Puerto Ricans of African descent were assigned to all-black units.

In 1916, the Third Battalion and the companies of service and machine-guns were integrated into the regiment.

When the United States declared war against Germany, the regiment was transferred to the regular Army and on May 3, 1917, recruited 1,969 men, considered at that time as war strength.

On May 14, 1917, the regiment was sent to Panama in defense of the Panama Canal Zone. The regiment returned to Puerto Rico in March 1919 and was renamed "The 65th Infantry Regiment" by the Reorganization Act of June 4, 1920.

During this period a young Puerto Rican officer of the Regular Army, Major Luis R. Esteves, was sent to Camp Las Casas to serve as an instructor in the preparation of Puerto Rican officers.

Major Luis R. Esteves became known as the <u>"Father of the Puerto Rican National Guard"</u>.

In 1923, the 65th provided personnel to the newly created 42nd Infantry Regiment.

CHAPTER 74

Second Nicaraguan Campaign 1926–1933

After World War I, Puerto Ricans fought on foreign shores as members of the United States Marine Corps.

Civil war broke out in Nicaragua during the first months of 1926, and upon the request of the Nicaraguan government, 3,000 U.S. Marines were sent ashore to establish a neutral zone for the protection of American citizens.

The American intervention was also known as the Banana Wars. Both Captain Pedro del Valle and Private Rafael Toro from Puerto Rico, participated in the Second Nicaraguan Campaign.

In 1926, Captain del Valle served with the Gendarmerie of Haiti for three years and during that time, he also became active in the war against Augusto Sandino in Nicaragua.

In 1927, Lieutenant Jaime Sabater, from San Juan, Puerto Rico graduated from United States Naval Academy.

Private Rafael Toro, from Humacao, Puerto Rico, was part of the U.S. Marine Corps occupation force in Nicaragua, serving with the Guardia Nacional de Nicaragua.

On July 25, 1927, Private Toro was assigned to advance guard duty in Nueva Segovia. As he rode into town, he was attacked; returning fire, he was able to hold back the enemy until reinforcements arrived. He was mortally wounded in this action for which he was posthumously awarded the Navy Cross.

Puerto Rico suffered greatly during the Great Depression of the 1930s, and many Puerto Ricans moved to the East Coast of the United States looking for jobs and a better way of life.

On the island, the unemployment rate continued to rise and many Puerto Ricans who were unable to find a job looked to the Armed Forces of the United States as a source of employment.

Not only were they paid better than at the few other available jobs, but they were also guaranteed three meals a day, clothing, and shelter.

CHAPTER 75

Salinas Puerto Rico Training Site

Soldiers of the 65th Infantry were training in Salinas, Puerto Rico as early as August 1941.

In 1942, the 65th Infantry underwent an extensive training program.

In 1943, they were sent to Panama to protect the Pacific and the Atlantic sides of the isthmus.

On November 25, 1943, <u>Colonel Antulio Segarra</u>, succeeded Col. John R. Menclenhall as commander the 65th Infantry. He became <u>the first Puerto Rican Regular Army officer to command a Regular Army regiment.</u>

In January 1944, the regiment was sent Jackson Barracks in New Orleans. Later, they were transferred to Fort Eustis in Newport News, Virginia in preparation for overseas deployment to North Africa.

They also served in Casablanca after the Naval Battle of Casablanca, where the regiment underwent amphibious training.

This enabled the 3rd Battalion to move on to Corsica, where it was attached to the 12th Air Force and tasked with guarding airfields.

Between March and April 1944, the 65th was reassigned to North Africa.

On May 3, 1944, the Third Battalion arrived at Napoles. The Battalion was then moved to Corsica and then to France. Salvador Roid commanded the 65th during this period in Europe, which earned him the Combat Infantryman Badge.

During this time, rumors swirled that the Regiment would be sent to live combat, while officers had already been moved to act as observers.

On September 22, 1944, the 65th Infantry landed in France. The Regiment was then moved to Peira Cava in the Maritime Alps, where it entered in action on December 13, 1944. This was the first time a Puerto Rican unit saw action in Europe.

The first offensive attack came the following day in response to enemy fire, with Col. Cordero allowing Capt. Efraín Sánchez and Company L to return fire.

The first casualty lost by the Regiment were <u>Sgt. Ángel Martínez and Sergio Sánchez.</u>

In total, in the border between France and Italy, the battalion lost 47 men, including its commander, Col. George Ford.

In November 1944, Company C provided security to the headquarters of the Seventh United States Army. The rest of the First Battalion was assigned_other tasks, such as defending the Command Center of the Sixth United States Army Group.

The Second and Third Battalions were assigned to defend communications.

In 1948, seven members received the Bronze Star for their service in World War II.

On 13 December 13, 1944, the 65th Infantry, under the command of <u>Lieutenant Colonel Juan César Cordero Dávila</u>, relieved the 2nd Battalion of the 442nd Infantry Regiment, a regiment which was made up of Japanese Americans under the command of Col. Virgil R. Miller, a native of San Germán, Puerto Rico and former member of the 65th Infantry Regiment.

In December 1944, the 3rd Battalion faced the German 34th Infantry Division's 107th Grenadier Regiment. They suffered a total of forty-seven battle casualties.

The first two Puerto Ricans to be killed in action from the 65th Infantry were Pvt. Sergio Sánchez-Sánchez and Sgt. Ángel_Martínez, from the town of Sabana Grande.

Upon arriving in the freezing and isolated outposts in the Maritime Alps, the unit's morale dropped severely. In an apparent effort to boost the unit's morale, its new commander, West Pointer Colonel George A.

Ford, personally led a patrol towards the German lines on January 4, 1945.

When they reached the German outposts, Colonel Ford was immediately shot and killed. In the firefight that followed, one of the enlisted men already mentioned was killed and several other were wounded, forcing the patrol to abandon the colonel's body.

On March 18, 1945, the regiment was sent to the District of Mannheim, Germany and assigned to Military Government activities, anti-sabotage, and security missions.

In all, the 65th Infantry participated in the campaigns of Rome-Arno, Rhineland, Ardennes-Alsace, and Central Europe.

On October 27, 1945, the regiment sailed from France arriving at Puerto Rico on November 9, 1945.

Operation "PORTREX"

65th Infantry troops convoyed through Isabel Segunda for PORTREX.

The 65th Infantry Regiment distinguished itself when the United States conducted a military exercise on the island of Vieques, on the eve of the Korean War.

This exercise was code named "Operation PORTREX," an acronym for "Puerto Rico Exercise." The objective was to see how the combined forces of the Army, Marines, Navy, and Air Force would do as "liberators" of an enemy captured territory, Vieques, against the "aggressors."

The core of the aggressor ground forces was made up of Puerto Rican soldiers, most of whom belonged to the 65th Infantry Regiment.

The liberators consisted of 32,600 combat troops from the 82nd Airborne Division's 504th Airborne Infantry Regiment and the Marine Corps, who received support from the Navy and Air Force.

Despite the large number of troops deployed, the 65th Infantry, the aggressor, was able to halt the offensive forces on the beaches of the island. Colonel William W. Harris, the commanding officer of the 65th, stated:

"Stopping the assault forces at the water's edge proved that the Puerto Ricans could hold their own against the best-trained soldiers that the United States Army could put into the field."

CHAPTER 76

Heroes vs. Cowards

The successful military maneuvers during PORTREX prompted the Army's leadership to deploy the 65th Infantry to Korea.

On August 27, 1950, the 65th Infantry, with 3,920 officers and men organized into three infantry battalions, one artillery battalion and a tank Company departed from Puerto Rico and arrived in Pusan, Korea on September 23, 1950.

It was during the long sea voyage that the men nicknamed the 65th Infantry as the "Borinqueneers." That was the name of the more peaceful of the two original Indian tribes that inhabited the island of Puerto Rico "Borinquen", and many of the men were direct descendants of that industrious race of people."

The men of the 65th, now attached to the Army's 3rd Infantry Division, were among the first infantrymen to meet the enemy on the battlefields of Korea.

After November 1950, they fought daily against units of the Chinese People's Liberation Army after the Chinese entered the war on the North Korean side. The 296th Regiment took its place at Puerto Rico.

In Korea, the regiment covered the retreat of the 1st Marine Division during the Battle of Chosin Reservoir.

One of the hardships suffered by the Puerto Ricans <u>was the lack of warm clothing during the cold, harsh winters.</u>

"Born in a semitropical climate- most of them had never seen snow-they had lived and fought through it all without complaint".

The U.S. always treated our soldiers as second-class citizen. When they reached Korea, they were not given the proper winter gears. Many did suffer of frost bite.

Then, look at what next happened...

The enemy made many attempts to encircle the regiment, but each time they failed because of the many casualties inflicted by the 65th. Because the 65th held their positions, that enabled the U.S. Marines to withdraw from the Chosin Reservoir in December 1950.

When the Marines were surrounded by the Chinese Communist troops close to the Manchurian border, they were ordered to retreat and work their way back to Hungnam.

The men of the 65th rushed to their defense and were ordered to stay behind and fight the enemy. As a result, the Marines were able to withdraw to their ships with the 65th holding the rear guard. The 65th, attached to the 1st Marine Division, was awarded the Navy Unit.

Commendation for their defense and were among the last units to embark from Hungnam.

Among the battles and operations in which the 65th participated was Operation Killer in January 1951, becoming the first regiment to cross the Han River in South Korea during the operation.

In April 1951, the regiment participated in the Uijonbu Corridor drives and in June 1951, the 65th was the third regiment to cross the Han Ton River. The 65th took and held Chorwon and they were also instrumental in breaking the Iron Triangle of Hill 717 in July 1951.

In November 1951, the regiment fought off an attack by two regimental size enemy units. Colonel Juan César Cordero Dávila of the 296th Regiment requested a transfer to active service in Korea.

In December 1951, Chief of Staff J. Lawton Collins visited Puerto Rico and granted the request, reassigning him to the 65th, replacing him with Lt. Col. Sepulveda.

Col. Cordero was formally named commander of the 65th Infantry on February 8, 1952, thus becoming one of the highest-ranking ethnic officers in the Army Brigadier William Warner Harris, USMA 1930, published a book that captured the distinguished history of the 65th while under his command.

When asked if the Puerto Ricans would fight when the time came, then Colonel_William Warner Harris' answer was just as direct: "My Puerto Ricans will fight anyone, anywhere."

Battles of Outpost Kelly and Jackson Heights

On 3 July 3. 1952, the regiment defended the main line of resistance (MLR) for 47 days and saw action at Cognac, King, and Queen with successful attacks on Chinese positions.

In September 1952, the 65th Infantry defended a hill known as "Outpost Kelly." Chinese Communist forces overran the hill in what became known as the Battle for Outpost Kelly. On two occasions, the 65th Regiment was overwhelmed by Chinese artillery and driven off.

2nd Platoon, Company C in 1952.

In October 1952, the regiment also saw action in the Chorwon Sector and on Iron Horse, Hill 391, whose lower part was called "Jackson Heights" in honor of Capt. George Jackson.

After enduring days of artillery bombardment with limited artillery support of their own, Company G withdrew to avoid being overrun by a numerically superior foe.

In June 1953, the 2nd Battalion conducted a series of successful raids about two and a half miles southeast of Jackson Heights and in November the regiment successfully counter-attacked enemy units in the Numsong Valley and held their positions until the armistice was reached.

Many non-Puerto Rican Hispanics served in the 65th Infantry during the war. Among those who distinguished themselves in combat and who served in the conflict as a member of the 65th Infantry was a young first lieutenant of <u>Mexican American descent whose name is Richard Edward Cavazos.</u>

Cavazos entered the military in Texas and served as Company Commander of Company E of the 2d Battalion.

Cavazos, who in 1982, became the first Hispanic to become a four-star general in the United States Army, was the recipient of the Distinguished Service Cross, the Silver Star Medal, and the Bronze Star Medal.

Mass court martial

Soldiers of the 65th, North of the Han River, Korea, June 1951.

Col. Cordero Dávila was relieved of his command by Col. Chester B. DeGavre, a West Point graduate and a "Continental," an officer from the mainland United States, and the officer staff of the 65th was replaced with non-Hispanic officers.

DeGavre, upset over the fact that "G" company did not hold on to Hill 391, ordered that the unit stop calling itself the "Borinqueneers," cut their special rations of rice and beans, ordered the men to shave off their mustaches, and had one of them wear a sign that read: "I am a coward. "The language barrier, an NCO shortage, and poor leadership were factors that influenced some of the men of Company L in their refusal to continue to fight.

One hundred and sixty-two Puerto Ricans of the 65th Infantry were arrested...

Between 23 November and 26 December 1952, ninety-five soldiers were court martialed and tried by General Court-Martial in fifteen separate trials. Ninety-one were found guilty and sentenced to prison terms ranging from one to 18 years of hard labor.

It was the largest mass court-martial of the Korean War. According to cultural historian Silvia Álvarez Curbelo, the government of Puerto Rico, caught in the middle of a potentially damaging affair that could jeopardize its political agenda, kept silent for nearly two months.

Finally, the incidents were made known by a local newspaper alerted by several letters written by the imprisoned soldiers to their families. Secret negotiations between the U.S. and Puerto Rican governments took place and the Secretary of the Army Robert T. Stevens moved quickly to remit the sentences and granted clemency and pardons to all those involved.

The breakdown of the 65th resulted from several factors: a shortage of officers and non-commissioned officers, a rotation policy that removed combat-experienced leaders and soldiers, tactical doctrine that led to high casualties, a shortage of artillery ammunition, communication problems between largely white, English-speaking officers and Spanish-speaking Puerto Rican enlisted men, and declining morale.

The report also found bias in the prosecution of the Puerto Ricans, citing instances of Continental soldiers who were not charged after refusing to fight in similar circumstances, before and after Jackson Heights.

Though the men who were court martialed were pardoned, a campaign for a formal exoneration was launched.

Awards in the Korean War

Master Sergeant Juan E. Negrón was awarded the Distinguished Service Cross for his courageous actions while serving as a member of Company L, 65th Infantry Regiment, 3d Infantry Division during combat operations against an armed enemy in Kalma-Eri, Korea on 28 April 1951. His award was upgraded to the Medal of Honor on 18 March 2014.

MASTER SERGEANT JUAN E NEGRON

For service as set forth in the following citation:
The Medal of Honor is posthumously presented to Juan E. Negrón. RA10406243), Master Sergeant, U.S. Army, for extraordinary heroism in connection with military operations against an armed enemy of the United Nations while serving with the 65th Infantry Regiment, 3d Infantry Division.

Master Sergeant Negrón distinguished himself by extraordinary heroism in action against enemy aggressor forces in the vicinity of Kalma-Eri, Korea, on 28 April 1951.

On that date, Sergeant Negrón took up the most vulnerable position on his company's exposed right flank after an enemy force had overrun a section of the line.

When notified that element of the company were withdrawing, Sergeant Negrón refused to leave his exposed_position, but delivered withering fire at hostile troops who had broken through a roadblock.

When the hostile troops approached his position, Sergeant Negrón accurately hurled hand grenades at short range, halting their attack.

Sergeant Negrón held the position throughout the night, while an allied counterattack was organized and launched.

After the enemy had been repulsed, fifteen enemy dead were found only a few feet from Sergeant Negrón's position.

The extraordinary heroism exhibited by Sergeant Negrón on this occasion reflects great credit on himself and is in keeping with the finest traditions of the military service.

A total of 61,000 Puerto Ricans served in the military during the Korean War. About 90% of the Puerto Ricans that saw action in Korea were volunteers.

The 65th Infantry was awarded battle participation credits for the following nine campaigns: UN Defense-1950, UN Offense-1950, CCF Intervention-1950, First UN Counterattack Offensive-1951, UN and CCF Spring Offensive-1951, UN Summer-Fall Offensive-1951, 2nd Korean Winter 1951–52, Korean Summer-Fall-1952 and 3rd Korean Winter-1952-53. They are credited with the last battalion-sized bayonet charge in U.S. Army history.

Individual awards in the Korean War Award

Ten Distinguished Service Crosses, 256 Silver Stars and 606 Bronze Stars for valor were awarded to the men of the 65th Infantry. Of the ten Distinguished Service Crosses that were awarded to the members of the 65th Infantry, five were awarded to Puerto Ricans:

Sergeant First Class Modesto Cartagena

Private Badal Hernández Guzmán

Master Sergeant Juan E. Negrón (upgraded to the Medal of Honor)

Corporal Fabián Nieves Laguer

Master Sergeant Belisario Noriega

According to El Nuevo Día newspaper, 30 May 2004, a total of 756 Puerto Ricans were killed in Korea, from all four branches of the U.S. armed forces. However, according to "All POW-MIA Korean War Casualties", the total amount of Puerto Rican casualties in the Korean War was 732. However, this total may vary slightly since some non-Puerto Ricans such as Captain James W. Conner were mistakenly included.

Out of the 700 plus casualties suffered in the war a total of 121 men were listed as missing in action.

The Battle of Outpost Kelly accounted for 73 of the men missing in action from the total of 121.

On 12 February 1951, General Douglas MacArthur, wrote in Tokyo:

The Puerto Ricans forming the ranks of the gallant 65th Infantry give daily proof on the battlefields of Korea of their courage, determination and resolute will to victory, their invincible loyalty to the United States and their fervent devotion to those immutable principles of human relations which the Americans of the Continent and of Puerto Rico have in common.

They are writing a brilliant record of heroism in battle, and I am indeed proud to have them under my command. I wish that we could count on many more like them.

CHAPTER 77

Post Korean War

General Richard E. Cavazos, the first Mexican American to reach the rank of brigadier general in the U.S. Army'.

The 65th Infantry was relieved from assignment to the 3d Infantry Division on 3 November 1954, and, returning to Puerto Rico, it was assigned on 2 December 1954, to the 23rd Infantry Division, which encompassed geographically separated units in the Caribbean region.

On 10 April 1956, it was inactivated at Losey Field, Puerto Rico, and relieved from assignment to the 23d, which itself was inactivated.

On 6 February 1959, the regiment was deactivated from the Regular Army, but the Puerto Rican Army National Guard soon adopted "65" as the identifying number for their existing 296th Regimental Combat Team at Losey Field, mainly composed of reserve component personnel.

On 15 February 1959, it was organized to consist of the 1st Battle Group, 65th Infantry, an element of the 92nd Infantry Brigade.

On February 21, 1960, commemorated as National Guard Day, the 65th Infantry Regiment was formally transferred from the Regular Army to the PRNG, in an activity where Gen. Cesár Cordero handed the units colors to Col. Rafael Rodríguez.

That same year, Company B of the 65th Regiment created Employer's Day, Día del Patrono in Spanish, where the employers of the volunteers that serve in the PRNG are instructed about the job that their employees do with the entity and participate in training of their own.

The idea behind the initiative was facilitating the processing of the request of leave-of-absence to train for two weeks during the summer.

On 1 May 1964, it was reorganized to consist of the 1st Battalion, 65th Infantry, and remained assigned to the 92nd. It was reorganized again on 1 April 1971, to consist of the 1st Battalion and the separate Company E.

This was followed by another reorganization on 1 September 1978, to consist of the 1st and 2nd Battalions within the 92nd, as well as the separate Company E.

Less than two years later another reorganization on 29 February 1980, eliminated the separate Company E while retaining the 1st and 2nd Battalions.

On 27 October 1987, the regiment was withdrawn from CARS and reorganized under the United States Army Regimental System with headquarters at Cayey.

It was reorganized on 1 September 1992, to consist of the 1st Battalion, 65th Infantry, and remained assigned to the 92nd Infantry Brigade.

On 14 February 2003, it was ordered into active federal service at home stations and released on 12 February 2005, reverting to territorial control.

On 1 October 2003, it was reorganized as the 65th Infantry Regiment in which only the 1st Battalion was active.

In 2009, Company C, 1st Battalion, 65th Infantry Regiment was deployed to the Horn of Africa and stationed at Camp Lemonier in Djibouti, after completing a 14-month deployment at Guantanamo Bay, Cuba. Company C carried the crew-served weapons to protect the camp.

It also operated the entry control checkpoints, protected U.S. and allied ships at the massive Djibouti Port and guarded the U.S. Embassy there.

By mid-2009, the rest of the battalion deployed there in case a larger combat maneuver element was needed to operate from the base. The area is the most unstable part of Africa, and the Somali border is less than 10 miles from Camp Lemonier.

Legacy

A monument dedicated to the 65th Infantry Regiment in Río Piedras, Puerto Rico.

During the Korean War, the Borinqueneers were awarded 10 Distinguished Service Crosses

Juan Negron was upgraded to the Medal of Honor
256 Silver Stars, 606 Bronze Stars, and 2,771 Purple Hearts.

Puerto Rico honored the unit by naming one of its principal avenues "Avenida 65 de Infantería" in San Juan.

The names of those killed in combat are inscribed in "El Monumento de la Recordación", Monument of Remembrance, which was unveiled on 19 May 1996 and is situated in front of the Capitol Building in San Juan, Puerto Rico.

In November 1999, Governor Pedro Rossello, along with the Senate of Puerto Rico, chartered the 65th Infantry Honor Task Force and appointed Anthony Mele as chairman to work with Major General Nels Running, Director, Committee of the 50th Anniversary of the Korean War to commemorate the 65th Infantry Regiment.

The 65th Infantry Honor Task Force is a coalition of individuals, veterans' organizations, and groups dedicated to advocate and preserve the legacy of the 65th Infantry Regiment.

The group organized tree planting and plaque commemoration ceremonies around the USA, to include Arlington National Cemetery in Virginia; Fort San Felipe del Morro in San Juan, Puerto Rico; and Fort Logan National Cemetery in Denver.

On 20 May 2001, the government of Puerto Rico unveiled a monument honoring the 65th Infantry Regiment. The monument was made by artist Sonny Rodríguez and is called "Mission Accomplished".

This monument contains a statue of a soldier wearing a poncho with his rifle in one hand and the regiment's flag in the other hand.

On 1 October 2013, the 65th Infantry Honor Task Force organized veterans from the 65th and their families to attend a salute to the regiment by the 3d US Infantry, The Old Guard, at Fort Myer, Virginia, a tour of the Tomb of the Unknown Soldiers, and wreath laying ceremony at the Korean War Combat Veterans Memorial in Washington, DC.

On March22–23 2014, the 65th Infantry Honor Task Force organized the salute of the first Medal of Honor awarded to a Borinqueneer; MSG Juan E. Negron in New York with Iris Negron, daughter of MSG Negron, and BG Jose Burgos.

In attendance were New York State Senators William E. Larkin, a Korean War combat veteran, and David Carlucci who presented a proclamation from the New York State Senate.

In 2014 the National Puerto Rican Day Parade, which is attended by nearly two million people and broadcast live on Fox TV, was dedicated to the Borinqueneers.

Congressional Gold Medal

Main article: Borinqueneers Congressional Gold Medal

Design of the Congressional Gold Medal which was awarded to the Borinqueneers of the 65th Infantry Regiment

A Congressional Gold Medal is an award bestowed by the United States Congress and is, along with the Presidential Medal of Freedom, the highest civilian award in the United States.

It is awarded to persons "who have performed an achievement that has an impact on American history and culture that is likely to be recognized as a major achievement in the recipient's field long after the achievement."

Congressional Gold Medals have also been awarded to: Native American code talkers; the Japanese American 100th Infantry Battalion and 442nd Infantry Regiment; the Tuskegee Airmen; the Montford Point Marines; the 1st Special Service Force, Devil's Brigade, and the Women Airforce Service Pilots, WASP.

S. 1726, the bill that would confer the Congressional Gold Medal on the 65th Infantry Regiment was introduced in Congress.

It was signed by President Barack Obama at a ceremony on June 10, 2014, becoming Public Law.

A decision on designs for a congressional gold medal being awarded in 2015 to the Borinqueneers of the 65th Infantry Regiment was selected by the Citizens Coinage Advisory Committee on June 16, 2015.

For the 65th Infantry Borinqueneers congressional gold medal, the CCAC recommended for the obverse a design depicting a close-up portrait of a unit staff sergeant, with three soldiers traversing rocky ground in the background.

The recommended reverse features an historic sentry box in Old San Juan, Puerto Rico, an olive branch, the 65th Infantry insignia patch and unit's motto, HONOR ET FIDELITAS, Honor and Fidelity.

On April 13, 2016, leaders of the United States House and Senate awarded the Congressional Gold Medal to the 65th Infantry Regiment.

65th Infantry Regiment United States

The 65th Infantry Regiment, nicknamed "The Borinqueneers" from the original Taíno name of the island, Borinquen, is a Puerto Rican regiment of the United States Army.

The regiment's motto is Honor et Fidelitas, Latin for Honor and Fidelity. The Army Appropriation Bill created by an act of Congress on 2 March 1898, authorized the creation of the first body of native troops in Puerto Rico.

On 30 June 1901, the "Porto Rico Provisional Regiment of Infantry" was organized.

On July 1, 1908, Congress incorporated the regiment into the Regular Army as the Puerto Rico Regiment of Infantry, United States Army.

On May 14, 1917, the Regiment was activated, and additional men were assigned, with the unit being sent to serve in Panama.

On June 4, 1920, the Regiment was renamed 65th Infantry.

During World War II, the Regiment saw action throughout Europe, especially France and Germany, participating in Naples-Foggia, Rome-Arno, and Rhin.

Several Purple Hearts were handed posthumously to members of the 65th Regiment, and the Medal of Honor was granted to Capt. Eurípides Rubio, Héctor Santiago, Carlos Lozada and Fernando García.

The 65th Infantry Regiment participated in World War I, World War II, the Korean War, and in what is known in the United States as the War on Terror.

On April 13, 2016, the 65th Infantry was awarded the Congressional Gold Medal.

CHAPTER 78

Our Son Weren't Cowards

Puerto Rican soldiers during the Korean War were not cowards. They had in experience leaders that led them to Courts Martial....

Puerto Rico Lt. John R. Wasson signaled to his men from the enemy side of the river. Night was falling over North Korea's Chorwon Valley, and Company L of the 65th Infantry Regiment, ordered into the darkness to track down and kill Chinese soldiers, had made it perhaps two miles into the no-man's land between the U.N. line and the communists.

Wasson, an officer fresh out of West Point, had crossed the river alone to inspect the rocky scrub on the other side. Now he was signaling his troops to follow.

The men of Company L paused. Only weeks earlier their regiment had been routed in the bloody battle for Outpost Kelly. They had not yet shaken the trauma of that slaughter.

The mortal screams of their friends and the sight, later, of what was left of their bodies: eyes gouged out of faces, limbs hacked from torsos.

In the aftermath of that defeat, the 3rd Division leadership relieved the regimental commander with whom many had trained. The new colonel ordered the soldiers to shave their mustaches until they proved their manhood and made some of them wear signs that read "I am a coward."

Now Wasson, new to the platoon, was calling them back into danger.

Instead, the men walked away. Back to their regiment and later to military prison. They were a few of the 91 soldiers sentenced to years of hard labor for refusing to fight in the weeks after the battle for Outpost Kelly.

It would be the largest mass court-martial of the Korean War.

By 1954, under mounting pressure, the Pentagon granted clemency or pardon to all the soldiers, and most were reinstated to service.

50 years later, a younger generation is campaigning to restore the once-celebrated name of the 65th. They blame the soldiers' disobedience not on cowardice but on a lack of training, poor leadership, and simple racial prejudice. They say the unit was singled out for prosecution because its members were Puerto Rican.

Bolstered by a new Army review that largely affirms their arguments and supported by a growing number of politicians on the island and in Congress, they are calling on President Bush to exonerate the court-martialed soldiers.

"It's left a scar on the honor of the Puerto Rican people," says Ernest Acosta Jr., director of the Puerto Rican-American Research Institute. "We're just trying to set the record straight."

Once, "El Sesenta y Cinco" was the pride of this U.S. territory, a rare institution in which Puerto Ricans could express patriotism for their island while arguing for their place within the larger United States.

"Those soldiers embodied the very Criollo tradition of courage," says Silvia Alvarez-Curbelo, a historian at the University of Puerto Rico. "They were a distinct symbol of the relationship between colony and empire, based on loyalty and service but with a high degree of pride and dignity."

In the early years, the 65th was given little opportunity to show it...

After whiling away all of World War I and most of World War II guarding the Panama Canal, the soldiers were thrown into action in Korea.

They were <u>Christened the Borinqueneers</u>. This name came from the native Tano word for their Caribbean homeland. They hit the ground fighting.

By the end of their first year, they had been credited with 15,787 enemy killed in action, more than 10 times their own casualty rate.

Members had won four Distinguished Service Crosses, 125 Silver Stars and the praise of the Far East Command.

"The Puerto Ricans forming the ranks of the gallant 65th Infantry give daily proof on the battlefields of Korea of their courage, determination and resolute will to victory, their invincible loyalty to the United States and their fervent devotion to those immutable principles of human relations which the Americans of the Continent and Puerto Rico have in common," Gen. Douglas MacArthur wrote in 1951.

"They are writing a brilliant record of heroism in battle, and I am indeed proud to have them under my command. I wish that we could count on many more like them."

CHAPTER 79

Tragedy hit the Borinqueneers

Then came the battle for Outpost Kelly. Elements of the 65th held the bare hill forward of the main U.S. line in September 1952 when the Chinese slammed in, driving the Puerto Ricans off. Twice the troops clawed their way back, only to be overwhelmed each time by Chinese artillery.

Sergio Lopez de Lopez, a 23-year-old private, was among those called to climb Kelly. "Thirty-eight men went up," he remembers. "Three came down."

By the end of September, Kelly was in enemy hands, the 65th had suffered 542 casualties and the 8th Army command was ordering changes.

Col. Juan Cesar Cordero Davila, the highest-ranking Puerto Rican in the Army, was replaced as regimental commander by Col. Chester B. DeGavre, a West Point graduate and a "continental," a white officer from the mainland United States.

DeGavre stripped the name Borinqueneers from the unit. He cut special rations of rice and beans. But what veterans remember most was his order that they shave their mustaches "until such a time as they gave proof of their manhood."

"Mine had to go also, after 22 years with me," wrote Maj. Silvestre E. Ortiz, the regimental adjutant. "All that the mustache means to a Puerto Rican, it is part of his personality, in many cases the product of

312

a religious vow, so much so that the three chaplains went to visit this gentleman and apprised him of its importance, unsuccessfully."

Barely a month after Kelly, soldiers of the 65th found themselves under fire again, now on an exposed rock slope in the no-man's land between the Chinese and U.S. lines called Jackson Heights.

For two days, the Chinese alternated pounding the outpost with heavy artillery and probing the wreckage with armed patrols.

Then they overran, but the Puerto Ricans fought back, retaking the hill briefly before fleeing under fire.

On the third day of battle, with casualties rising, a group of 80 men from the 65th gathered away from Jackson Heights and was refusing orders to go back. The next day more soldiers dropped out of the fighting.

Finally, the unit was ordered away from the outpost, back to the main U.S. line.

By the end of October, the 65th had suffered 259 more casualties, most of them at Jackson Heights. In the aftermath, 123 men were charged with disobeying orders.

In early November, a platoon from Company L was on patrol when 39 more men refused to follow Wasson across the river.

They too were arrested.

One hundred sixty-two Puerto Ricans crowded the division stockade. The courts-martial began in December. Ninety-five soldiers were tried. Ninety-one were found guilty and sentenced to prison terms ranging from one to 18 years of hard labor.

The news reached Puerto Rico and the mainland in early 1953. Families, Congress, and the press demanded explanations. "Nuestros hijos no son cobardes!" the San Juan newspaper El Imparcial protested in one headline: "Our sons are not cowards!"

Under growing pressure, the Pentagon responded. In February 1953, Army Chief of Staff Gen. J. Lawton Collins told the House Armed Services Committee the 65th had distinguished itself in battle but had broken down because of inexperienced officers and the inability of the troops to speak English.

"The Puerto Ricans have proven in action in early fighting in Korea that they are a gallant people and that they will fight just as well as anyone else if they are properly trained and properly led," Collins said.

Language difficulties became the official explanation for the failure of the 65th, and Army Secretary Robert Stevens moved quickly to overturn the sentences, and most of the soldiers were reinstated.

Meanwhile, the Army was reconstituting the regiment, with continental soldiers assigned in the same proportion as in other units. By the end of spring the unit had lost its Puerto Rican identity. The Borinqueneers faded into history, little known to subsequent generations of Puerto Ricans.

Ernest Acosta Jr. had not heard of the regiment in 1995 when he happened upon a copy of "Puerto Rico's Fighting 65th U.S. Infantry." Retired Gen. W.W. Harris, commander of the regiment during its first year in Korea, called his men "the best damn soldiers in that war." Rotated out of command before Outpost Kelly and Jackson Heights, Harris avoided mention of the courts-martial.

Acosta, a computer systems analyst for the federal government, had founded the Puerto Rican-American Research Institute years earlier to respond to negative images of Puerto Ricans in the media.

A peacetime veteran of the Army himself, the Maryland man prevailed on U.S. Rep. Nydia Velazquez, D-N.Y., to introduce bills to recognize and honor the 65th. Then, at a 1998 conference of the National Puerto Rican Coalition in Washington, someone mentioned the courts- martial.

"Knowing what we knew about the 65th, something seemed wrong here," Acosta remembers. "How could soldiers that had been so highly praised suddenly be court-martialed in such high numbers? Something must have happened."

Working with friends Guillermo Rodriguez and Baltazar Soto, Army colonels whose fathers had been at Jackson Heights, he pored over yellowing military records, newspaper stories, letters written by soldiers.

After reading of the accomplishments of the 65th, the disaster at Outpost Kelly, and the humiliation of the men by DeGavre, they asked Army Secretary Louis Caldera in 1999 to review the courts-martial. Caldera referred the project to the Center for Military History.

The Army report, released last year, blames the breakdown of the 65th on a shortage of officers and noncommissioned officers, a rotation policy that removed combat-experienced leaders and soldiers, tactics that led to high casualties, an ammunition shortage, communication problems between largely white, English- speaking officers and Spanish-speaking Puerto Rican enlisted men, and declining morale.

"The heavy cumulative effects of all these influences was simply too great a burden for the 65th to bear," the report concludes. "It is a tribute to the dedication and perseverance of the men of the 65th that, considering all this, they attacked as many times as they did and were able to advance as far as they did. As happens too often in war, they were let down by their leaders at all levels."

The report also finds bias in the prosecution of the Puerto Ricans, citing instances of continental soldiers who were not charged after refusing to fight in similar circumstances, before and after Jackson Heights.

Believing the convictions and subsequent pardons and clemency still taint the soldiers with guilt, Acosta is using the report to campaign for formal exoneration, a declaration of their innocence.

That campaign is gaining support. Resident Commissioner Anibal Acevedo Vila last month asked Bush "to correct a historic injustice committed by the U.S. Army against a group of brave Puerto Ricans."

Gov. Sila M. Calderon also has lent her support, saying it is the policy of her administration "to recognize the valor and the honorable service realized by the 65th Infantry in the North American wars."

Acosta and Rodriguez planned to meet with Acevedo to discuss strategy for a campaign that would involve the Puerto Rican members of Congress to urge Bush to act.

Acosta sees the experience of the 65th as one of several long-festering resentments now gaining attention, including Naval practice bombing on Vieques, images of Puerto Ricans presented in the often-produced musical "West Side Story" and the still- unresolved question of the island's political status in relation to the United States.

"The Puerto Rican community is finally coming of age, it's finally beginning to protest," he says. "The community wants equality. It wants to be treated like everyone else."

De Lopez is reluctant to talk about his wartime experiences. Lying awake at night, he remembers the human gore that littered Outpost Kelly, the hacked-off arms and legs of his friends and comrades.

The retired printer sips a Coke in his cool, comfortable, one- story home in the Puerto Rican interior. Virginia Aviles Robles, the woman he married two weeks before shipping out to Korea, prepares dinner; their granddaughters giggle and play in the driveway out front. A hand-tinted portrait of the soldier as a young man, taken before Outpost Kelly, dominates the front hall.

"It's still difficult to think of these things," he says. "I know so many people who were killed like animals."

Surviving court-martialed veterans have not been closely involved in the drive for exoneration. Francisco Alicia, president of the 65th Infantry Veterans and Retirees Association in San Juan, says the

225-member organization supports the effort, but has little information about Outpost Kelly, Jackson Heights, or the courts- martial.

De Lopez was one of the soldiers of Company L court-martialed for refusing to follow Wasson across the river. He was sentenced to two years of hard labor and dishonorable discharge, then pardoned, freed, and reinstated six months later.

He says now that exoneration is "not so important."

"It would be something," he said. "But it's already been 50 years. All those years we suffered."

Silvia Alvarez-Curbelo, the historian, says there still is value to revisiting the 65th.

"It's never too late for justice," she says. You must revisit the past. Not for wanting to find the guilty or the innocent or anything like that but to have a clear picture of who you are. You have to go to the past."

CHAPTER 80

Fort Allen Army Base Juana Diaz, Puerto Rico

Fort Allen Army Base is a United States Army Installation located on the southern coast of Puerto Rico. It was established just prior to U.S. involvement in World War II. The base has also been a hub of Untied States Navy communication centers.

Today, they are no active-duty units stationed at the base, but it serves an active role in the training and education of United States Army Reserve and Puerto Rico Army National Guard soldiers on the island.

Most Fort Allen's facilities are dedicated only to the training of soldiers with a few being used for administrative, temporary lodging, support, storage, and maintenance.

Here is some History about Fort Allen

In 1941, the United States Department of The Army began expressing interest in establishing an additional U.S. military installation in Puerto Rico.

Losey Army Airfield, an existing airfield near Juana Diaz was already in full use, but additional assets in the area were needed.

Losey Army Airfield was named for aeronautical meteorologist Captain Robert M. Losey, who unfortunately was to become the first

U.S. combat death of World War II after being killed by German bombs in Norway.

The 32nd Fighter Squadron, 20th Troop Carrier Squadron, 4th Tactical Reconnaissance Squadron, 417th Bombardment Squadron, 36th Fighter Group and the 23rd Fighter Squadron all found a home in the area during World War II.

The base was then transferred from the control of the United States Army Air Corps to the regular Army and renamed to the Camp Losey in 1949.

The facility was renamed to Fort Allen in late 1950 and would provide operational support for U.S. and NATO troops in the Korean War.

Fort Allen Army Base is a United States Army Installation located on the southern coast of Puerto Rico. Established in the years just prior to US involvement in World War II.

The base has also been a hub of Untied States Navy communication centers. Today, they are no active-duty units stationed at the base, but it serves an active role in the training and education of United States Army Reserve and Puerto Rico Army National Guard soldiers on the island.

Most Fort Allen's facilities are dedicated solely to the training of soldiers with a few being used for administrative, temporary lodging, support, storage, and maintenance.

In 1963 the United States Navy took control of Fort Allen and US Naval Radio Station was constructed at the base. Additionally, the world's largest radio telescope facility at the time, the Arecibo Observatory was opened.

The next twenty years would see the base become a stronghold of United States Navy communications in the area with the addition of a nearby high frequency transmitter site in Isabela.

In 1979 both the high frequency transmitter site in Isabela and the nearby area of Sabana Seca would both be attacked by terrorists.

Activity at Fort Allen quickly outgrew the capacity of the base and, in 1980 operations were moved to the newly established Naval Communication Station Puerto Rico.

The following year, a U.S. Immigration and Naturalization Service processing station was erected at Fort Allen to deal with the influx of Cuban and Haitian refugees fleeing conflict in the area.

Over the next few years, control of the base was transitioned to the Puerto Rico Army National Guard, who had already been using the base for training for the past several years.

In 1983, Fort Allen began gaining large permanent units, including the 35th Signal Battalion and other components of the United States Army Reserve.

Two years later, the Puerto National Guard Language Center moved to Fort Allen, further boosting its size. The early 1990's saw almost 600 ships stationed in the Fort Allen area because of technological leaps in communication and radio technology that allowed Army and Navy units to greatly expand mission capacities.

In 2007, Fort Allen saw several units, deployed to Iraq and Afghanistan in support of Operation Iraqi Freedom and Operation Enduring Freedom.

Present day Fort Allen continues to be a stronghold of communications and operational support for the Fort Allen Armed Forces Reserve, Puerto Rico National Guard, United States Navy, and the United States Army Reserves. There are also several detachments at Fort Allen that operate to support the National Guard Youth Challenge Program.

Despite being primarily an education and training facility, Fort Allen does have several other recreational and multi-use buildings. The base boasts a pool, barracks, security office, barber shop and a chow hall.

The PRNG LANGUAGE CENTER

Every year, students from the Rutherford B. Hayes Elementary School, comes to the PRNG Language Center to celebrate its traditional _Special Christmas their Children. It is a beautiful Christmas Activity for the gifted children Of the Rutherford B. Hayes Elementary School in Juana Diaz.

The students and teachers of the Language Center work very hard to get this activity going. The money for the food and toys come from a candy store in the Language Center. Also, chocolate, and other items are sold to get funds for this beautiful event.

Youth Challenge Program

Established in 1999, the National Guard Youth Challenge Program at Fort Allen is a community outreach program geared towards at risk youth. The program provides a structured program for high school dropout's ages 16 to 18.

The National Guard personnel help instill discipline, values, life skills and education in hopes of giving the youth a new track on life.

Current Units

Fort Allen is home to several both Army Reserve and Army National Guard units. The base also regularly plays host to US Navy units.

Current United States Army Reserve Units include the 276th Ordnance Company, 35th Signal Battalion, 613th Military Policy Company, 941st Quartermaster Company and the 807th Signal Company.

Current Fort Allen United States Army National Guard units include the 219th Quartermaster detachment, 192nd Support Battalion C Company and the 240th Military Policy Company.

Fort Allen also houses the retention office of the United States Army Reserve, Armed Forces Reserve Center,180th Division and the US Army Reserve 8th Multifunctional.

CHAPTER 81

The Language Center, Fort Allen Juana Diaz PR

Before I begin writing about my work at the Language Center, I will narrate a few facts of this wonderful 2nd to none institution.

The Puerto Rico National Guard Language Center was established in 1976. It has performed its mission of providing English language training to non-prior service Warriors, Airmen, military families, and Puerto Rico National Guard citizen Warriors.

It was originally founded as the English Technical Language School. This school was located at Camp Santiago Training Site in Salinas, Puerto Rico. It has been functioning as a State-operated educational program within the Puerto Rico Army National Guard for over 44 yrs.

It aimed at reducing the number of trainees returning from Basic Training. The problem was that if the new applicants didn't go to the Language Center, they would be returning from the United States due to lack of proficiency in the English language.

The Defense Language Institute English Language Center at Lackland, Air Force Base, in Texas approved the Puerto Rico National Guard Language Center as a non-resident English Language Training Pro-gram in 1979.

It wasn't until 1984 that the National Guard Bureau approved federal funding to operate the Language Center.

The following year, in May 1985, the Language Center relocated to its present site at Fort Allen, Juana Diaz, and PR.

The Language Center has a very important vision. The vision is that it must be an accredited, prestigious institution. The school would facilitate language acquisition and military skills. I know it can be done because all instructors are fully qualified. It is also aiming in the transformation, readiness and retention of Warriors and Airmen for America's Army and Joint Forces.

The PUERTO RICO NATIONAL GUARD LANGUAGE CENTER conducts an intensive full-time ENGLISH LANGUAGE TRAINING program consisting of seven hours daily of English instruction, five days a week.

In addition, students are normally assigned two hours of homework/ study hall daily. The AMERI-CAN LANGUAGE COURSE curriculum consists of a combination of classroom learning and individual language laboratory instruction. They also receive military classes.

The students don't go home on weekends; therefore, they are speaking English 24/7. Family members are allowed to come for visits on Sunday afternoons.

During some holidays, students pack their belonging and head home.

When I began teaching at the Language Center, what I like best was the discipline. Every day I looked forward on going into a classroom where students are there to learn.

All instructors at the Language Center are well qualified. They all have a secondary level or adult education certifications. Our academic background is from B.A. or master's degree.

It didn't matter what level of teaching I received; I was always ready. It was challenging teaching a slow student. Some didn't like to study. They came in with a bad attitude; however, after an hour of teaching them, they changed. They were even willing to participate in a conversation.

At beginning of a new lesson, I introduced the swim or sink method of learning. They were impressed. The following hour they were ready with no negative attitude. I used to start the morning with a famous quotation or idiom. They learned those crazy idioms.

Sometimes, I even took a chance of talking about Ebonics. They wanted more......

As every English teacher knows, Ebonics are not taught in the classroom. I taught it because that is the only way students will learn the difference between an idiomatic expression and Ebonics.

Idiomatic expression is mastering the language. Ebonics should be taught to show that it is only street language.

I taught some of my classes through music. A slow student or even an advanced student enjoyed them. Why, because music is the universal language....

After lunch, the students were usually sleepy; therefore, I took them out of the classroom to show them sounds associating them with our environment.

There were many funny and sad situations in the classroom. I treated each situation with kindness. The students knew that no one was supposed to make fun of the other.

The saddest day for me was retiring from the Language Center. The staff is part of my extended family. The students were my children because I took them with no English whatsoever to a fully bilingual individual.

The staff at the Language Center is part of me. I consider them my extended family.

Mr. Eliu Rivera and Myrna Rolon were always there to give me a helping hand when I was going to introduce a new lesson. I learned a lot from them. They had a unique way of teaching. Some students used to tell me that I taught just like Mr. Rivera. Others stated that I even had corny jokes like Ms. Rolon.

Let me also mention Ms. Awilda Quinones, Ms. Nitza Santiago, Mr. Julio Gonzalez, Ms. Gladys Sanchez, and Mr. Luis Rivera. They always had kind words for me.

I want to thank my supervisor, Maj. Noris Rodriguez. She was always there when my mom was in the hospital. When mom died, Noris and all the instructors were at my side on that sad day.

My buddies, Iris Quijano and Saul Ortiz went to the cemetery and stayed with me even after my mom was buried.

The military side was also very helpful. They made sure that the warriors treated the instructors with respect. Many thanks to:

Col. Efrain Soto	Maj. Noris Rodriguez	CW4 Willie Hernandez
First Sgt. Tony Latayari	CSM Soroya Suarez	D.I. Sharon Acosta
Sgt. Salvador Santiago	Maj. Arnold Rivera	CWO4 Ivelisse Ortiz
CWO4 Nelson Pomades	Sgt. Julio Chacon	Sgt. Juan Lopez
Sgt. Cabrera	Sgt. Guzman	Sgt. Mora
Maj. Millie Rosa	D.I. Wendy Montero	D.I. Noemi Tricoche
Maj. Doris Acevedo	D.I. David Childs	Maj. Yesenia Rosa
CSM. Luis Cora	CWO Luis Hernandez	D.I. Juan Lopez

My thanks to the Puerto Rico National Guard for giving me the opportunity to teach at the Language Center. I am sorry to inform you that the Puerto Rico Army National Guard Language Center closed its doors on September 30, 2018.

CHAPTER 82

Rafael Hernandez

WORLD WAR 1

During World War I, many Puerto Ricans were drafted, recruited, or volunteered while residing in the continental United States. They were sent to either black or white units depending on their skin color.

A curious case is that of James Reese Europe, a distinguished African American jazz musician who obtained an officer, lieutenant, commission with the New York National Guard and served with the 369th Colored Infantry Regiment.

The 369th would be known as the "Harlem Hell fighters" for their distinguished role in France.

Europe visited Puerto Rico and recruited some two dozen Puerto Ricans for his band. Among them were brothers Rafael and Jesús Hernández. Rafael Hernandez is considered by many as Puerto Rico's greatest composer.

Besides the 18 Puerto Ricans recruited for the regimental band, about a dozen Afro-Puerto Ricans from New York joined or were drafted into this regiment. Unlike most black units, the 369th saw combat because it was placed under French command.

Due to the high casualties suffered by the French Army since 1914, losing a whole generation of men by the end of the war, and because they were fighting in their own country, the French command was no longer sick about who they allowed to fight to save France from defeat.

Jorge Otero Barreto
'Puerto Rican Rambo'

Jorge Otero Barreto was born on April 7, 1937, in Vega Baja, Puerto Rico. His parent are Eloy Otero Bruno and Crispina Barreto Torres.

Eloy Otero Bruno, Jorge's father, had an admiration for America's first president, George Washington. The family had no idea that little Jorge would one day be something of an American icon in his own right. a status earned after becoming one of the most decorated soldiers of the Vietnam War.

After pursuing biology studies for three years in college, Jorge Otero-Barreto joined the Army in 1959. One year later, he made history when he became the first Puerto Rican to ever graduate from the Army's Air Assault School.

Within a year of completing training, Otero was volunteering to go to Vietnam, the first of five deployments he would make between 1961 and 1970, during which time he would serve with the 101st Airborne, the 82nd Airborne, and the 25th Infantry Division, among others.

Otero would volunteer for approximately 200 combat missions during his five deployments, a lofty number that eventually earned him the moniker, "The Puerto Rican Rambo," after the fictional death-dealing character made famous by actor Sylvester Stallone.

Over the course of five deployments, Otero-Barreto would earn 38 commendations, including three Silver Stars, five Purple Hearts, five Bronze Stars, five Air Medals and four Army Commendation Medals.

One commendation was earned for actions on May 1, 1968, when the platoon sergeant, along with men from the 101st Air Cavalry Division, was occupying positions designed to pin down a North Vietnamese regiment in a village near the deadly city of Hue.

Early that morning, Otero and his men began getting bombarded by a series of charges by enemy soldiers desperate to rid themselves of their predicament.

Two charges by enemy soldiers were repelled by U.S. troops. Fifty-eight enemies were killed in the charges, and the assailants were forced to limp back to the village.

This Marine stroked a Taliban fighter to death with the enemy's own weapon,

The Marine was awarded the Navy Cross for his actions.

Rather than wait for another assault, Otero took 1st Platoon, Company A, to the point position to lead an assault on the village.

Quickly into their advance, first platoon began taking machine gun, small arms, and rocket-propelled grenade fire from a scattering of spider holes and bunkers.

The Puerto Rican Rambo wasted no time in going to work. Otero sprinted to the nearest machine gun bunker and quickly killed the three men manning the position.

Gathering the rest of his squad, Otero then moved through three more fortified enemy bunkers, going from one to the next until all that remained was a trail of destruction.

The assault by Otero, which allowed the rest of Company A's platoons to maneuver into advantageous positions and overrun the enemy, would earn him one of his three Silver Stars.

While the conclusion of Vietnam would mark the end of his career in combat, it would not be the last of Otero's many lifetime achievements.

In 2006, he was named the recipient of the National Puerto Rican Coalition's Lifetime Achievement Award. Since then, he has had veterans' homes and museums named for him, and in 2011, was honored in his hometown when the city named the Puerto Rican Rambo its citizen of the year.

Chapter 83

SFC Gil Ramos Rivera

Korea & Vietnam War Heroes

Lt. Gil Ramos Rivera was born on September 5, 1925, in Cayey, PR. His parents were Segundo Ramos, a US soldier, and Paula Rivera de Ramos.

Gil Ramos Rivera had four siblings. His older sister was Merida, two older brothers Jose and Jorge. He also had a younger sister Nazarea.

The United States gained control of Puerto Rico from the declining Spanish Empire after the Spanish-American War in 1898.

The Jones Act of 1916, implemented in March of 1917, granted American citizenship to all residents of Puerto Rico. While Puerto Rico's previous territorial status allowed the military to conscript them into service, since gaining citizenship, even larger numbers of Puerto Ricans, including Ramos-Rivera's father Segundo, served in the United States military.

Ramos Rivera grew up with his family in Cayey, PR. Cayey served as the location of a Naval facility, the El Cayey Naval Radio Station, and Henry Barracks, an Army post.

Soldiers like Ramos Rivera's father served in the military for two reasons: to provide their family with steady income, and for the prestige of serving as a soldier in "being a cut above other men in society."

By 1920, the base served as the home of several regiments including the Puerto Rican 65th Infantry Regiment. Puerto Rican troops aided the United States' interventions in Central America and the Caribbean in the early years of the twentieth century-known as the Banana Wars.

As such, the 1930 Census shows Segundo Ramos as a soldier stationed at Henry Barracks. Three-year-old Gil and his family depended solely on his father Segundo's salary as a soldier as the rest of the family listed no occupation.

By the 1935 Puerto Rican Territorial Census, Gil, now ten and a fluent English speaker, continued to live at Henry Barracks with his family.

In May of 1937, Ramos Rivera's father retired from the military with the rank of first lieutenant.

After his retirement, the 1940 Census shows Gil and his family continue to reside in Cayey, in the city of Monte Llano.

Following in his father's footsteps, on October 10, 1950, Ramos Rivera enlisted in the United States Army. His entry into the military coincided with the beginnings of the Korean War.

The conflict began as North Korea, supported by the communist countries of the Soviet Union and China, invaded South Korea on June 25, 1950.

The United States led the efforts of the United Nations in supporting the South Koreans, providing over ninety percent of the troops of the United Nations' forces, military equipment, and supplies.

As a result of the end of racial segregation during the early 1950s, more English-speaking Puerto Ricans like Ramos-Rivera began to serve in non-Puerto Rican units.

As the war continued, the United Nations' troops advanced into North Korea before the Chinese pushed them back into South Korea, eventually turning the war into a stalemate reminiscent of World War I with trench warfare in France.

Ultimately, an armistice stopped the open conflict in 1953, though skirmishes presently continue.

In all, a total of over 43,000 Puerto Ricans like Ramos-Rivera served in the Korean War.

Ramos Rivera continued his service in the Vietnam War. The North Vietnamese Communists fought against the anti-Communist South Vietnamese supported by the United States.

While Americans served in a limited capacity in the 1950s with only 700 troops, by 1969, American forces reached their peak of over 543,000 soldiers in Vietnam.

Counting Puerto Ricans living in their native country, over 48,000 troops served in Vietnam.

While Ramos-Rivera spoke fluent English, the desperate need for recruits saw the Defense Department relax their policy of enforcing an English immersion course for Puerto Ricans, thus sending many Puerto Rican recruits to Vietnam without proper language skills.

15th Medical Battalion Valorous Unit Award, Quan Loi, Vietnam

Ramos Rivera saw firsthand the heat of battle during Vietnam. Many infantry troops often moved in a "long green line", meaning that the unit marched in a single file line.

On one occasion during the 1969–1970-time frame, one such unit came under heavy fire by the North Vietnamese Army. The 15th Medical Battalion within the Airmobile 1st Cavalry Division sought to recover and treat casualties, placing themselves in danger as the enemy encroached on their perimeter.

Ramos Rivera, now a sergeant first class, and other non-medical personnel sought to protect the battalion as the doctors worked to care for the casualties.

Fortunately, no injuries occurred for members of the medical company who received a Valorous Unit Award in 1970.

In addition, sometime during his twenty-year career in the Army, he received a Purple Heart. The predecessor award, the Badge of Military Merit issued by then General George Washington in 1782, fell into disuse until 1932 when General Douglas MacArthur revived the award as the Purple Heart in honor of the bicentennial of Washington's birthday.

At the beginning of 1942, during World War II, the military awarded the medal to soldiers wounded or killed in combat. Typically, the military issues the award to soldiers like Ramos Rivera who met certain criteria of injury that occurred during hostilities and documented by a medical officer.

These honors and recognition reveal the quality of Ramos-Rivera's service to this country.

Completing his twenty years of service, Ramos Rivera retired from the Army on November 1, 1970. After his retirement, Ramos-Rivera eventually moved to Florida.

From the 1940s to 1980s, large numbers of Puerto Ricans migrated to the United States mainland for better opportunities and to escape the poverty that existed in Puerto Rico.

Ramos Rivera settled in Orlando where he lived for the rest of his life. On March 17, 1996, Ramos-Rivera passed away at the age of seventy. Florida National Cemetery in Bushnell, Florida placed a memorial headstone in honor of Ramos Rivera and his service to this country. His service in the heat of intense battle and the affirmation of his service by the military deserves praise and gratitude.

CHAPTER 84

Summary of Past, Present, Future

The Puerto Rico National Guard ARMY/AIRFORCE

The Puerto Rico National Guard (PRNG) is the national guard of the U.S. Commonwealth of Puerto Rico. The Constitution of the United States specifically charges the National Guard with <u>dual federal and state missions</u>, which includes to provide soldiers and airmen to the United States Army and U.S. Air Force in national emergencies or when requested by the president of the United States, and to perform military operations at the state level or any other lawful service as requested by the governor of Puerto Rico.

The PRNG responds to the governor of Puerto Rico, who serves as its commander in chief and imparts orders with the Puerto Rico adjutant general acting as conduit, and its local mission is to respond as requested in military or civilian tasks.

Abroad, its main function is to train a reserve capable of providing additional personnel in a war scenario.

THE PAST

The PRNG traces its roots back to the first Puerto Rican militias founded by Juan Ponce de León during the 16th century and prides itself in the battles that its predecessor won against the Taíno, enemy navies, pirates, privateers, and buccaneers, such as Francis Drake, Cumberland

and Baldiuino Henrico, centuries before from strongholds such as Castillo San Felipe del Morro.

These forces which preceded by operated similarly to the Minutemen, were involved in several military and piratical incursions during the Spanish colonial period.

Due to this, the PRNG claims to be the only member of the National Guard of the United States to be a product of two distinct lineages.

The individual claims a unique tradition that unlike the rest of the state national guards, also includes the early American period that preceded the creation of the Thirteen Colonies.

This claim is reflected in its first coat of arms which depicts the defeat of the British in the second Battle of San Juan and the patch worn by the 295th Regiment, designed by John Roqueña in 1953, which features a man wearing a morion.

The first coat of arms of the PRNG featured a lion guarding a tower on top of an isle located in the middle of a blue field representing the ocean, the beast representing the militia guarding San Juan, three sailboats that represent the defeated British float in 1798, and a sheep next to a red book representing Puerto Rico as seen in the coat of arms.

Since its early days, the units stationed in Puerto Rico used a yellow and red patch that features a garita, like those at El Morro.

After the Spanish American War in 1898, Spain ceded Puerto Rico to the United States. US military authorities discussed Puerto Rico's military value. It offered tremendous commercial value in expanding commerce among the US, Central and South America.

Because of the political changes in the beginning of the 20th century, the strategic military importance of Puerto Rico grew.

In 1906, a group of Puerto Ricans met with Governor Winthrop, and the commissioner of interior, Lawrence H. Graham, to organize a National Guard of Puerto Rico.

The public supported this effort, and some companies were organized, in different towns around the island: Yauco under the command of Captain Santiago Vivaldi; Juana Díaz, commanded by Captain Diaz-Brik, Peñuelas by Captain Gabino Balasquide, and two in Ponce by Pedro Juan Armstrong, Mario Belaval, J. Oppenheimer, F. del Valle and Doctor Laguna.

In San Juan three companies were organized under Federico Val-Spinosa, Justo Barros, J. del Barril, R. Swigett, J. Deere, Lugo Vinas, and F. Fano.

As the companies were being formed, all the officers and soldiers had to purchase their own uniforms and supplies, since there was no government funding for the enterprise.

This organization failed due to existing US federal law, which prohibited the formation of any armed force within the United States and its territories without authorization from Congress.

During World War I, Puerto Ricans served in the 373d, 374th, and 375th Infantry Regiments of the National Army and the Puerto Rican Regiment of the Regular Army.

Approximately 20,000 troops were trained at Camp Las Casas. The young Puerto Rican officer, Luis Raúl Estevez, thought a Puerto Rican National Guard was needed.

As the first Puerto Rican to graduate from the US Military Academy at West Point, he had learned about military units in other states. He discussed the issue with the governor of Puerto Rico, Arthur Yager, soon after the conclusion of World War I.

The governor, Legislature of Puerto Rico, and US Congress approved the plan, and the National Guard was organized in 1919.

In 1938, Luis R. Esteves was promoted to Major General and appointed as Adjutant General of the Puerto Rican National Guard.

The first regiment of the Puerto Rico National Guard, "First Infantry Regiment", was organized on June 2, 1920, and reorganized on December 26, 1922, as the 295th Infantry Regiment.

On March 1, 1936, the 296th Infantry Regiment was organized. Before, the 296th existed as a battalion of the 295th Infantry Regiment.

On October 30, 1950, the Puerto Rican Nationalist Party organized a series of uprisings in numerous cities in Puerto Rico against United States rule and the Puerto Rican commonwealth government in what is known as the Puerto Rican Nationalist Party Revolts of the 1950s.

The Puerto Rico National Guard was mobilized under the command of Puerto Rico adjutant general Luis R. Esteves by orders of Governor Luis Muñoz Marín and sent to confront the Nationalists in various towns such Jayuya, Toabaja and San Juan.

Due to the lack of belligerent invaders, the PRNG has participated in several functions such as coordination during natural disasters.

It was mainly tropical storms, hurricanes, floods, and droughts. The PRNG use to repair roads, bridges, telecommunication arrays and aqueducts.

The PRNG also hosts other disciplines, including a band and a religious services branch that includes personal if different credos.

Through these, the organization also related with other government agencies and entities, occasionally organizing parades or friendly competitions or entertainment through its artistic unit, Banda 248.

Otherwise, the organization makes donations to other initiatives, mainly the Red Cross and similar entities.

THE PRNG NEW STRUCTURE
Guardsmen at the 58th Presidential Inauguration

The Puerto Rico National Guard comprises both Army and Air National Guard components, namely the Puerto Rico Army National Guard and the Puerto Rico Air National Guard respectively, with a total authorized strength of 8,400 citizen-soldiers and airmen.

The Constitution of the United States specifically charges the different National Guards with dual federal and state missions.

The Puerto Rico National Guard is the only United States military force empowered to function in a state/territorial status within Puerto Rico. Those functions range from limited actions during non-emergency situations to full-scale law enforcement of martial law when local law enforcement officials can no longer maintain civil control.

The Puerto Rico National Guard may be called into federal service in response to a call by the president of the United States or Congress, usually at the request of the governor of Puerto Rico.

When under state/territory control, the governor serves as commander-in-chief. When troops from the Puerto Rico National Guard are called to federal service, the president serves as commander-in-chief. The federal mission assigned to the different National Guards is: "To provide properly trained and equipped units for prompt mobilization for war, national emergency or as otherwise needed."

The governor of Puerto Rico may call individuals or units of the Puerto Rico National Guard into state service during emergencies or to assist in special situations in which National Guard use is appropriate. The state mission assigned to the National Guard is: "To provide trained and disciplined forces for domestic emergencies or as otherwise provided by state law."

CHAPTER 85

History Summary

Spanish colonial period 1510–1898

The PRNG claims direct descent from the Puerto Rican militias that were founded after the Spanish Empire granted the island a Governor and General captain.

Its first large conflict emerged from the response to the Spanish–Taíno War of San Juan–Borikén, only years after the arrival of Juan Ponce de León and before the totality of Puerto Rico was under Spanish sovereignty.

The Taínos of Borikén, led by Agüeybaná II were forced into labor and their territory threatened by the Spanish expansionism in the region, consequently deciding to begin a counteroffensive by killing Cristóbal de Sotomayor, the leader of a settlement built in southern Puerto Rico.

Lacking a formal structure during the initial stages of the colonization, the Spanish settlers were forced to adopt a military initiative and organize these militias, while also continuing their main jobs, giving rise to the first civilian reserves.

Additional native attacks took place in 1514 and 1520, by which point they had been driven into exile in the Lesser Antilles.

During this decade, French buccaneers would also become a threat, attacking the archipelago in 1528, only for more exiled Taínos to attack the following year.

Hostile adversaries would make a single incursion during the following decade, one was an attack attributed to island Caribs, in 1556 and the other a French attack, the only reported during the following thirty years.

However, the 1570s saw a surge in activity, with buccaneers attacking in 1570 and 1576 and the natives in 1573.

Puerto Rico was considered a strong strategic point by the Spanish Empire due to its location as the last bastion before taking the transatlantic voyage to Europe, and due to this fortification of its ports began during the second half of the 16th century.

The first major attack faced by the militias was led by Francis Drake in 1595, leading thousands of men in the Battle of San Juan but being repelled.

In 1598, George Clifford, 3rd Earl of Cumberland managed to take the city in the second Battle of San Juan after battling his way through the local militias but was forced to leave two months later due to an epidemic.

Despite this setback, the local militias earned enough of a reputation for the next governor, Alonso de Mercado, to reportedly send back most of the soldiers that accompanied him in his voyage and rely on them for defensive purposes.

The main fortress of San Juan Bay, El Morro, was finished by 1608 and additional fortifications such as San Cristóbal soon followed.

The next major engagement took part 27 years later, when Netherlands lead another failed invasion in the third Battle of San Juan. The militias would also participate in military incursions in other adjacent islands, including some that are now part of the Puerto Rican archipelago.

In 1765, Marshall Alejandro O'Reilly who would later become known as "El Padre de las Milicias", reorganized the militias and created a group that was disciplined enough to fight in regular combat at the Anglo-Spanish War and be commended by the crown.

In 1797, the British attempted another invasion, this time led by Ralph Abercrombie, but were defeated by a force that heavily depended on the local militias in the fourth Battle of San Juan.

In 1868, amidst a growing pro-independence in the population that eventually lead to the Grito de Lares, the Spanish government decided to replace the mostly Puerto Rican quorum of the militias with an Institute of Volunteers that was completely composed of Spanish-born citizens.

During the decades that followed, the loss of several former colonies and of influence in the continent affected the maintenance of the local military installations and of the force, leading to an ill-prepared force with which to face the Hispano-American War.

Early American colonial period 1898–1938

In 1906, a group of men led by Commissioner of Interior Lawrence H. Grahame decided that there was a need to create a national guard that mirrored those in the states to replace the militias.

Companies were created in Yauco, Juana Díaz, Peñuelas, Ponce and San Juan. This entity was initially dependent on volunteers that were trained in El Morro, none of which received a salary.

However, the colonial legislature failed to approve a project that was meant to authorize the organization and seek funding, causing the initiative to be halted.

Cadet Luis R. Esteves, 1915

With the onset of World War, I and the mobilization of the 373rd, 374th and 375th regiments of the Regular Army, the need for a local military force became evident as some 20,000 men were trained in Camp Las Casas.

As soon as the war concluded, a local officer, Luis Raúl Estevez, inquired colonial governor Arthur Yager about reactivating the national guard, an initiative that gained the support of the official and the colonial legislature.

On July 19, 1919, Congress passed a law approving the budget for the following year to meet the requirements of the National Defense Act of 1916.

Adjutant General John Wilson was given command over the nascent organization.

On July 19, 1919, the United States Department of War informed Yager about the administration's intention of supporting a local reserve pursuant to the statutes of this law to create a permanent national guard that could assist the other branches of the military or working independently.

The entity resumed operation and was meant to receive an infantry brigade, with artillery, cavalry, engineering, and specialized troops.

Esteves became the first commander of the current interaction of the PRNG.

Company A was organized under Cpt. Luis Irizarry on November 23, 1919.

The unit was trained in terrains and buildings that were lent by Carmelo Alomar of the Agricultural Experimental Station.

Company B was organized on February 1, 1920 and was separated a week later in two companies stationed in San Sebastián, Company M and Company L, which were later formally organized.

On February 7, 1920, several new companies were organized, including Company E in Ponce, Company G in Yauco.

On February 25, 1920, the First Regiment Puerto Rico Infantry was provisionally organized under Mayor Luis Esteves, receiving Companies A, B, M, L, E, G and Headquarters.

Company F was organized on March 7, 1920, in Peñuelas.

The following week, Company I was organized at Arecibo.

On April 13, 1920, Company C was organized in Cabo Rojo.

On April 25, 1920, Company H was organized at Sabana Grande.

On April 30, 1920, the First Regiment received command of several headquarters at San Juan, Mayagüez and Sabana Grande.

On May 9, 1920, Company D was organized at San Germán. Towards the month's end, Company K was organized at Bayamón.

On May 30, 1920, the designation of Company B was reassigned to a company in Maricao.

That same day, Troop A of the First Squadron P.R. Cavalry was organized in Mayagüez.

The First Infantry Regiment was formally recognized on June 2, 1920, before becoming the 295th Infantry Regiment two years later.

With Esteves as its senior instructor, the regiment is symbolically considered the older within the structure of the US national guards due to its claim.

On June 14, 1920, the First Infantry Medical Detachment was organized in Mayagüez.

On June 17, 1923, the 296th was separated as a splinter, with its first Battalion winning recognition for best company in the national guard twice.

The First Regiment's First Headquarters Company was organized in Bayamón three days later.

Later that week, the first PRNG band was organized at Mayagüez.

The First Regiment's Machine Gun Company was organized at San Juan on September 19, 1920.

More than two months later, its Supply Company was organized at San Juan.

The first annual exercises began on December 6, 1920, at Salinas, during the following years this camp would be moved throughout_the camps.

In the 1920s, several groups dedicated to target shooting were scattered throughout Puerto Rico, with the PRNG deciding to organize competitions.

On November 24, 1930, personnel from the entity founded the Ponce Rifle and Sporting Club, later affiliating itself with the National Rifle Association.

The PRNG itself would promote these events, forming the Puerto Rico National Guard Shooting Club presided by Salvador Roig.

The national guard was mobilized after the passing of hurricane San Felipe in 1928 and San Ciprián in 1932.

During these disasters, they were assigned civil assistance.

Similar interventions took place in the Dominican Republic and Haiti.

In 1933, the 296th First Battalion won the Harrison Cup.

On May 3, colonial governor Winship argued for a light artillery unit.

On March 16, 1936, the PRNG underwent a reorganization.

In February 1934, Gen. George Leach, who oversaw Company A of the 295th, visited Puerto Rico and was surprised to see that the bayonets had been repaired motu proprio with local resources and their discipline, promoting him to pronounce during a speech that he had "inspected the national guards of the 48 states" and not seen one better prepared than the PRNG, going to the extent that if the president asked which was the best regiment for defense, it would be the 295th.

The 296th remained under the supervision of the 295th until June 1, 1936, when it was designated as a regiment under Col. Luis Irizarry.

In 1937, the 296th first Battalion was reassigned to the 295th as Company A.

In 1938, the PRNG joined the 65th Infantry Regiment and participated in exercises supervised by Gen. Frank Ross Mckoy.

On July 25, 1938, Irizarry was killed during an assassination attempt against colonial governor Winship in one of several confrontations between the government and the Puerto Rican Nationalist Party following the events of the Ponce massacre.

Col. José Enrique Colom took over the 296th Regiment...

In 1938, the 295th, 65th and 296th Regiments and other personnel from the PRNG joined the Regular Army in several military exercises also involving the Navy.

The three regiments formed a brigade that was led by brigadier general Walter Short and was given jurisdiction over Puerto Rico in case of military action.

The following two years, annual training was held in Arecibo and Tortuguero in anticipation to the impending activation in the newly declared World War II.

Wilson died in December 1938, and months later Luis Raúl Esteves was given command of the PRNG.

On August 3, 1939, the National Guard paid homage to the colonel of the 296th, José Colom, who was serving as interim governor of Puerto Rico, with a mass march, the first of this kind held under the colonial administration, to commemorate Governor's Day.

In turn, Colom handed several recognitions to the companies and soldiers that distinguished themselves during the year.

On January 8, 1940, an emergency camp was held and a training exercise where an invasion of the northern coast of Puerto Rico was being invaded, the municipalities of Arecibo and Vega Baja, and the 295th and 296th were tasked with repelling it.

Both were placed in charge of solving a tactical exercise, code named MUSKETRY, which involved a sudden appearance by a hostile force. [61] In March 1940, a new military code for Puerto Rico was presented to the colonial legislature along other initiatives related to the PRNG.

The final annual camp prior to activation in World War II was the longest yet, lasting three weeks.

On May 19, 1940, the PRNG was mobilized to attend the flooding caused by Rivera Portugués and Bucaná in Ponce.

During this time, the PRNG underwent a reorganization that led to the transfer of guardsmen and units, as well as the creation of new units.

In June 1940, the 162nd Battalion of Field Artillery was first organized, with its batteries, A through C, being assigned to San Juan, Río Piedras and Ponce.

This same year, the 130th Engineering Regiment received authorization to organize its 1st Battalion, with its companies being assigned to San Juan, Mayagüez and Guayama.

The 295th's Company A was reassigned as the 296th's Company K. This reorganization led to the ascension of several officers to accommodate the new units.

CHAPTER 86

World War II and reorganization 1938–1950

On October 15, 1940, the PRNG was activated pursuant to Executive Order 3551.[69] A group of 1,359 belonging to 295th Infantry Regiment were assigned to Campeonato Tortuguero in Vega Alta, Puerto Rico where training was under seen by Esteves under Col. Miguel A. Muñoz.

The 296th had a force of 1,363 and joined the 295th at Tortuguero. [70][71] The other units, which included those that received formal recognition on this date, were the 92nd Brigade, 47 men, the 162nd Artillery Battalion, 274 men, the 130th Engineering Battalion 193 men, the 253rd Artillery Battalion 175 men and the 201st/123rd Artillery Battalion 323 men.

Besides San Juan, the municipalities of Ponce, Mayagüez, Vega Baja, Manatí, Arecibo, Bayamón, Caguas, Fajardo, Humacao, Cayey, San Germán, Maricao, Cabo Rojo, Sabana Grande, Penuelas, Yauco, Aibonito, Coamo, Juana Díaz, Río Piedras, Guayama and Aguadilla had personnel assigned to them.

The 130th Regiment was placed under the Regular Army and trained by the 27th Combat Engineering Regiment at Tortuguero, where its Company A was charged with additional constructions.

On March 19, 1941, additional personnel were assigned to the 295th Regiment, and shortly afterwards it was moved to Salinas, Puerto Rico, for further training.

On August 12, 1941, Colom left the 296th Regiment and was replaced by Col. Antulio Segarra. The 130th and 27th Engineering were reorganized in a Combat Engineering Regiment in charge of Lt. Col. Sylvester Nordner and continued working on the infrastructure of the local bases.

Engineers of the 65th Infantry Regiment in Korea

On December 7, 1941, the PRNG was assigned to surveillance and monitoring operations throughout Puerto Rico.

After more than a year performing this task, the 295th Infantry Regiment was separated in two battalions and reassigned to operate in Aruba and Curazao, while the rest of the personnel was placed on detachments and sent in operations that took place in Surinam, Trinidad, Jamaica, and Cuba.

On January 7, 1943, the 65th Infantry Regiment was assigned to Panama led by Commander Salvador Roig, with 300 men being transferred from the 296th to complement its force.

The remainder of that regiment remained at Camp O'Reilly in Gurabo...

On October 30, 1943, Col. Eduardo Andini took over the 296th Regiment.

In December 1943 the 295th Infantry Regiment was reorganized in Puerto Rico and the following month began replacement operations in Campamento Tortuguero.

That same month, Col. Andrés López Antongiorgi took over the 296th Regiment and its battalions were systematically transported to Panama where it took over the work previously done by the 65th, which was reassigned to North Africa.

The regiment also provided 400 men and a Cannon Company to the parting unit.

The 266th Regiment was given the task of guarding the Panama Canal Zone, both in the Atlantic and Pacific coasts, and participated in missions in Peru, Galapagos, and Ecuador under Col. Francisco Parra Toro.

It served in the Mobile Forces, in jungle training and performed before visiting Latin American officials.

Three months later, the 295th Regiment began training at Camp O'Reilly and was later translated to Losey Field.

On May 13, 1943, the 162nd Battalion traveled to Panama, where it replaced the 2nd Field Artillery Battalion and was assigned the medical detachment two months later.

During the summer, the 295th was assigned to Panama, where replaced the 296th Regiment in the Mobile Force and surveillance operations under Col. Ramón Nadal.

There the battalions underwent jungle setting training along Latin American personnel and participated in monitoring of the Atlantic and Pacific oceans.

The 130th was re designated 130 Engineer Battalion Combat and placed under Lt. Col. Walter Torres.

In June 1943, a large portion of the 130th Puerto Rican officers were sent to Fort Belvoir for training.

Later in the year, the 130th was reassigned to Panama and given the task of building a landing strip in the jungle and a bridge between Piña Island and the Panamanian mainland, for which it was commended. [

On June 27, 1944, the 162nd Battalion returned to the United States and was assigned to Camp Burtner and later to Hampton Road and Fort Jackson.

The 296th was reassigned to serve in the Pacific, and on November 11, 1944, Col. Ramón Nadal took over it.

In January 1945, Col. Amaury Gandía took over and lead the 295th Regiment until it was demobilized and returned to Puerto Rico.

In Hawaii and accompanied by the 1558th Engineering and the 1114th Artillery, the unit took charge of training at camps Aiea and Kahuco, where the first, second and third battalions were assigned to different locations.

The 296th Regiment was trained in anticipation for an impending invasion of Japan but was later reassigned to work as occupation troops.

On April 19, 1945, the 162nd Battalion arrived at France, where it participated in operations held along the Seventh Army, the Sixth Group, 63rd Infantry, VI Army Corps, 84th Army Division and the Third Army.

In October it was returned to Puerto Rico, where it remained until its demobilization seven month later. The 130th was sent to Camp Bowie, where they would complete further training an await further mobilization, but the war would end before.

In March 1946, they were returned to Puerto Rico, where it was demobilized shortly after arrival.

On May 6, 1946, the 162nd was demobilized and reorganized under Lt. Col. Jaime Fullana, with its batteries being granted recognition between 1947 and 1948.

The conclusion of the war lead to the license and honorable discharge of several members of the PRNG, who wanted to continue their civilian lives.

During the summer of 1946, Esteves reorganized the 295th and 296th Infantry Regiments.

The Department of War issued a plan where the PRNG would be reorganized into headquarters, two units 295th and 296th, an anti-air group, and numerous battalions, detachments, companies, and other specialty groups at a cost of 2.5 million per year.

Secretary Patterson, who was once a member of his local national guard, felt an urgency to reorganize the civil guard as soon as possible.

In the recruitment initiative that followed, the PRNG would finish second among the 51 national guards affiliated to the USNG, only behind Wyoming, surpassing pre-established goals for a 204% of the total.

The most successful recruiter, Arturo Romañat, received a commendation and traveled to Washington where he met several high-ranking officials.

The 296th was placed in charge of Col. Juan Cordero. Company Headquarters for the first and second natal lions were in Mayagüez and Ponce, with Lieutenant Colonels Rafael Sepúlveda, Manuel Nazario and Ivan Domínguez.

The 296th's Company A, based in San Germán, became the first unit to complete quorum among all national guards affiliated to the

United States following the war and won the Eisenhower Trophy in consecutive years.

Between October and December 1946, other companies were scattered throughout Puerto Rico.

On September 15, 1946, the 295th Infantry Regiment was taken over by Col. Wilson Colberg.

This coincided with the establishment of Company Headquarters led by Cpt. Ramón Cantero.

The 295th held its first Annual Training under this new regime in August.

On November 3, 1946, the first set of commissions were awarded to the new PRNG.

Black men were not allowed to enlist in the PRNG until December 3, 1946, when colonial governor Jesús T. Piñero authorized it.

On February 9, 1947, the 482nd Artillery Battalion was organized under Lt. Col. Jacinto Hidalgo, its batteries were organized in San Juan and Cayey throughout the year and one in 1948.

Along the 225th Engineering Battalion, reorganized on January 22, 1948, the 296th was fully reorganized.

In May 1947, Esteves re-designated several companies of the 295th and 296th to facilitate their training with tanks and mortars.

In the summer of 1947, the 296th traveled to Tortuguero to attend its first training camp after reorganizing.

The following year, it held its first training at full force.

The 296th Regiment received Class A recognition, earning priority status in order of activation.

On June 15, 1947, Company K of the 295th was reorganized at Ceiba under Lt. Alejo Rivera, moving from its previous base in Fajardo.

On August 11, 1947, a parade led by the 295th was held in honor of Col. Miguel Muñoz.

During the following years, the national guard was involved in training, with Company I of the 296th hosting visiting officers.

On September 16, 1948, colonial governor Piñero and President Truman proclaimed the celebration of National Guard Day.

During this year, seven U.S. officials were commended by Gen. Ray Porter for their performance at Panama.

Korean War, Jayuya Uprising 1950–1953

Shortly after war was declared in Korea, the 65th regiment was activated, with the 296th Regiment taking its place at Puerto Rico on August 11, 1950.

Led by Col. César Cordero, who was given control of Camp Tortuguero, the regiment was assigned for training in anticipation for future deployment and waiting for orders from the General Headquarters of the Antilles Department.

During the following months, its battalions were scattered throughout Puerto Rico.

On September 8, 1950, the municipality of Sabana Grande held an activity in homage of the PRNG.

During the following years, the contradiction between the government of Luis Muñoz Marín and the Nationalist Party was widened over the Commonwealth that was being negotiated in Congress.

On October 30, 1950, these differences materialized in the Jayuya Uprising.

The 295th Infantry Regiment was mobilized from the beginning of the insurrection until November 6, 1950.

In the crossfire that took place at Utuado, Corporal José Rodríguez Alicea of H Unit in Arecibo was killed.

The 296th's First Battalion was mobilized under Lt. Col. Rafael Sepúlveda, was moved to forts Brooke and Buchanan.

This revolution was quelled after the Puerto Rico Air National Guard bombed the municipalities of Jayuya and Utuado, the first and so far, only time that the United States military has bombed a locale under the jurisdiction of the federal government.

Following the crossfire, the PRNG confiscated a flag of Puerto Rico that had been placed before the Jayuya Police Headquarters.

For its participation in this conflict, the entity received letters of gratification from the Puerto Rico Police Department and other organizations affiliated to the government such as the Puerto Rico Water Resources Authority.

In turn, Esteves commended several officers for their coordination.

On January 22, 1951, the 296th Regiment was moved to Camp Losey under Col. Cordero.

On February 1, 1951, the 296th was formally reorganized.

Its units systematically operated at Salinas and training continued in expectation.

During this time, the 296th replaced personnel for the 65th Regiment.

Chief of Staff J. Lawton Collins visited Puerto Rico and transferred Col. Cordero to the 65th, replacing him with Lt. Col. Sepúlveda.

Company D of Yauco was the first to complete its quorum, being recognized by the Army on February 15, 1953.

On September 14, 1952, the 296th's Headquarters Company was organized.[109] In 1953, the 296th Annual Training was heavily affected by the moves to service.

The PRNG also promoted assistance by awarding a golden cup to units with perfect assistance.

Battery B of the 482nd was returned to the jurisdiction of Puerto Rico and received a recognition by the Army.

CHAPTER 87

Cold War and Governor Assignments 1954–1991

Brigadier Gen. Kenneth Sweany attended the summer training in July 1954, expressing satisfaction following the Governor's Day parade that culminated it.

On November 19, 1954, the Regular Army formally returned the designation of 296th Regiment to the PRNG in an activity hosted by Muñoz Marín, this under new administrative personnel due to several former members remaining in active service.

Detachments were then assigned to several municipalities. The Regiment was able to gather enough troops, but the officers were scarce due to active service and the Inactive Reserve.

Other moves included the adoption of a fighting cock as new insignia and the establishment of a periodical. The efficiency of the personnel was gauged in shooting competitions, with the results being sent back to the USNG for comparison with other national guards.

In 1955, a Commission of the House of Representatives supervised the PRNG's exercises to gauge the entity's efficiency.

During the passing of Hurricane Santa Clara, the 296th's Company I provided support to the government.

The 296th's Engineering Company 225 was tasked with the construction of a bridge.

The PRNG underwent another reorganization on February 15, 1959. The tank companies of the 295th and 296th Regiments were assigned to the first battalion in Ponce.

Several pre-existing companies were reassigned into the creation of the new Group 65.

Several other companies were reassigned new names and purpose, including the 162nd, 482nd and 123rd Battalions.

On February 15, 1959, the 296th was assigned to Mayagüez under Col. Raúl Mercado.

This same date the 92nd Brigade was returned to the PRNG, after having been formed from the 295th and the 296th in 1940 and reassigned to the Puerto Rico Military Department the following years.

The 295th and 296th Regiments, 192nd Battalion, 162nd Second Support Battalion, 892nd Engineering Company, Rangers E Company, and Troop E of the signaling platoon were placed under it.

In 1955, the 296th's Company G won the local National Guard Trophy and the Pershing Trophy, beating other national guards in the Third Area of the South.

On April 30, 1957, Esteves retired from service due to health concerns. Gen. Juan Cordero took office on October 1, 1958 and was ascended to the rank of Brigadier General.

On February 21, 1960, commemorated as National Guard Day, the 65th Infantry Regiment was transferred from the Regular Army to the PRNG, in an activity where Gen. Cesár Cordero handed the unit's colors to Col. Rafael Rodríguez. During this time, Governor Luis Muñoz Marín took over the office of adjutant general.

On September 5, 1960, the PRNG was activated to attend a series of building and bridge collapses caused by floods brought by the adjacent passing of Hurricane Donna, which lead to the deaths of 149 civilians.

In December 1961, the PRNG was involved in the reception of John F. Kennedy during his visit to Puerto Rico.

CHAPTER 88

Puerto Rico National Guardsmen in 2012

The Military Academy of the Puerto Rico National Guard was established on June 1, 1963, at Camp Tortuguero on an initiative of César Cordero.

Its curriculum was equivalent to Fort Benning's and lasted for a year and 15 days, at which point graduates received their certification. The institution was subsequently changed to the Henry Barracks in Cayey and from there to Campamento Santiago.

On May 1, 1964, the PRNG underwent another reorganization, the second under Gen. Cordero.

On March 20, 1966, Salvador Roig was placed in charge of the PRNG by Roberto Sánchez Vilella. The PRNG also engaged in other civil activities, such as cooperativism, several becoming involved with Cooperativa El Sentinela and inter-agency softball tournaments.

In 1968 and 1969, Gen. Alberto Picó created the Civic Medical Service Program led by Support Battalion 192's Company B and the 201 Surgery Hospital of the Mobile Army, first offering service to the communities of Salinas.

The initiative then moved to the municipality of Culebra. Other municipalities treated during this time include Aibonito, Coamo, Orovovis, Vega Baja, Guánica, Ponce, San Juan, as part of yearly trainings, requests, or emergent circumstances.

Similar operations held at Utuado in 1974, led to a recognition by the House of Representatives.

On January 10, 1969, Picó was promoted to Adjutant General.

The Civic Action and Rehabilitation from Disaster and Rescue Program was established parallel to this, with the expressed intention of aiding civic organizations_in non-intrusive ways following natural disasters.

Under this initiative, the 892nd Company and personnel from the 130th of Engineering was engaged in projects such as reconstructing damaged roads, the removal of debris and replacing bridges.

They also attended some civic and government requests, particularly during training exercises.

The PRNG was also involved in the activities of Constitution Day on July 25, 1970.

Other activities included raising funds for civic organizations, specific constructions, disposing of garbage, building restorations, and cooperating with the Boy Scouts of America.

On October 9, 1970, the PRNG was activated to attend a series of floods, mobilizing 265 men which remained in service for a period of ten days.

The entity's role in this event was mostly focused on the evacuation of victims and providing supplies in cooperation with other government agencies.

For these efforts, several government functionaries sent letter to Gen. Picó, in which they thanked him for the services provided.

On February 1, 1973, Chardón was named Adjutant General and ascended to the rank of Brigadier General.

On July 6, 1973, Rafael Hernández Colón activated the PRNG in response to a strike being declared in the Autor dad de Fuentes Fluviales. The 92nd Brigade and other units were in service for a week under Brigadier General Salvador Padilla.

On November 28, 1974, Hernández Colón activated the national guard again, this time in response to a strike being declared in the Puerto Rico Aqueducts and Sewers Authority.

This time, the PRNG remained in service for two weeks.

On September 6, 1975, Salvador Padilla was named Adjutant General of the PRNG.

The following month, Tropical Storm Eloise passed near the North Coast of Puerto Rico, with many guardsmen voluntarily joining the Civil Defense in the evacuation, clearing of garbage, transportation and the management of Assistance Centers that followed.

Military Installations

Camp Santiago Joint Maneuver Training Center on 16,000 acres of land located in Salinas, Puerto Rico is the island's premier National Guard training facility.

Though it has no permanent residents, Camp Santiago can house thousands of troops on a temporary basis.

Some old barracks are being replaced with new two-level barracks. In addition to rifle and small arm ranges, a leadership reaction course, and dining facilities and classrooms, Camp Santiago houses a Puerto Rico National Guard Museum, a theater, a Class Six Shoppette and, since 2009, a post exchange on base.

A $1.7 million Urban Assault Course is to be constructed at Camp Santiago.

The National Guard units from other states also come to Camp Santiago for their two weeks annual training.

In 1975 the facility was renamed from Camp Salinas to Camp Santiago in honor of Specialist Four Héctor Santiago-Colón, who received the Medal of Honor during the Vietnam War. Salinas was Santiago's birthplace.

Fort Allen, located 4 miles, 6.4 km, south of Juana Díaz, is the site of the Puerto Rico National Guard Language Center.

Many PRNG and U.S. Army Reserve units are stationed at Fort Allen. The National Guard's Youth Challenge Program operates at Fort Allen, graduating hundreds of high school students each year who had formerly dropped out of school.

The Relocatable over the Horizon ROTHR, receiver site has operated at Fort Allen since the 1990s; it is part of a surveillance network designed to monitor flights over an area encompassing more than 1,000,000 square miles, 2,600,000 km2, in South America.

The ROTHR radar consists of 34 antennas and support structure from 71 to 123 feet, 37 m, tall.

Barracks can house military personnel on a temporary basis, NGX has a post exchange on base, and an Armed Forces Reserve Center is under construction.

Previously Fort Allen was used by the US Army as the Losey Army Airfield during WWII, and later used as a U.S. Navy communications center.

Since 1980, Fort Allen has been under control of the Puerto Rico National Guard.

Muñiz Air National Guard Base in Carolina is the home of the Puerto Rico Air National Guard 156th Airlift Wing and the 198th Airlift Squadron. Also, at Muñiz ANGB are located the headquarters of the 1st Air Base Group, the air support division of the Puerto Rico State Guard.

Muñiz ANGB has hangars, command offices, a recruiting office, classrooms, maintenance shops, a community club, a Family Readiness Center, a post barbershop, and NGX has a post exchange on base. Muñiz ANGB is also the home of the STARBASE youth program in Puerto Rico.

Operation Coronet Oak shares Muñiz ANGB flight line with the 156th Airlift Wing, which also flies C-130 military transport airplanes.

In 1963 this Air base was renamed Muñiz Air National Guard Base while commemorating the 20th year of its federal recognition.

Punta Borinquen Radar Station located next to Punta Borinquen Golf Course at the former Ramey Air Force Base is home for the Puerto Rico Air National Guard's 141st Air Control Squadron.

Punta Salinas Radar Site

The Puerto Rico Air National Guard's operate Punta Salinas Radar Site in Toa Baja 140th Air Defense Support Squadron. Its mission is to provide air traffic control to the Federal Aviation Administration and provide support for military and law enforcement operations.

Isla Grande Aviation Support Facility is located at the Fernando Luis Ribas Dominica Airport in San Juan. Its mission is to support the Puerto Rico Army National Guard aviation units.

Watercraft Support Maintenance Center at the former Naval Station Roosevelt Roads in Ceiba, Puerto Rico is home for the Puerto Rico Army National Guard Landing Craft Detachment, 191st Regional Support Group.

Puerto Rico Army National Guard armories are in Aibonito, Aguadilla, Arecibo, Arroyo, Cabo Rojo, Caguas, Cayey, Ceiba, Coamo, Guayama, Gurabo, Humacao, Juncos, Mayaguez, Peñuelas, Ponce, Sabana Grande, San German, Utuado, Vega Baja and San Juan.

Some of these armories might close and units will move into new Armed Forces Reserve Centers in Ceiba, Mayaguez, Fort Allen and to a new Puerto Rico National Guard Readiness Center in Fort Buchanan.

Community outreach programs
Drug Demand Reduction Program

The National Guard uses its resources to help the island's youth to be drug-free. The Drug Demand Reduction Program works closely with local law enforcement, education, and community-based organizations to reduce the chances of exposure of illegal drugs to American children. They also provide National Guard-led education-based, leadership and motivational programs.

Drug Demand Reduction directly interacts with children through their KEY National Initiative, Drug Free Starts with Me. The program visits local schools and communities around the island to increase awareness and motivation, and provide leadership, guidance, and support to adolescents about their choice to remain drug-free.

Youth Challenge Program

This program intervenes with 16- to 18-year-old high school dropouts to help them reclaim their lives; it helps them graduate with the values, life skills, education, and self-discipline necessary to succeed as productive citizens.

Founded in the 1990s during the administration of Governor Pedro Rosselló, the program has had thousands of dropouts participate and graduate.

STARBASE Youth Program

As an acronym of Science and Technology Academies Reinforcing Basic Aviation and Space Education, this youth program is intended to help students from 4th–12th grade to improve their math and science skills through aviation.

The program starts in elementary school to attract and prepare students at an early age for careers in engineering and other science-related fields of study.

The program principally exposes at-risk children and their teachers to real-world applications of math and science; it includes experiential learning, simulations, and experiments in aviation and space-related fields.

The program also addresses drug use prevention, health, self-esteem, and life skills within a math-and science-based program. Founded in 1995 by SSgt Elaine Montgomery, the program celebrates its 15th anniversary in May 2010.

CHAPTER 90

Additional Military Knowledge

Phonetic Alphabet

A - alpha	N - november
B - bravo	O - oscar
C - charlie	P - papa
D - delta	Q - quebec
E - echo	R - romeo
F - foxtrot	S - sierra
G - golf	T - tango
H - hotel	U - uniform
I - india	V - victor
J - juliet	W - wiskey
K - kilo	X - x-ray
L - lima	Y - yankee
M - mike	Z - zulu

U.S. ARMY RANKS

The Army profession is a unique vocation of experts who are entrusted to defend the Constitution and the rights and interests of the American people.

More than an indication of pay grade, Army ranks provide a system of leadership that indicates a Soldier's level of expertise, responsibility, and authority inside that profession.

Regardless of rank, every Soldier has a significant role in the total Army mission.

They plan missions, give orders and assign Soldiers tasks.

Second Lieutenant. Typically, the entry-level rank for most commissioned officers. ...

First Lieutenant A seasoned lieutenant with 18 to 24 months of service

Major

Lieutenant Colonel

Colonel

Brigadier General

Major General

OFFICER RANKS

Commissioned officers are the managers, problem solvers, key influencers and planners who lead enlisted Soldiers in all situations. They plan missions, give orders, and assign Soldiers tasks.

ENLISTED RANKS

Enlisted Soldiers are the backbone of the Army. They have specific specialties within an Army unit, perform specific job functions and have the knowledge that ensures the success of their unit's current mission within the Army. THE SERGENTS

WARRANT OFFICER RANKS

The adaptive technical expert, combat leader, trainer, and advisor. Through progressive levels of expertise in assignments, training, and education, the warrant officer administers, manages, maintains, operates and integrates systems and equipment across the full spectrum of operations.

CORPS AND DIVISION OPERATIONS

The U.S. Army is the largest branch of service with a greater variety of units than the other services, each with a different organization and purpose.

Therefore, the Army provides the combatant commander with an interlocking array of higher headquarters trained and equipped to apply land power from the theater level, through the operational level, and down to the tactical employment of various brigades, groups, and battalions.

Together the theater Army, corps, and division give the combatant commander several options necessary for the employment of land power in an interdependent joint force.

Military/Civilian Time

Military = Civilian	Military = Civilian
0001 = 12:01 am	1300 = 1:00 pm
0100 – 1:00 am	1400 – 2:00 pm
0200 – 2:00 am	1500 – 3:00 pm
0300 = 3:00 am	1600 = 4:00 pm
0400 = 4:00 am	1700 = 5:00 pm
0500 – 5:00 am	1800 – 6:00 pm
0600 – 6:00 am	1900 – 7:00 pm
0700 = 7:00 am	2000 = 8:00 pm
0800 = 8:00 am	2100 = 9:00 pm
0900 – 9:00 am	2200 – 10:00 pm
1000 – 10:00 am	2300 – 11:00 pm
1100 = 11:00 am	2400 = 12 Midnight
1200 = Noon	

MILITARY VOCABULARY
MOSTLY IDIOMATIC EXPRESSIONS AND EBONICS/SLANG

Air Picket -- Any airborne system tasked with detecting, reporting and tracking enemy aerial movements within a certain area of operation.

Alpha Charlie -- Military alphabet used to represent ass chewing. Defines getting verbally reprimanded. Recommended by user Joe Trejo.

Any mouse -- A lockbox on Navy ships where sailors may drop anonymous suggestions.

Ass -- Armored vehicles such as Stryker's and Tanks.

Ate-Up -- Describes a service member who follows regulations so closely that they disregard the context of the situation. Conversely, may describe a service member who doesn't understand regulations at all.

B

Band-Aid -- A Vietnam-era term for a medic.

Bang-bang -- An Army term describing a pistol or rifle.

Big Voice -- Term used to describe the loudspeaker on a military base. The Big Voice warns of everything from incoming attacks to scheduled ordnance disposal.

Bird -- Slang for helicopter.

Bitchin' Betty -- Most U.S. military aircraft feature warning systems that frequently utilize female voices. The phrase is derived from the same anthropomorphizing applied to GPS units in cars, only Bitchin' Betty's alert pilots to life-threatening situations.

'Black' on ammo, fuel, water, etc. -- A common phrase denoting a particular resource is gone.

Blowed up -- The state of being hit by an IED.

Blue Falcon -- A euphemism for buddy **** or buddy ****er, which is slang for a backstabber. Recommended by user chopper.

Bolo -- A derogatory remark for recruits who cannot pass marksmanship training. The idea being that if one cannot use a rifle, one must resort to a bolo.

Bone -- A B-1 bomber.

Bull**** Bomb -- A package intended to disperse propaganda leaflets. Recommended by user Steve Neal.

Bullwinkle Badge -- Another name for the Air Assault Badge. Recommended by user David E Windsor II.

Burn Bag -- A bag used to hold shredded documents, designed to be burned. May also refer to a useless person. Recommended by user Gregory Waugh.

C

Cannibalize -- The act of taking workable parts of one item and using them in another.

Chancre Mechanic -- Medical officer who checks service members for venereal diseases.

Charlie Foxtrot -- Commonly used expression utilizing the military alphabet to stand for cluster***.

Chem-Light Batteries -- A mythical object that would be extremely, functionally pointless. Often the source of fruitless hunts embarked upon by hapless privates.

Chest Candy -- Slang for ribbons and medals worn on a uniform. Can be insulting or applauding.

Chicken plates -- Sheets of protective material, called Small Arms Protective Inserts, which are used in the Interceptor body armor system.

Comics -- Term used to describe maps presented by military intelligence. The term is insulting in nature as a slight against the accuracy of the maps. It also refers to the brightly colored layouts and symbols usually included.

Commo -- Communications equipment or the individuals who operate it. Usually given to communications officers on U.S. Navy vessels.

Crank -- Navy term for a sailor pulling temporary duty in the galley.

Crumb Catcher -- Military slang describing the mouth.

Crusher -- Hats worn by pilots during World War II. The hat's wide top brim would need to be crushed down to allow for headsets to be worn.

D

Dear John -- Common term referring to a significant other breaking up with a service member through a letter. Recommended by user wilburbythepsea.

Demilitarized Zone -- A specific area in which any type of military force -- including but not limited to personnel, hardware, and infrastructure -- are banned.

Digit Midget -- Usually used with a number as a prefix. X digit midget refers to the number of days till an individual goes on leave or retires. Recommended by user Steve Pinder.

Digies -- Digital camouflage worn by soldiers and Marines.

Ditty bopper -- A term in the Army referring to signals intelligence radio operators trained to utilize Morse code. Also used as a verb to describe soldiers marching out of synch with a cadence.

Dope on a Rope -- Derogatory term used for air-assault soldiers.

Dust-off -- Specifically, a medical evacuation by helicopter.

Dynamited Chicken -- Term originating in the Navy referring to chicken cacciatore or chicken a la king.

E

Embed -- When a reporter stays with the military to conduct journalistic business. They typically are provided with security and necessities provided by the unit they are embedded with.

Expectant -- A casualty who is expected to pass die.

Eagle Keeper -- Maintenance crew chief of an F-15.

F

Fang -- A verb to describe being rebuked, called out or otherwise disparaged.

Fangs -- A Marine Corps term for one's teeth.

Fart Sack -- Refers to a sleeping bag or an airman's flight suit.

Farts and Darts -- Refers to the clouds and lightning bolt embellishments found on Air Force officer caps. Recommended by user NGH144.

Fashion Show -- A Naval punishment where a sailor is required to dress in each of his uniforms over a period of several hours.

Fast Mover -- Slang for a jet fighter. Aptly named due to the rapidity of a jet fighter's movement.

First Light -- The time of nautical twilight when the sun is 12 degrees below the horizon.

Flaming ***hole -- An Air Force term to describe the fiery effect of a jet plane turning on its afterburners during combat or any other military operation.

Flight Suit Insert -- Air Force slang for a pilot.

Fitty -- Slang for an M2 .50 caliber machine gun.

Five-Sided Puzzle Palace -- Slang for the Pentagon.

Football Bat -- An individual or way of doing things that is particularly odd.

Force Projection -- The ability of a nation-state to extend military force beyond their borders.

Fourth Point of Contact -- From rolling after a successful parachute drop: a term to describe an individual's buttocks. The first three points are feet, calves and back of the thigh. Recommended by user Elise Morgan.

Fruit Salad -- Slang for a service member's display of medals and ribbons on a dress uniform. Recommended by user DL_in _DEN.

Fugazi -- Completely out of whack, ****ed up, screwy. This term originated during the Vietnam War and experienced limited use by civilians.

G

Galloping Dandruff -- An Army term used since World War I to refer to crab lice.

Geardo -- An Army term for a soldier who spends an inordinate amount of money on gear, regardless of actual need.

Gedunk -- Refers to snack foods, such as candy and chips, as well as the place they're sold. Associated with the Navy and can be used in the phrase "gedunk sailor" as a pejorative remark for inexperienced sailors. Recommended by user Benson McCloud.

Go fasters -- A term for sneakers used in the Army, Navy, and Marine Corps.

GOFO -- Literally stands for "grasp of the ****ing obvious."

Gone Elvis -- A service member who is missing in action.

Grape -- A term with two meanings; one for the Air Force and one for the Navy. A Navy Grape is an individual who refuels aircraft. An Air Force Grape, on the other hand, refers to an easy assignment and can be used as a compliment when a service member makes something look easy.

Great Mistakes -- The name sailors have given the Great Lakes Naval Training Center north of Chicago. It references the closing of two other training facilities in San Diego and Orlando, which both feature far more enjoyable weather.

Grid Squares -- A nonexistent item recruits typically are told to go find.

Groundhog Day -- Term originating from the titular movie that refers to deployments that seem to proceed in the exact same way despite attempts to change them.

Gum Shoe -- Navy slang for a sailor cryptology technician. The first CT school was located on top of a building where tar would get stuck to the bottom of students' shoes.

Gun -- Term for a mortar or artillery piece. Must never be used within the military to describe a pistol or rifle.

Gunner -- A service member who operates a crew-served weapon, such as a piece of artillery or ship's cannon. Recommended by user John Alfred.

H

Hangar Queen -- An aircraft that is used primarily for spare parts to repair other planes. Recommended by Steve Pinder.

Hardball -- A hard-surfaced road.

Hardened Site -- A structure usually built under rock or concrete designed to withstand conventional, nuclear, biological, and chemical attack.

Hat Up -- To change one's location. Refers to the need to wear a hat for the intended destination. Recommended by user JimBrown1946.

Hawk -- Term for cold weather. Commonly referred to as "the hawk."

Helo -- Short-hand term for a helicopter.

High Speed -- An individual who is highly motivated and at or near peak efficacy. Can be used sarcastically. Recommended by user sara.

Hit the Silk -- Ejecting from an aircraft and utilizing a parachute.

I

Inactive Status -- Members of the Reserves who are unable to train for points, receive pay and cannot be considered for promotion.

Ink Stick -- Marine Corps term for a pen.

Iron Rations -- Rations used in an emergency survival situation.

J

Jawa -- Term for an Army soldier who is stationed in a desert area, named after the desert-dwelling aliens of "Star Wars."

Jesus Slippers -- Military-issued shower footwear.

Jockstrap Medal -- Derogatory term for medals given by the military to active CIA members.

Joe -- Army term for a soldier. Shortened from G.I. Joe.

Joint Operation Planning -- All type of planning involving joint military forces regarding military operations, including, but not limited to, mobilization, deployment, and sustainment.

K

Kinetic -- Slang adjective meaning violent.

Klicks -- Kilometers.

L

Latrine Queen -- Air Force specific term for a trainee in basic who oversees the team responsible for cleaning bathrooms.

Left-Handed Monkey Wrench -- A nonexistent tool. Often the object of fruitless searches undertaken by recruits at the behest of more experienced service members. Recommended by user John Alfred.

Long Pig -- Slang for when a human being is used as a source of food. Typically, this happens in extremely desperate situations.

M

Major Nuclear Power -- Any nation-state with a nuclear arsenal capable of being delivered to any other nation in the world.

Meat Identifier -- A dish or sauce that identifies what type of meat is being served. For example, cranberry sauce indicates turkey while applesauce indicates pork chops.

Meat Wagon -- Slang for an ambulance or any other medical emergency vehicle. Recommended by user 5712540.

Moonbeam -- Marine term for flashlight.

Moving Like Pond Water -- Moving so slowly that a unique term is required to describe it. Recommended by user 31320680.

Mustang -- Term referring to any officer who was promoted from the enlisted ranks. Can be used respectfully or pejoratively.

N

Nut to Butt -- The instruction used to tell soldiers to line up in a tight, forward-facing line wherein one's nuts are in extreme proximity to the butt of the soldier before them.

O

Officer's Candy -- Navy term used by sailors to describe the scented cake placed in urinals.

Officer of the Deck -- Any officer charged with the operation of a ship. Reports to the commanding officer, executive officer and navigator for relevant issues and concerns.

Over the Hill -- Missing in action or someone who officially has gone missing from their post.

Oxygen Thief -- A biting piece of slang for someone who's useless or talks too much.

P

Pad Eye Remover -- A nonexistent item used by sailors to trick new service members into a fruitless search. Pad-eyes are used to secure airplanes with chains.

People Tank -- A U.S. Navy term for the inner hull of a submarine.

Pill Pusher -- A U.S. Navy term for a hospital corpsman.

Pink Mist -- A distinct effect created by certain types of gunshot wounds.

Pogey Bait -- Snack food. A "pogue" is an individual who does not serve on the frontlines and performs non-combat-oriented roles. "Pogey bait" is, subsequently, a bribe given to these individuals in exchange for expedited or high-quality services.

Pollywog -- A sailor who has not crossed the equator on a U.S. Navy ship. Recommended by user Terry Thomason.

Puddle Pirate -- Member of the Coast Guard. So called due to a fallacious belief that the Coast Guard never operates in deep water.

PX Ranger -- An individual who purchases, from the Post Exchange, paraphernalia unique to certain prestigious ranks or occupations and passes them off as though they earned the items. Recommended by mw1968.

Q

Quay -- A man-made structure between a shore and land that can be used by ships to berth and is typically an area for handling cargo.

R

Rainbow -- A recruit in basic training. Recommended by user wilburbythespea.

Red Team -- A body of experts on a specific topic who are instructed to research and suggest alternative methods regarding a planned course of action.

Remington Raider -- A somewhat derogatory term used for Marines given the harrowing task of performing office duties.

Rocks and Shoals -- U.S. Navy rules and regulations.

Rotor head -- Slang for a helicopter pilot. Recommended by user Bob Panted.

Ruck Up -- "Ruck" is short for "ruck sack," which refers to backpacks service members sometimes wear. To "ruck up" is to get through a particularly challenging or stressful situation. Recommended by mw1968.

S

Salad Bar -- References the service ribbons found on a military uniform.

Scrambled Eggs -- Refers to the embellishments found on some officer's caps. Recommended by user NGH144.

Self-Propelled Sandbags -- A derogatory term for a Marine based on their emphasis on fighting on the front lines. Recommended by user Nathan King.

Shavetail -- A term referring to second lieutenants in the U.S. Army. It primarily refers to the haircuts received in Officer Candidate School. The term's origins date to the time when the Army used pack animals, and handlers shaved the tail of newly broken animals to distinguish them from those more seasoned.

Shellback -- A sailor who has crossed the equator on a U.S. Navy ship. Responsible for turning all Pollywogs into Shellbacks once they cross the equator themselves. Recommended by user Terry Thomason.

Snake Eater -- Member of the U.S. Army Special Forces.

S*** on a Shingle -- Slang for a piece of toast with gravy. Recommended by user Mike W.

Sky Blossom -- A deployed parachute.

Slick Sleeve -- Refers to a sailor who has not yet earned a rank that requires decoration on the sleeves.

Smoke -- To punish a service member with excessive physical work due to a minor infraction.

Snivel Gear -- Any equipment meant for use in cold weather. Recommended by mw1968.

Soap chips -- A psychological operations (PSYOPS) tactic where fake letters from an enemy's home country are written and placed on bodies and battle wreckage. They include sentimental content, hint at the infidelity of loved ones back home and are designed to demoralize combatants.

Soup Sandwich -- Used to describe an individual, object, situation or mission that has gone horribly wrong. The thrust of the term's meaning derives from the fact that it is incredibly difficult, some would say impossible, to make a sandwich out of soup. Recommended by user David E Windsor II.

Swoop -- Marine term for a weekend trip off base.

T

Taco -- An Air Force term for receiving an "unsatisfactory" grade on a training exercise due to the vague taco-shape of the letter "u."

Tango Uniform -- Slang for "tits up," which is the position dead bodies tend to face. The term can be applied to the deceased as well as broken pieces of equipment. Recommended by users 10741875 and iaff.

Target Discrimination -- The capability of a surveillance or guidance system to choose certain targets when multiple options are presented.

Trench Monkey -- A derogatory term referring to a member of the U.S. Army.

Twidget -- A sailor who repairs electronic equipment. Suggested by user X-USN-DS1.

U

Un-Ass -- To move immediately or leave one's current position.

Uncle Sam's Canoe Club -- A U.S. Navy term for the U.S. Coast Guard.

Unit Identification Code -- An alphanumeric, six-character string that identifies all active, reserve, and guard units of the United States military.

V

Voice in the Sky -- Term referring to military base announcements broadcast over speakers. Recommended by user SMSgt.

Voluntold -- An assignment that is technically voluntary but understood to be mandatory.

W

Weapons of Mass Destruction -- Weapons that can cause destruction or death beyond the ability of conventional weapons. These typically are nuclear, biological, chemical, radiological or high-yield explosive in nature. This definition does not include the vehicle, or transportation method, of delivering the weapon.

Z

Zone of Action -- A smaller section of a larger area. Typically, these are under the purview of a tactical unit, usually during an offensive maneuver.

Zoomie -- Term used by non-flying service members for anyone who operates a flying vehicle.

REFERENCE

Whalen, Carmen Teresa; Vázquez-Hernández, Víctor (2005). The Puerto Rican Diaspora Historical Perspectives. p. 176. ISBN 978-1-59213-413-7.

Morris, Nancy (1995). Puerto Rico Culture, Politics, and Identity. Praeger. p. 31. ISBN 978-0-275-95228-0.

Obama honors Puerto Rican Infantry Regiment with Congressional Gold Medal, Washington Post, June 10, 2014.

«¿Taínos mansos? ¡Piénselo otra vez!». Periodicolaperla.com. Archived from the original on 2016-04-03. Retrieved 2016-05-28.

"Ponce de Len, Juan | Infoplease". www.infoplease.com.

Puerto Rico Reconstruction Administration (1940). "History from Puerto Rico: A Guide to the Island of Borinquen". The University Society. Archived from the original on 2009-03-04. Retrieved 2009-03-12.

"Historia De Utuado". Ortizal.com. 2011-11-05. Archived from the original on 2016-04-22. Retrieved 2016-05-28.

"A Historical Overview of Colonial Puerto Rico: The Importance of San Juan as a Military Outpost". Archived from the original on 2009-05-31. Retrieved 2009-03-12.

Narraciones históricas by Cayetano Coll y Toste, Pub. Editorial Cultural 1976. P. 57. ISBN 84-399-5350-X.

New York Magazine. New York Media, LLC. 11 November 1991. p. 84. Retrieved 2021-03-27.

Soto, Marie Cruz (2008). Inhabiting Isla Nena, 1514-2003: Island Narrations, Imperial Dramas and Vieques, Puerto Rico (PhD). University of Michigan. pp. 90–91.

Historias de Puerto Rico by Paul G. Miller, (1947) pp. 221–237.

The Athenaeum. J. Lection. 1899. p. 33. Retrieved 2021-03-27.
de Hostos 1949, pp. 303–305.
Brau 1975, p. 111.
"Haro, Juan de [administrador colonial español] (ca. 1550–1631)". MCNBiografias.com (in Spanish). Retrieved 2016-05-28.
Middeldyk, R.A. Van, The History of Puerto Rico from the Spanish Discovery to the American Occupation, archived from the original on 2008-01-22
Balletto, Barbara (2003). Insight Guide Puerto Rico. Insight Guides. p. 32. ISBN 978-981-234-949-1.
"Puerto Rican Ancestors in Spanish and American Military Records". Archived from the original on March 28, 2012. Retrieved February 22, 2012.
Santiago Maunez Vizcarrondo. "Centro Cultural" (in Spanish). Dra. Antonia Sáez. Archived from the original on May 5, 2006. Retrieved October 22, 2006.
"Arecibo, Puerto Rico". Welcome.topuertorico.org. Retrieved 2016-05-28.
"Regimento Fijo de Puerto Rico". Archived from the original on October 6, 2006. Retrieved October 6, 2006.
Instituto de Cultura Puertorriqueña
"The Celtic Connection". Archived from the original on August 13, 2006. Retrieved October 6, 2006.
"Something Sweet Like Mango in the Air: A Primer on Mayagüez". Puerto Rico Herald. Retrieved 2016-05-28.
"Gálvez and the other forgotten Heroes of the American Revolution"; Thomas Ellingwood Fortin, Producer, New Albion Pictures
"Cajun and Cajuns: Genealogy site for Cajun, Acadian and Louisiana genealogy, history and culture". Thecajuns.com. Retrieved 2016-05-28.
LaFarelle, Lorenzo G. (1992). Bernardo de Gálvez Hero of the American Revolution. Marion Koogler McNay Art Museum. p. 57. ISBN 978-0-89015-849-4.
Hector Díaz (March 16, 1996). "Maryland State Resolution on the Role Played by Hispanics In The Achievement of American

Independence". Lasculturas.com. Archived from the original on March 8, 2004. Retrieved October 7, 2006.

Denis-Rosario, Milagros (2011). "The Silence of the Black Militia: Socio-Historical Analysis of the British Attack to Puerto Rico of 179". Memorias: Revista Digital de Historia y Arqueología desde el Caribe [Memories: Digital Magazine of History and Archeology from the Caribbean]. No. 14 (January – July). ISSN 1794-8886. Retrieved March 18, 2021.

"Myths, Legends, and Superstitions of Puerto Rico". Gopuertorico. about.com. Retrieved 2016-05-28.

"La Rogativa Details". Lindsaydaen.com. Archived from the original on 2015-06-11. Retrieved 2016-05-28.

Municipio de San Juan. Actas del Cabildo 1792–1798., San Juan: M. Pareja, 1967, 287.

Brau 1975, p. 214.

"History: Power y Giralt, Ramón". Enciclopediapr.org. 2014-09-12. Archived from the original on 2016-03-04. Retrieved 2016-05-28.

"Benefactores y Hombres Notables de Puerto Rico"; by Eduardo Neumann Gandia; published 1896 National Library of Spain.

Negroni, Héctor Andrés (1992). Historia militar de Puerto Rico (in Spanish). Sociedad Estatal Quinto Centenario. ISBN 978-84-7844-138-9.

Baralt, Guillermo A. (2007). Slave Revolts in Puerto Rico Conspiracies and Uprisings, 1795–1873. Markus Wiener Publishers. p. 5. ISBN 978-1-55876-463-7.

Baralt, Guillermo A. (2007). Slave Revolts in Puerto Rico Conspiracies and Uprisings, 1795–1873. Markus Wiener Publishing. ISBN 978-1-55876-463-7.

"MayagÃ¼ez Capital ULT" (PDF). Mayaguezsabeaman RENCE

Hispanic link weekly report, Volume 6, Page 122

The Contributions of Hispanic Servicewomen--Written by: Judith Bellafaire, Ph.D., Curator Archived 2004-03-14 at the Wayback Machine

Puerto Rican Woman in Defense of our country Archived 2016-03-03 at the Wayback Machine

"LAS WACS"-Participacion de la Mujer Boricua En la Segunda Guerra
Mundial; by: Carmen Garcia Rosado; Page 79; 1ra. Edicion
publicada En Octubre de 2006; 2da Edicion revisada 2007; Registro
de Propiedad Intelectual ELA (Government of Puerto Rico) #06-
13P-)1A-399; Library of Congress TXY 1-312-685

ABOUT THE AUTHOR

Norma Iris Pagan Morales was born in Ponce, Puerto Rico. She comes from a very lovable family. Her parents, Juan Jose Pagan Rodriguez, and Digna Morales Figueroa, now deceased, always helped her with her projects as a writer and teaching career.

Norma has three siblings, Adelin Milagros Pagan Morales, Juan Jose Pagan Morales, and Julio Manuel Pagan Morales. Julio Manuel Pagan Morales died on September 19, 1998. He was also known for his writing/composer skills.

Norma did all her academic studies in New York City, Puerto Rico and Canada. She worked in the City of New York Police Department. As an Educator, she worked in New York City Bd. of Education, in Puerto Rico Bd. of Education. Puerto Rico Army National Language Center as an English Instructor/Lab Instructor.

She has teaching certifications and licenses for the following:

1. English Teacher (Literature High School and adults Level)
2. English as a Second Language (Elementary and High School)
3. Teaching English as a Foreign Language and Spanish
4. Communications skills (includes office procedures, and business for today's work force)
5. Computers in the classroom
6. Long distance teaching

She has published seven books: Proud of My Puerto Rican Bequest, ¿Porque Soy Boricua? Poemas del Alma, Art in Written Form,

A Baffling Short Stories Collection, On the Job in the Big Apple and Nature's Rage in the Caribbean.

www.ingramcontent.com/pod-product-compliance
Lightning Source LLC
Chambersburg PA
CBHW021607120626
46545CB00001B/104